ORGANIZING THE
SPONTANEOUS

ORGANIZING THE

SPONTANEOUS

CITIZEN PROTEST IN

POSTWAR JAPAN

BY WESLEY SASAKI-UEMURA

UNIVERSITY OF HAWAI'I PRESS

HONOLULU

© 2001 University of Hawai'i Press

Printed in the United States of America

06 05 04 03 02 01   6 5 4 3 2 1

Library of Congress Cataloging-in-Publication Data
Sasaki-Uemura, Wesley Makoto.
    Organizing the spontaneous: citizen protest in postwar Japan /
Wesley Sasaki-Uemura.
    p. cm.
    Includes bibliographical references and index.
    ISBN 0–8248–2311–7 (cloth : alk. paper) —
ISBN 0–8248–2439–3 (paper : alk. paper)
    1. Social movements—Japan—History—20th century. 2. Protest
movements—Japan—History—20th century. 3. Citizen participation.
4. Japan—Social conditions—1945– 5. Japan—History—1945– I. Title.

HN727 .S245   2001
303.48'4'09520904—dc21   00–067502

University of Hawai'i Press books are printed on acid-free
paper and meet the guidelines for permanence and
durability of the Council on Library Resources.

Designed by Trina Stahl

Printed by The Maple-Vail Book Manufacturing Group

To the loving memory of
Maye Mitsuye Oye Uemura,
for the debt that can never be repaid

CONTENTS

ACKNOWLEDGMENTS

ONE OF THE phrases I had to memorize in college was "ontogeny recapitulates phylogeny." The way I met the people who helped me on this project recapitulates the networks of personal relations among citizens' movements that are the subject of this book. The first step of this journey came years before graduate school when I worked at the Pacific-Asia Resource Center, a Japanese citizens' movement that focused on connections with people's movements abroad. When I first came to PARC in 1980, those who sat on its board and worked in its office ranged from disaffected former members of the Communist Party to New Left student activists, former anti–Vietnam war protesters, YWCA and Christian activists, independent laborites, antinuclear protesters and environmentalists concerned about Japan's export of polluting industries, economists researching the effects of Japanese businesses in Southeast Asia, volunteers working for human rights in Korea, Thailand, and the Philippines, and supporters of the Sanrizuka farmers' protest against the Narita airport.

The international emphasis of the group was unusual for Japanese movements, but its principles of organization and the way it networked with other groups were not. PARC did not insist that its members subscribe to a particular ideological perspective, preferring a commitment to action. The group saw its role as facilitating dialogue between like-minded bodies rather than overseeing or directing other movements. People belonged to different movements and organizations at the same time they were members of PARC, and they participated in each group as individuals rather than as official representatives. They recognized the autonomy of other movements and carefully guarded their own.

I am therefore deeply indebted to the staff of PARC for providing me with my first experience of postwar citizens' movements, and I wish to mention specifically, in alphabetical order, Inoue Reiko, Kaji Etsuko, Kōmoto Yōichi, Douglas Lummis, Mutō Ichiyo, Ōhashi Seiko, Okada Osamu, Robert Ricketts, Sasahara Kyōko, Watanabe Ben, Yamaka Junko, and Yoshikawa Yūichi, although there are many others.

It was through individuals at PARC that I met others who encouraged me to pursue graduate studies at Cornell University. Professors such as J. Victor Koschmann, Robert J. Smith, Sherman Cochran, and Brett deBary suffered many long years teaching me and broadening my understanding of Japan and the rest of East Asia. They were all extremely generous intellectually, and I was very fortunate that they were willing to spend many hours talking with me outside of class as well. Equally appreciated are the discussions and debates I had with my graduate student colleagues such as Guy Yasko, Joanne Izbicki, Tim Diener, Yoko Miyakawa, Gordon Matthews, Phil Gabriel, Sarah Pradt, and others to be mentioned subsequently. Several visiting professors at Cornell provided further intellectual and material support. Miriam Silverberg was one of the most dynamic and stimulating teachers I have known, and I am deeply indebted to her for the staunch support she has given me over the years. Torigoe Hiroyuki made me think about the question of mentalité and methodological approaches, and he provided me with a feel for the sixties. Matsuzawa Hiroaki's seminar forced me to think more deeply about the nature of labor, the structure of leftist thought, and concomitant issues of organization. He also provided personal information about his experiences related to the Anpo struggle. Hamashita Takeshi expressed interest in my topic from the start and gave me both encouragement and a sorely needed sounding board for my ideas.

The first day I arrived back in Japan on the Fulbright program in 1990, I was introduced to Laura Hein, who graciously shared her expertise, enthusiastically read and critiqued my work, and included me on a panel at the Association for Asian Studies conference. Through her introduction, I was also able to participate in a graduate student reading group being directed by Andrew Gordon in Tokyo while I was doing dissertation research; that group provided an opportunity to test out our ideas on one another. Laura has continued to comment astutely on my work and to prod me onward over the years.

Rikkyō (St. Paul's) University and the international student center provided an institutional base during my dissertation research. The international center arranged a get-together with the Rikkyō Ladies Club, whose members had spent time overseas and were now returning the favor by volunteering to tutor international students in Japanese. In my case, Ugawa Miyoko spent a great deal of time and effort during that year guiding me through history texts and sharing her personal experiences of the early sixties. She, in turn, introduced me to Matsumoto Seiji, who related his experiences as a subleader in the student movement and the effect that the Anpo demonstrations had on his later community activities.

Professor Kurihara Akira directed my studies at Rikkyō and provided me with access to the research materials in his office. His sense of who and what were most crucial to investigate was invaluable and saved me from many hours of aimless searching. He continually introduced me to citizen movements as well as intellectuals researching postwar history, such as professors Igarashi Akio and Tsuzuki Tsutomu, who were especially helpful in discussing citizen and student movements, the thought of Maruyama Masao, and the question of nationalism. Kurihara also introduced me to Professor Takabatake Michitoshi, an early member of the Voiceless Voices (Koe Naki Koe no Kai) whose insights are key to the analysis here. The title of this book comes from the subtitle of his article in the collection *Authority and the Individual in Japan*. Takabatake in turn arranged for me to interview Kobayashi Tomi, the mainstay of the Voiceless Voices over the decades, and she then set up a meeting with other members of the group.

Kurihara was also active in setting up networking conferences for citizens' movements, and through him I met activists such as Maruyama Hisashi and the staff of the Residents' (Movements) Library, who devote their efforts to archiving and exchanging the small-scale publications that various citizens' movements produce. Maruyama complained that there were two things he never had enough of—time and money—but he was very generous in offering his time to explain to me the significance of the 1960 Anpo protests as they related to citizen movements and the proliferation of their small-scale publications in the following decades. Kurihara and fellow Cornellian Rebecca Jennison provided introductions to Ōsawa Shinichirō, who generously shared his personal history and taught me about the problems of the student-worker alliance at the time of the Anpo protests. He was also a valuable source of information on Tsurumi Shunsuke, another key figure in the Voiceless Voices and Beheiren.

On my second research trip, in 1996, Ōsawa introduced me to Inaba Yoshikazu and Nakamura Kiyoshi from the Poets of Ōi (Ōi Shijin) circle and the office staff of the National Congress of Culture. Inaba and Nakamura were very generous with their time and their resources, but I am especially grateful for their perspective and insight as ordinary workers with extraordinary gifts. The staff of the National Congress of Culture (Kokumin Bunka Kaigi) also spent a good deal of time explaining their views on labor culture and its relation to the culture circles, and the antibases and ban-the-bomb movements of the late 1950s. They also introduced me to Nakajima Makoto, who gave a lengthy formal discourse on the relationship between labor and citizens' movements and chatted informally at equal length on personal reflections.

During my 1996 visit, my web of connections spread to include the women of the Grass Seeds (Kusa no Mi Kai), and I would like to extend special thanks to Kageyama Fumi for handling correspondence and arranging a group interview that included Imai Yaeko, Ishizaki Atsuko, Nakanishi Masako, Numabe Tamiko, and Saitō Tsuruko. These women also provided research materials and in return asked only that I distribute free copies of Japan's constitution to any Japanese students I might have in class.

Araya Makoto from the Mountain Range (Yamanami no Kai) also gave me several relevant issues of their magazine that were not available elsewhere as well as a pirate edition of a festschrift the group had compiled for Shiratori Kunio. I would also like to thank Araya for arranging another meeting with two others from the Tokyo group, Shigenaga Hiromichi and Kimura Seiya, who gave further insight into this unusual movement.

Librarians Hosoya Akio at the Japan Foundation in Tokyo and Koide Izumi at the International House of Japan were helpful in tracking down resources and also in making suggestions when the materials I sought were not part of their holdings. I would also like to thank the staff of the Science of Thought (Shisō no Kagaku) office for their help in obtaining research materials. I am deeply indebted to Sasaki Makiko, who devoted countless hours of volunteer work transcribing the interviews I conducted and made numerous suggestions about form and content.

At the University of Utah, Anand Yang constantly spurred and prodded me, and this project would not have been completed without him. An early conversation with colleague Jim Lehning prompted me to think about my subject more broadly when he remarked that I might analyze my material in terms of a genealogy of postwar social movements. The theory reading group organized by Dorothee Kocks at Utah also provided a great deal of intellectual stimulation that helped me conceptualize my own project. I am also very grateful to Anne Walthall, fellow Cornellian Susan Klein, and Utah colleagues Janet Theiss and Eric Hinderaker, who took time to read portions of this manuscript and provide me with feedback on the work.

I would also like to thank my editor, Patricia Crosby, for her patient help in editing and publishing this manuscript. I especially appreciate the efforts she made to accommodate my situation and the professionalism with which she handled things. Special thanks go to Susan Stone for her judicious copyediting. Finally, I would be remiss if I did not thank the readers for the University of Hawaiʻi Press for their comments and criticisms.

Throughout the process of writing this book, I have received generous support from the following agencies. The Fulbright program provided a dissertation research grant in 1990–1991. I am very grateful to the Tokyo staff of the Japan–United States Educational Commission, especially Matsushima Mikako, for helping with my arrangements and providing further educational and social opportunities. Cornell University's East Asia Program funded a follow-up research trip to Japan in the summer of 1992, and a Mellon Completion Fellowship from the graduate school in 1992–1993 allowed me to complete my dissertation that year. At the University of Utah, the College of Humanities Career Development Committee provided me release time from teaching in the spring of 1996 for research preparation and writing. A grant from the university's Faculty Research Committee provided release time and funding for the research I carried out in Japan in the fall of 1996. This grant allowed me to conduct numerous interviews with both activists and intellectuals who appear in this book.

Aspects of this work were presented at the 1992 Columbia University Graduate Student Conference on East Asia; the 1993 Association for Asian Studies annual conference; a University of California, Los Angeles, Center for Japanese Studies Colloquium in February 1994; and the 1997 Association for Asian Studies annual conference.

Japanese names in the text are written according to the East Asian custom of listing family name first and given name last. Japanese words appear with diacritical marks except for well-known place names such as Tokyo or Osaka. Unless otherwise noted, the author is responsible for the translations of Japanese writings and interviews, and for any mistakes appearing in those passages.

1

INTRODUCTION

C ERTAIN CRUCIAL DATES in history become wellsprings of collective memory. In Japan, one only has to mention August 15, for example, to prompt a chain of reflections about the 1945 radio broadcast announcing Japan's surrender in World War II, the transition from the old imperial system to the new postwar democracy, "Year Zero"[1] and the "good defeat"[2] that resulted in the postwar economic miracle, and the irrevocable changes that this day brought to everyone's life.

May 19 and June 15, although less ubiquitous, evoke a similar stream of memories from 1960, when hundreds of thousands of Japanese across the country took to the streets to protest the revised U.S.-Japan Security Treaty, or Anpo as it is abbreviated in Japanese. The two dates mark the peak of the demonstrations. On May 19, Prime Minister Kishi Nobusuke used police force to secure passage of the treaty, provoking a storm of popular reaction against his regime. The date, therefore, elicits memories of people rushing to defend Japan's fragile new democracy, a month of daily meetings and rallies and demonstrations, and the awe participants felt at seeing such a vast range of people who had gathered for a common purpose.

June 15, in contrast, evokes bitter memories among those who took part in the protests. That day, right-wing groups violently attacked citizen marchers, and a clash between students and riot police at the National Diet building resulted in the death of a university coed, the first fatality of the protests. Those events, in turn, prompt angry reflections on the state's suppression of dissent and the mass media's capitulation to the ruling party when they blamed the demonstrators for the violence. People recall mourning for the student at her memorial service a few days later and mourning for the movement at the Diet building as the treaty went into effect.

The chain of memories extends further to how the prime minister ultimately resigned in disgrace and the ruling party ended its high profile attempts to revive prewar structures and turned its attention to promoting economic prosperity instead. Some participants recall feeling enervated and disillusioned in the aftermath of the struggle as the movement fragmented and the general public became quiescent, while others were energized by the level of activism during the protests and entertained hopes of recapturing its potential for social and political change.

Even today, the 1960 Anpo protests are described as a major historical watershed that set the course of postwar democracy. Participants and analysts alike trace the protest movement against the Vietnam War that started in Japan in 1965, the campus revolts of the late 1960s, the environmental movements of local residents that proliferated in the 1970s, the grassroots networking of citizens' groups, and the consumer movements of the 1980s and 1990s all back to Anpo. The 1960 protests mark a paradigm shift in social movements away from ideologies of class struggle and mass movements dominated by workers and the opposition parties to smaller, diverse movements based on citizens as the main actor.

However, May 19 and June 15 were not just lines of demarcation; they also stood at the peak of an arc of protests that built up over the latter half of the 1950s and waned in the first half of the 1960s until the Vietnam War and campus unrest set off another major wave. The Anpo struggle was the culmination of years of activity among groups trying to resist the state's drive to restore prewar structures and create alternative visions for postwar democracy. Citizens' movements articulated new ideas of political subjectivity through both their organization and their social and political praxis, and these ideas had important consequences for future movements. Thus, the Anpo protests need to be seen as an extended process rather than a single, limited event.

This book seeks to present a fundamentally different perspective on the process than seen in previous analyses by examining four citizens' groups that took part in the Anpo protests—the Mountain Range, the Poets of Ōi, the Grass Seeds, and the Voiceless Voices. It looks at the origins, structures, and activities of these groups from the participants' point of view in order to comprehend better how and why these massive protests occurred. From their perspective, the protests were a struggle over the form Japanese democracy would take rather than a critique of international relations. Despite the Japanese government's image of closely managing and controlling social and political conflict, significant ruptures have continued to appear, and an analysis of these Anpo era movements provides insight into how citizens have challenged state control throughout the postwar period.

The discussion of each group focuses on a key context or aspect of the Anpo protests. The Mountain Range shows the importance of the historical context and, more specifically, the specter of World War II to the protesters. The group was formed by people who wanted to reassess their experiences of the war at a time when the ruling party seemed intent on bringing the war days back. The key struggle here was over historical memory and assuming personal responsibility for the past. The question of war responsibility has recurred down to the present, as evidenced by the textbook controversies in the 1980s, in which the Ministry of Education attempted to remove or soften references in school history texts to Japan's aggression in Asia, and the recent movement by "comfort women" to extract an official apology from the gov-

ernment for its abuse and exploitation of them during the Pacific
War. The government's failure to engage in a sincere and genuine
"settling of accounts" from World War II still affects Japan's
economic and political relations with the rest of Asia.

The Poets of Ōi illustrate a crucial organizational context
for the movements of the Anpo era. The foundations for grassroots activism lay in the face-to-face interaction and debate that
occurred in small groups known as culture circles. Circles were
egalitarian groups formed around people's own interests and
related to their daily lives. They stood at the junction between culture and politics and played an important role in people's political
socialization. The Poets of Ōi were a poetry circle at a large industrial factory, and they illustrate how workers imbued their work
with new meaning by creating their own workplace culture. The
group also shows the crucial transition that labor was undergoing
and the waning influence that a bureaucratic, ideologically based
labor movement would have in the coming years.

The Grass Seeds show the importance of new sectors and constituencies that had been politically enfranchised under the postwar constitution, especially women. The question of gender is
crucial to the development of citizens' movements and the subsequent residence-based environmental movements of the 1970s.
The heavy identification of women with the domestic sphere
affected the style and content of groups they formed or joined.
The Grass Seeds organized themselves to tackle problems of their
daily lives and thought of themselves as a kind of gossip session
around the village well (idobata kaigi), an informal circle of
friends who gather to discuss village affairs in exhaustive detail.
Thus, their political involvement grew out of everyday concerns
and the need to express themselves. The group also illustrates the
way citizens' movements dealt with the problem of free expression
by developing "mini-communications" networks to address the
limitations of the centralized mass media.

The Voiceless Voices show the importance of ideas and values
in mobilizing protesters. The Anpo protests manifested a political

philosophy based on the citizen as the subject of political engagement, and groups such as the Voiceless Voices refined this philosophy through social praxis. Citizens' movements strengthened the idea of direct democracy and shifted the emphasis from ideology to action as an organizational principle. Unlike the other groups discussed, the Voiceless Voices formed in the midst of the Anpo protests and had a fairly high profile in the press during this period. Their influence extended beyond their numbers, and their name is often mentioned as a precursor to citizen movements of the 1970s and 1980s.

The four groups examined here do not exhaust the types of groups engaged in the demonstrations. This book does not, for example, focus on the Japan Communist Party or its organs, because there is considerable material written by or about them, and they represented the old paradigm that citizens' movements were beginning to displace. The student movement is another aspect of the protests that is not analyzed in detail because it has been covered extensively in other works. Nor should the four groups covered here be considered ideal archetypes against which other groups should be measured. The Anpo protests encompassed a wide variety of movements, and other groups could certainly be used to illustrate the same aspects discussed here. Indeed, this is part of the point. The participants were a diverse collection of bodies that displayed numerous variations on the themes discussed in this book. So even though the movements discussed here were comparatively small, they were important for the themes they illustrate. As Fernando Calderón, Alejandro Piscitelli, and José Luis Reyna have written about recent social movements in Latin America, "the multiplicity of practices by the new social actors in the region—stimulating, colorful, and polyvalent—teaches us that 'small' does not amount to 'insignificant.'"[3]

The analysis presented here begins with the premise that the Anpo protests, like other large-scale movements, were not monolithic or homogeneous. The demonstrations comprised several diverse elements, some of which conflicted with others (especially the opposition parties), and although the massive marches around the Diet drew the most attention, protesters engaged in a variety of actions. They held rallies and meetings, set up debates, put on lectures, and engaged in petition drives and letter-writing campaigns, working on a variety of levels to encourage broad participation in the movement. In other words, the Anpo protests were ideologically and organizationally diverse.

Because of the cold war context and the prominence of the Japan Socialist Party and the Japan Communist Party in the protests, the Kishi administration consistently portrayed the protesters as a single-minded mob in the grip of outside Soviet agitators. Some scholars have perpetuated the claim that the protesters were controlled by the opposition parties,[4] and, indeed, the party leaders did try to enforce ideological and organizational unity. However, a deeper examination of the protests shows that the participants were conscious political actors, not an unconscious mass. When they described their actions as spontaneous, protesters were asserting that their movements were self-generated entities rather than externally formed and directed.

Therefore, accounts that focus on so-called great men of history (and all too many of these histories are gender exclusive) as the prime movers and shapers of movements and events fail to explain these events adequately. Western and Japanese scholars who concentrate on government or party leaders and party politics in their accounts of Anpo find it difficult to explain why a seemingly contained policy dispute suddenly turned into a crisis of democracy that brought hundreds of thousands of workers and citizens into the streets. While much of the writing about Anpo minutely dissects the provisions of the treaty or details the complex behind-the-scenes strategies and maneuvers by politicians, government leaders in Japan and the United States had no major disagreements over the treaty. Diplomatic history, therefore, cannot explain the size and vehemence of the protests. Instead, the protests need to be seen as a struggle by ordinary Japanese to consolidate participatory rights in both state and society rather than as a conflict between the leaders of Japan's political parties or as an international dispute between Japan and the United States.

This account, then, does not rely on official communiques or military records or party documents, but instead tries to present the participants' own voices. Over and over throughout the Anpo protests, participants said they could no longer stand by and watch silently; they felt compelled to demonstrate their will (*ishi hyōji*). The image used by student poet Kishigami Daisaku to open his lengthy poem on the Anpo protests is suggestive: "I simply strike the match in my hand as voiceless voices at my back demand to show their will."[5] All of the groups examined in this book considered their newsletters and writings to be crucial elements of a democratic social praxis, but their words have often been excluded from previous accounts of the protests. Thus, this book relies heavily on the groups' own publications, participant-observer accounts, and interviews with members.

Finally, this analysis ties the philosophies and organizational characteristics of Anpo era movements to others that developed in later decades, often referred to as new social movements. Movement participants frequently described their groups as underground streams that came together during the Anpo protests in a giant whirlpool or vortex that engulfed the Diet but then afterward quietly slipped below the surface, where they joined other streams later on. The progressive journal *Science of Thought (Shisō no kagaku)* even carried a column titled "Japan's Underground Streams" (Nihon no chikasui) dedicated to providing information on the activities of various small citizens' movements. The imagery suggests a Daoist respect for water's power while also implying a flexible, pliable form that adapts to the land's contours as it flows along. The analogy implies that these movements think of themselves as small grassroots groups with fluid organization and fluctuating memberships that alternate between periods of high and low activity. The streams are not confined within the banks of artificial channels, forced to adhere to a particular ideological position. They freely link up with other streams according to mutual concerns and feed new streams of activity. The groups see themselves as having left legacies for the new social movements in terms of shared characteristics, especially those of personal autonomy and the "autonomy of struggle."[6] In light of this perceived connection, it is useful to review recent social movement theory in evaluating the historical continuities and differences between the earlier progenitors and the movements that surfaced in the subsequent waves of protest in Japan.

Theoretical Considerations

MANY THEORISTS acknowledge the difficulty of defining the characteristics of new social movements. There are two major reasons for this. One is the wide range of groups that are placed in the category and the extreme diversity of issues around which they have formed.[7] The variety of issues and groups is even taken as a defining characteristic that distinguishes new social movements from previous ones. This assumption of diversity, or, to put it another way, the more specific, specialized focus of each group, may have led theorists to emphasize the form these groups take more than the content of their philosophies. They describe organization, membership, modes of collective activities, and a general antiestablishment disposition.

However, as Alan Scott points out, using organizational form as the major criterion for distinguishing new social movements is problematic because those groups display a broad range of forms, which, moreover, often change over time.[8] Some groups that are categorized as new social movements may not even see themselves as "new." They may not be oppositional but may advocate the defense of parts of the social or political order.[9] Given the tendency to define social movements as antiestablishment, the question arises as to whether or not a right-wing group can legitimately be considered a new social movement. Certainly some of the usual organizational characteristics could be applied to conservative or reactionary groups. This is why it is necessary to examine the values that each group promotes through its organization and actions.

The other difficulty in defining such movements is that the major paradigm in new social movement theory has shifted over the past three decades, so the theories themselves must be historicized. New social movement theory was prompted by a sense that in the late 1960s and 1970s protest movements had become very different from previous ones based on socialist ideologies. These new groups were suspicious of united front protest movements led by left-wing vanguard political parties that insisted on ideological conformity. The appearance of new social movements has been taken as an indication that, as Stuart Hall writes, "Socialist Man with one mind, one set of interests, one project, is dead. And good riddance."[10] In the case of Japan, Kurihara Akira sees the emergence of new social movements in the 1960s as a rejection of "old paradigm" social movements that identified the main actor or subject as the proletariat, engaged in struggle dichotomized as progressive (or left-wing) versus conservative (or right-wing), and that were organizationally based on Marxist-oriented political parties.[11]

The new social movements, by contrast, identify different subjects—whether citizens, local residents, or people who suffer discrimination—and reject the ideological orientation of "old" movements in forming their own autonomous groups. As they did in Europe and North America, new social movements in Japan developed around a plethora of issues, but residence-based environmentalist movements of the late 1960s and 1970s are most often cited as typical examples. These residents' movements arose in response to the contradictions of Japan's state-directed rapid economic growth and in response to the state's attempt to establish a "managed society" (*kanri shakai*), integrating systems of production and information and exerting central control over them.

New social movement theory, then, needs to be approached historically as a multivalenced response to both Marxism and functionalism (which takes a positivist, objectivist approach and focuses on institutionalized relations), one that may have neo-Marxist or postmodern as well as neoconservative impulses. Carol McClurg Mueller presents a succinct, useful intellectual history of new social movement theory.[12] Her description provides a framework for situating some notable works on social movements in Asia and places the analysis of this book in perspective.

Mueller notes that the grievance model was the key paradigm in social movement theory up to the 1970s. This model sees protest movements as arising mainly from severe deprivation and the accumulated grievances of those who suffer from major structural changes in society but lack channels for expressing their discontent or addressing their problems. Although theorists were divided as to the origins of the grievances, they generally stressed mentality and social psychology in explaining movements.

The resource mobilization paradigm developed in response to the grievance model and emphasized the acquisition of material resources and political opportunity to explain why some movements developed with relatively light grievances while other groups with seemingly much greater reason to protest did not. This theoretical approach quickly came to dominate the academic literature on social movements during the 1970s and early '80s,[13] and it was applied in research on Japan as well. Krauss and Simcock wrote their analysis of resident-based environmental movements in the heyday of resource mobilization theory, and they explicitly emphasize that theory as a corrective to the grievance model.[14] The residents' movements often used existing local organizations and government connections, so they were not seriously alienated from their communities, and their constituencies cut across class lines and status boundaries.

Samual Popkin's 1979 book *The Rational Peasant* attempted to apply these notions of resource mobilization and rational choice to the case of peasant protests in Vietnam. Popkin was responding specifically to James Scott's *Moral Economy of the Peasant*, which Popkin casts as a variation on the grievance model. Popkin asserts that peasants make individual, rational choices (albeit in the context of their immediate families) to maximize their positions, and they base the decision on whether or not to join a protest movement or revolt on this calculation.[15] He presents this theory as an explanation of why areas with more "modern" (i.e., capitalist) forms of agriculture were the sites of revolt rather than places with much more severe conditions of exploitation and deprivation, and therefore supposedly greater grievances. That is, peasants decide that they can better maximize their profits in areas with more "modern" agriculture than in traditional areas with much more limited growth potential.

The problem with Popkin's analysis was that it misrepresented Scott's argument, which although written before Popkin's book actually constituted a response to problems with the resource mobilization paradigm. Scott's analysis begins from the position of the peasant embedded within the cultural context of the village and the historical context of colonialism's disruption of traditional social arrangements. His hypothesis of peasants' "subsistence ethic" is used to show why peasants may prefer traditional landlord arrangements over the more "modern" capitalistic ones that came with the colonial period. That is, peasants may prefer an admittedly exploitative situation over one that potentially brings greater profits because the former provides a stable livelihood at or above subsistence level and offers relief through community relationships when peasants dip below subsistence level.[16]

Scott's work presaged the critiques of the resource mobilization paradigm that developed in the 1980s by emphasizing the social embeddedness of the peasants. Popkin's characterization of Southeast Asian peasants shows a tendency to presume that the actor in social movements is a universal but atomized, self-interested individual without giving sufficient weight to the variety of social networks and cultural contexts in which a person is embedded. Feminists, for example, quickly pointed out that resource mobilization theory presumed the social actor to be male and that if one presumed a mother, that is, a woman with a particular social relation, as the actor, the analysis would differ greatly. In addition to gender, identities and networks of race and ethnicity, nationality, class, and religion all affect the notions of grievances one has and choices one can make.[17] Further, "resource mobilization theory, as originally conceived, self-consciously minimized the role of ideas and beliefs and their elaboration. Like grievances, the cultural configurations that legitimate and make collective action meaningful were taken as givens."[18]

Identity-centered theories that "emphasize the processes by which social actors constitute collective identities as a means to create democratic spaces for more autonomous action" quickly became dominant in social movement theory ouside of North America and England.[19] For example, Latin American scholarship in the 1980s was so heavily weighted toward a focus on identity that the concerns of the resource mobilization approach, such as concrete practices and resource constraints, were neglected.[20] Being outside of the North American context made the presumptions of the social actor in the resource mobilization paradigm clear to the Latin Americanists, and America- or Eurocentrism is a problem that sociologists, anthropologists, and political scientists working on non-Western regions have had to tackle.

For example, Robin LeBlanc criticizes the application of new social movement theory to a consumer cooperative, because it obscures the distinctive nature of the Japanese housewives' movements she investigates and does not pay enough attention to how members of those movements perceive their own identities.[21] The groups, like their European or American counterparts, are constituted almost entirely of women with "concerns for peace, a clean environment, and a greater degree of political and economic self-determination."[22] However, LeBlanc considers the particular images associated with housewives in the Japanese context to be crucial to their political positions and strategies. Although housewives are acutely aware that their image of being political amateurs often results in exclusion from the political process, the image can be useful in the public political sphere, because women are seen as less corrupt than men, without vested interests in the system. Housewives are seen as more altruistic because Japanese women are identified with being caregivers in the domestic sphere.

Jeffrey Broadbent also finds resource mobilization theory inadequate in explaining the development of environmental protest movements in Japan. In the cases he examined, he says, "new material resources did not play an important role in sparking protest mobilization" nor did new political opportunities account for the protests.[23] He disputes the assumption of Western theories that collective action in Japan arises when atomized individuals come together in a liberal, pluralist political system, arguing that Japanese society has not been atomized, and the persistence of old collective organizations has led to a different process of movement formation.[24] In emphasizing particular social and cultural contexts, Broadbent eventually suggests that social movements cannot be accounted for with a fixed general theory. "Rather, they are exceedingly contingent upon the ontological quality of the structure of power, which they take shape within and against."[25]

Nancy Abelmann takes a somewhat different approach in her use of social movement theory to inform her ethnography of the Koch'ang Tenant Farmers Movement in South Korea in the late 1980s. Drawing from Alberto Melucci, Alain Touraine, and Arturo Escobar, Abelmann stresses identity formation without making an explicit critique of resource mobilization theory. She sees social movements as networks, rather than as unitary entities with a single mind, engaged in a discursive process of self-production. That is, social movements interact, negotiate, and conflict with social, political, economic, cultural, and historical contexts. Abelmann is especially concerned with the context of historicity and points to the implicitly Eurocentric assumption that self-producing, self-aware movements are possible only in a postindustrial society.[26] In Touraine's formulation, the Koch'ang movement could not be a new social movement, because South Korea had not achieved the same stage of development as Europe. Abelmann thus agrees with "Escobar's corrective that historicities are multiple and that they emerge in heterogeneous idioms and metaphors in different historical moments and cultural milieus."[27]

The question of multiple historicities is important to the formation and activities of the groups examined in this book. Protests also imply a struggle over histories and who will be the custodians of the past, in Carol Gluck's words.[28] In order for movements to construct collective identities, they must historicize their situation.

Works by LeBlanc, Broadbent, and Abelmann reflect a recent reconsideration of the resource mobilization paradigm as applied to East Asia that parallels a shift in theoretical emphasis among commentators on Western movements, as Mueller notes. Mueller sees these reconsiderations as centering on three elements: "a reconceptualization of the actor, the extension of the central role of micromobilization in face-to-face interaction within a variety of group contexts, and the specification of meaning generating oppositional elements within sociopolitical cultures at varying levels of temporal extensity, formality, and instrumental appropriation."[29] Theorists have reasserted the importance of values and philosophies in producing movements and have turned their attention to fairly circumscribed "collective action frames" that focus on the concerns of daily life and take personal contacts as the key to forming groups and identities. This book also takes these as major focal points and like Abelmann sees the contest over historicities as crucial to understanding the Anpo era movements.

2

UNDERCURRENTS OF CITIZEN PROTEST

"1960 was a year of political turmoil. It was the year of Anpo."

Kōsai Yutaka, *The Era of High-Speed Growth*

CONTEMPORARY JAPAN FROM the 1970s has often been touted as an efficient, harmonious society with a consensual political system that featured a cozy relationship between business and government. This generally placid image of postwar society, however, ignores powerful undercurrents that challenged the state's visions for Japan from the 1950s onward. Present-day society was born from sharp contention between the government and its citizens, and this contention hit its first peak in 1960. The most prominent event in which these conflicts played themselves out was the protest against the renewal of the revised U.S.-Japan Security Treaty (Anpo).

The original treaty had been signed in conjunction with the San Francisco Peace Treaty on September 8, 1951, as a trade-off for ending the occupation of Japan. Its five articles provided for U.S. military bases in Japan and the continued presence of American troops as well as the right of the United States to intervene in internal disturbances. It also required Japan to receive U.S. consent before granting any third party military bases and privileges, and stipulated that the treaty could not be terminated without mutual consent. Japan also developed its postwar military, the Self-Defense Forces, under the auspices of the Security Treaty despite its legal contradictions with the constitution.[1] The threat of remilitarization, the restrictions the treaty imposed on Japan's sovereignty, and the various social problems surrounding the U.S. military bases, especially with regard to their extraterritoriality, all served to make Anpo unpopular even with the revisions that the conservative government proposed. Nevertheless, Prime Minister Kishi Nobusuke pushed for ratification of the revised treaty in order to cement relations with America. He vastly underestimated the depth of the opposition to the treaty and his administration.

From the spring of 1959 to the fall of 1960, an estimated sixteen million Japanese engaged in protests against the Security Treaty. Over the course of the opposition, more than ten million people signed petitions against the treaty's renewal, some six million laborers engaged in sympathy strikes, and hundreds of thousands of citizens marched in the streets of Tokyo and other major cities around the country.[2]

Political activity reached a crescendo in May and June of 1960 after Kishi mobilized the police on May 19 to expel opposition party members from the parliament and forcibly ratify the treaty, turning a limited diplomatic controversy into a general crisis of democracy. Protesters saw the ratification of the Security Treaty as the culmination of years of government initiatives to reverse the democratic reforms of the Allied Occupation and revive prewar fascist institutions. Thus, the movement against Anpo included, among others, those who fought the ruling party's efforts to revise the constitution, especially Article 9 renouncing war and military forces; those who opposed the state's drive to exert greater centralized control over the educational system; those who struggled against the government's efforts to undermine the power of organized labor; and those who rejected Kishi's proposed bill to expand the powers of the police. These people were joined by peace activists opposing nuclear weapons, local residents adversely affected by the military bases, associations promoting the normalization of relations with China and Korea, labor unions, women's groups, student organizations, merchant associations, Christian groups, modern theater troupes and artists, progressive public intellectuals, minority groups who sought an end to legal and social discrimination, and other citizen movements.[3] Anpo was the umbrella under which this broad range of concerns were gathered.

The Anpo protests have been called the most important postwar confrontation between democratic forces and traditional paternalism in Japanese politics.[4] Ishida Takeshi and Ellis Krauss have referred to them as "the high water mark for the student movement and the left in general, who were never to reach the same level of popular support again."[5] Although the opposition failed to get the treaty rescinded, the massive protests forced the government to cancel President Eisenhower's state visit to Japan and caused Kishi to resign as prime minister. Historian Ienaga Saburō has noted that it was one of the few instances in modern Japanese history where a popular movement directly toppled an authoritarian regime.[6] In the long run, the protests forced the ruling Liberal Democratic Party to give up the confrontational tactics it had employed in trying to resuscitate the prewar system and to acknowledge the overwhelming sentiment for retaining the reforms of the Occupation era. The new prime minister, Ikeda Hayato, adopted a low-key political profile that emphasized economic programs rather than ideological rhetoric, a stance that the Liberal Democratic Party maintained for decades to come.

The protests also changed the nature of the political opposition, which began to fragment into more specialized independent interests as groups reevaluated the conceptual basis for their actions. The influence of the Japan Socialist Party and the Japan Communist Party declined after parallel defeats in 1960 of the Anpo movement and the coal miners' strike at Miike in Kyushu, the most protracted strike in postwar history. The labor federations affiliated with the opposition parties also lost militancy and strength, especially after the Miike strike failed to wrest any major concessions from the Mitsui mine owners. The opposition's united front strategy proved inadequate in the Anpo struggle, and partici-pants questioned the ideological orthodoxy that the two parties tried to impose on the movement despite key differences among the participating groups. Student organizations in particular chafed under Socialist and Communist party directives and challenged the parties' claim to being the revolutionary vanguard. Large num-bers of student activists eventually severed their ties to the parties and formed new alliances, giving rise to the New Left. In general, the mass participation in the Anpo protests represented a para-digm shift away from the idea of a unified class-based struggle in which the workers were considered the primary actors to a model of political engagement through loose, horizontal networks of autonomous local movements in which citizens were the principal subjects.[7]

Many commentators have also ascribed broad social signifi-cance to the upheavals of 1960 that went beyond the realm of partisan politics. Some saw the protests as the pivotal moment in turning away from the problems of the prewar system and war-time devastation toward the "bright life" (akarui seikatsu) of the postwar economic miracle. Anpo stands roughly midway between the government's 1956 declaration that the postwar era was over, since economic production had surpassed prewar levels,[8] and the early achievement of Ikeda's plan to double people's income by the end of the 1960s. Particularly during the last half of the 1950s, the pace of industrialization quickened, spurring major migra-tions of people from rural to urban areas and expanding the influence of mass communications. According to mass society theorist Matsushita Keiichi, these processes atomized and leveled old forms of community and prompted new demands for inclusion and participatory rights.[9] Masumi and Scalapino hold that the Anpo protests opened up possibilities for the broad-scale democ-ratization of society because, given the essentially closed nature of the political process, protesters were forced to operate outside of parliamentary channels and create variant theories of democracy.[10] Kōsai Yutaka considers the Anpo and Miike protests to be inevitable conflicts that Japan had to endure in order to become an "advanced" country. The protests were "rites of passage in Japan's period of modernization in the 1960s; they were an exorcism for that purpose, a rite of purification."[11] This, he claims, enabled Japan to purge statism and class ideology from the emergent middle-class society so it could converge with its American counterpart.

Such characterizations, however, represent the protesters and the Japanese public in general as being swept along by the tide of the times rather than as self-conscious actors trying to realize alternate visions of society. This perception is often reinforced by some of the photographs and TV broadcasts of the demonstrations, especially those around the Diet building in Tokyo. In order to convey the scale of the protests, which sometimes involved hundreds of thousands of protesters, photographers and camera crews took wide-angle aerial shots from helicopters and other elevated sites. The very perspective of these images tends to lump all of the demonstrators together and portray them as an untamed force of nature, a thunderstorm or volcanic eruption of outrage at the government. In fact, the government, mass media, and protesters themselves commonly referred to the waves of demonstrators swirling around the parliament as a whirlpool or vortex (*uzumaki*), pulling people centripetally to the site with irresistible force.

Kishi and his administration took this "god's eye" view in order to dismiss the opposition and assert their own position. They disparaged the protests as "riots" and characterized the demonstrators as a violent, irrational "mob." State officials claimed that the protests were the result of an international communist conspiracy and implied that the participants were unwittingly duped and manipulated by the Japan Communist Party and Moscow.[12] Kishi further claimed that the majority of Japanese supported him, and, therefore, he would listen only to the "voiceless voices," or "silent majority," rather than the "vocal minority" calling for his resignation. Kishi's level of rhetoric not only reflected the cold war atmosphere but was also an attempt to retain American support despite his overwhelming unpopularity. The Eisenhower administration and the American press tended to cast the protests in the same light. When Eisenhower's press secretary, James Hagerty, had his car blockaded and jostled by student protesters on his arrival in Japan on June 10, he implied that it was the work of foreign agents. The *New York Times* editorialized on June 13, "In point of fact, the real authors of these demonstrations have been hard-core Communists and Left-Wing Socialists mouthing ultra-Communist slogans who are able to manipulate student and labor organizations for their revolutionary purposes."[13]

The leaders of the Communist and Socialist parties were not entirely averse to being portrayed as the ones responsible for the mass uprising. This portrayal ascribed greater power and influence to them than they could otherwise claim. The party leaders certainly tried to coordinate and direct the disparate elements of the protests and to unify their ideological perspective, believing that a united front strategy would gain wider support and exert greater pressure on the government. However, despite their attempts to cast the protesters as a unified mass lining up behind the revolutionary vanguard, the bulk of the protesters did not adhere to Marxist ideology, and even those who did, like some student groups, refused to bow to the party line when the leadership attempted to suppress contrary viewpoints.

The perspective at street level was considerably more complex than the aerial shots. Photographs taken from this angle tended to catalog the wide variety of groups involved in the protests. Newspapers and weekly magazines carried pictures of "parasol parades" by housewives, noodle-shop owners carrying their shop curtains to identify themselves, artists and actors, farmers hoisting straw mat banners (*mushirobata*) traditionally used to display demands in peasant uprisings, laborers in work uniforms marching under their union flags, and so on.[14] This human-scale perspective revealed the demonstrators as conscious actors with diverse points of view rather than as an elemental, irrational force. The vortex encircling the Diet comprised countless smaller movements that had decided to join the cause. Citizen movement activists often described their small-scale movements as underground streams (*chikasui* or *fukuryūsui*) that usually flowed unobtrusively through daily life, only to well up to the surface and merge with other streams at critical junctures such as the Anpo protests. Participants in these movements saw themselves as engaged in a deliberate process of reshaping their political subjectivity and transforming democratic praxis in Japan.

Paradoxically, citizen groups often referred to their own participation in the Anpo protests as "spontaneous" (*jihatsuteki*), but this self-ascription was meant to denote that they were self-motivated rather than impulsive or instinctual. They were pointing to their autonomy by claiming "spontaneous or natural generation," the definition of the compound term "*shizen hassei,*" from which the word "*jihatsu*" was derived. These citizens' movements took pains to show that they had developed independently rather than by executive design of the Japan Communist Party or the Japan Socialist Party. They also wanted to distinguish themselves from organizations whose leadership committed all members of the group to engage in activities without consulting them beforehand (*gurumi soshiki*). Thus, they used the word "spontaneous" to indicate that their political engagement arose from each individual's own volition and concerns.

It was the influx of ordinary citizens and their movements that accounted for the sudden, enormous increase in the size of the demonstrations after May 19. Citizen participation was the driving force behind the opposition to the treaty, but most English-language accounts do not analyze this distinctive feature of the protests or differentiate the various strains of participating citizen movements. They tend to focus on party politics and key leaders or on the relationship between Japan and the United States. However, the Anpo protests were more important for their social consequences than for their diplomatic implications. They were the peak in a long arc of debates over redefining the body politic and the nature of social relations within the "imagined community" of Japan, not a brief event that began and ended with an outburst of street demonstrations.

After the protests ended, many citizens' movements continued their activities at a more unobtrusive local level, returning to their primary concerns or shifting their focus to other relevant issues. Some participants moved on to other organizations, bringing with them ideas and strategies from their previous groups. The 1960 Anpo movements thus influenced environmental and social movements decades later.

The image of several underground streams converging to create a ground swell at certain historical junctures also points to a more general approach to examining how large-scale movements of social protest develop. Such movements are never unitary in character but comprise diverse elements that are able to establish equivalences between their various subject positions in order to work together.[15] Moreover, while these movements appear to burst forth out of nowhere, they are the culmination of long-standing efforts at the community level that preceded the more visible mass events.

Two other major protests in contemporary Asia have also shown this pattern—the People's Power movement in the Philippines that ousted longtime dictator Ferdinand Marcos at the end of February 1986 and the South Korean movement for democratization in 1987 that pressured Chun Doo Hwan to step down as president and hold the first direct elections for the office. The mass protests at the Presidential Palace and other places in Manila were more than an emotional outburst against Marcos' election fraud in the Snap Election of February 7 or his refusal to step down from the presidency even though he lacked a popular mandate. The Filipinos were responding to the accumulated weight of history, and the groundwork for the protests had been laid over decades of grassroots organizing throughout various sectors of society.[16] Similarly, the outbreak of huge protests across South Korea in June of 1987 cannot be comprehended without looking at the various types of movements that came together and examining their extended histories. A broad range of long-standing religious, civil, human rights, academic, farmer, labor and student groups had formed a loosely organized national coalition a few months earlier in order to press for an end to the military dictatorship and promote constitutional reform and direct presidential elections. As with the Anpo protests, the participation of middle-class citizens was an important key to the effectiveness of both of these movements, and while an authoritarian right-wing dictator was a major target of the protests in both the Philippines and Korea, the movements also aimed at broader transformations of their closed political systems. In both of these cases, "we are confronted with the emergence of a plurality of subjects, whose forms of constitution and diversity it is only possible to think if we relinquish the category of 'subject' as a unified and unifying essence."[17]

Citizen Participation

FOUR FACTORS that have not received enough attention in the past should be highlighted to account for the level of citizen participation in the Anpo protests. First of all, the specter of World War II was still prominent in people's minds. People remained acutely aware of the costs of war and were highly sensitive to the threat of wartime revivals. Second, new channels for involvement had arisen during the 1950s that helped socialize people in political activities. Many of the participants came out of the circle movements, which were small, grassroots bodies organized at people's place of work or residence and often centered on cultural activities. Such groups continued to spring up after the Anpo protests but were increasingly based on place of residence and oriented toward environmental concerns. The third major factor in the strength of citizens' movements was the increasing presence of women. Postwar political changes afforded women new opportunities for involvement in social movements. The development of consumer society during the late 1950s meant that women's everyday domestic concerns also had political implications. A fourth factor was the development of a citizen ethos that placed the citizen rather than the proletariat as the subject or agent of historical change. The development of this ethos was intimately related to the debates over subjectivity that had taken place among intellectuals on the left during the early 1950s, but citizen activists also sought to revamp their theories according to actual practice within their circles and other social movements.

The Specter of World War II

IN 1960, the Japanese public was still very conscious of World War II and the disastrous effects it had on their country. Treaty negotiations for Anpo began less than fifteen years after Japan's defeat, less than a decade after the Occupation and the Korean War had ended and less than five years after the government had declared that the postwar era had ended. Numerous movements helped maintain an ongoing dialogue about the war, such as the reading groups that looked at letters that soldiers had written as they were being sent off to die in battle.[18] Throughout the 1950s, people continued to grapple with the issues of survivors' guilt, personal accountability, and war responsibility, and to debate how to avoid repeating the same mistakes that led to war.

Moreover, living reminders of the prewar fascist system continued not only to survive but to dominate politics and society. Kishi was only the most visible symbol of this. He had been an elite government bureaucrat during the war and was indicted as a Class A war criminal by the Far East Military Tribunal at the beginning of the Occupation. However, during the the two-year trial, SCAP (Supreme Commander of the Allied Powers) "reversed course" owing to increasing cold war tensions. Occupation officials became more concerned with suppressing supposed Communist influences than with purging wartime officials, and so two days after seven of the most high profile Class A war criminals were executed, Kishi was released along with eighteen others in the 1948 Christmas amnesty.

Through personal connections and backroom dealings, Kishi became the head of the Liberal Democratic Party, which formed in 1955 by merging two conservative prewar parties that had been renamed after World War II. In 1957, he rose to the office of prime minister without having to stand for popular election. Despite his claims of having transformed himself into a true democrat, Kishi's program clearly aimed at rescinding the postwar reforms and strengthening the power of the state over the citizens. He felt that the ratification of the revised Security Treaty would be the crowning touch to his administration, because the new treaty would remove provisions that the government felt violated Japan's sovereignty and would make the relationship between America and Japan more equal. The treaty also committed Japan firmly to the Western bloc in the cold war and raised the specter of war by obligating Japan to support the United States militarily even in conflicts where Japan had no direct interest or involvement. The United States retained its rights to station troops and maintain military bases in Japan, which were key outposts for its China containment strategy.

It was, however, the manner in which the treaty was ratified that did the most to raise fears of a fascist revival. When Kishi went to Washington in January of 1960 to initial the treaty agreement, he was confident that he could easily get it passed in the parliament even though a broad coalition called the People's Council to Stop the Revised Security Treaty (Anpo Kaitei Soshi Kokumin Kaigi) had been building a ground swell of opinion against the treaty for nearly ten months. The opposition parties managed to bottle up the treaty in committee, and by the spring, Kishi was losing patience. He had already extended an invitation to President Eisenhower for a state visit in June, during which he intended to present the ratified treaty as a gift. If he used the constitutional stipulation that bills or treaties could "automatically" take force without Upper House approval one month after being passed by the Lower House, provided that the Diet was still in session,[19] then Kishi would have to get the treaty ratified by May 19 to meet his schedule.

As that date approached, it seemed that Kishi would fail in his attempt. On the evening of the nineteenth, Japan Socialist Party members staged a sit-in in the halls of the Diet to prevent the Lower House Speaker from going to the Lower House chambers and extending the legislative session at the last minute. But since Kishi had vowed to ratify the pact at all costs, he called in the police to haul out all of the opposition party representatives physically and escort House Speaker Kiyose Ichirō, another official who had been indicted as a war criminal and then received amnesty, into the chambers. The old man was jostled about, and amidst all the shouting few people in the chambers could actually hear him call for a fifty-day extension of the Diet session. However, it was clear what he wanted, and just a few minutes past midnight, the Lower House reconvened and in the absence of any opposition members took just fifteen minutes to approve the treaty by voice vote.[20] Following hard on the heels of Kishi's attempt to increase the powers of the police, the forcible ratification suddenly made palpable the threat of a return to the state's violent oppression and shifted the focus of the protests. The key issue now was choosing between democracy or dictatorship, as the noted China scholar Takeuchi Yoshimi put it when he asserted that "until the dictatorship is overthrown, it is useless to argue about whether one opposes or supports the Anpo treaty."[21]

New Modes of Participation

A SECOND reason that so many citizens took to the streets in protest was that groundwork for grassroots political activism had already been laid by various circle movements that had formed in the 1950s. These were small, informal, voluntary organizations whose face-to-face contact may have been their most salient characteristic.[22] Scholars and activists have found precedents for these postwar movements in premodern social organs such as communal gossip sessions around the village well (*idobata kaigi*), village youth groups, mutual aid societies, and pilgrimage groups.[23] One Kyushu movement described itself and other circles as a transitional form between "the fragments of the old community that were broken apart by capitalism" and newly emerging community organs.[24] Therefore, they asserted that the proliferation of circles in the 1950s was not necessarily evidence of how much "progress" Japan had made toward modernity or how "healthy" its society was. Circles adapted older egalitarian forms to counteract the centralized hierarchies that still remained from the prewar period. Unlike political parties, which were created by elite executives with long-term objectives and platforms, they sprang up at the local level outside of official channels and organized themselves around people's common interests.

These grassroots movements encompassed a wide range of activities. Some were communal self-help societies that formed to combat the physical deprivation of the immediate postwar period. Numerous study circles sprang up around the country to read works on subjects that had been officially discouraged or restricted during the war, and students formed their own study circles as a supplement or alternative to the education they were getting at school. Another popular trend was circles devoted to recording what had happened in ordinary people's lives (*seikatsu kiroku*), whether through self-reflective writings or third-party transcriptions of conversations (*kikigaki*).[25]

Circles were perhaps most often organized around some cultural activity such as singing choral works or folksongs, performing drama, dancing, producing art or learning art appreciation, writing poetry, and so on. Pursuits such as hiking and nature clubs were also common. These groups often sprang up at people's place of work, owing in part to the efforts of Japan Communist Party organizers who attempted to raise the political consciousness of the laborers and build mass organizations that could be mobilized for political action. Party organizers who formed circles to document people's lives were supposed to guide members to write about their exploitation as members of the proletariat in order to motivate them to action.[26] Communist leaders considered such circles to be cells of the party, and in the last half of the 1950s they tried to incorporate these movements into mass organizations under their leadership. The Japan Socialist Party and their labor federation Sōhyō also formed their own alliance of circles called the National Congress of Culture (Kokumin Bunka Kaigi). However, as the choral (utagoe) movement showed, even circles that had been organized by the Communist Party did not necessarily consider themselves to be communist cells and often did not follow the central leadership's policies and directives.

Such movements wanted a greater degree of local autonomy, and they held a fundamentally different idea of labor from Communist Party ideologues, most of whom could only conceive of labor in terms of suffering. The party line, represented by Kurahara Korehito's notion of social realism in literature, saw the cultural pursuits of these circles simply as a means of making the proletariat comprehend the conditions of their class exploitation and alienation.[27] However, the workers themselves did not perceive their labor entirely negatively even while acknowledging the conditions of their exploitation. Work itself had intrinsic value, and their circle activities were not merely leisure-time escape from the drudgery of their jobs. Rather, the circles were an extension of their work, a means of expressing the value of their jobs and enriching their relations with fellow workers. Therefore, they pursued the self-expressive activities of their circles for their own sake.

They were also reluctant to comply with party demands for self-sacrifice, which smacked of the prewar state's slogan "messhi hōkō," which implied sacrificing oneself physically and spiritually for the sake of the nation as embodied in the emperor. Within the context of the postwar Occupation, the pursuit of individual interests gained a stronger appeal. What distinguished circles from other social relations was that people created and maintained them on the basis of common personal interests. The impact of circle movements on the Anpo protests, then, was not that the established opposition parties could mobilize protesters through their control of the mass organs to which large numbers of circles belonged. Instead, the proliferation of these movements indicates the degree to which self-motivated grassroots organizations could become actively engaged in the political realm.

New Constituencies

NOT ONLY did new types of social movements appear in the early postwar years, but certain key constituencies that previously had been excluded from politics gained a significant presence. Organized labor was one such constituency, but one group that has not received enough attention in this context is women. As more and more citizens' movements sprang up, women came to play an increasingly prominent role in them so that by the 1970s gender was often considered a defining characteristic of these groups. Whereas the organized labor movement was seen as basically male, in part owing to discriminatory employment structures, citizens' movements were increasingly identified with residential issues, in which women generally had a greater stake.

Women were a newly enfranchised political constituency in postwar Japan, having been denied the vote under the prewar system and discouraged from any public political presence. Women's rights were severely constrained under the prewar Civil Code, and during the war years the state promoted the ideology that a woman's place was in the home as a "good wife, wise mother" (ryōsai kenbo). The new postwar constitution not only gave women the right to vote, but also revamped the Civil Code to provide them rights within the family, such as the right to inherit property, and labor protection, such as maternity leave.[28] These rights helped legitimate their efforts to carve out social spaces in which to voice their concerns.

Women's postwar activism began with reassessing their wartime experiences, often in circles devoted to recording their lives. As Tsurumi Kazuko noted, for women in particular, "speaking out in public about their sufferings during the war is a first step towards the redefinition of their roles."[29] Their reflections were frequently self-critical regarding their acceptance of the "good wife, wise mother" ideology and their willingness to send off their husbands and sons to die in the war. Women who became involved in these movements felt that their task was to make sure that such things never happened again.

One avenue of political engagement that was relatively comfortable and socially acceptable for women was consumer issues. Because they continued to be heavily identified with the domestic sphere, consumer concerns were a key motivation in getting women involved. The most prominent example in the 1950s was the development of the ban-the-bomb movement in Japan, in which housewives played a crucial role.

Ironically, the mass movement against nuclear weapons was sparked more by the March 1, 1954, H-bomb test that the United States conducted on Bikini atoll than by the Hiroshima and Nagasaki bombings at the end of World War II. SCAP censorship laws had both forbidden publication of the medical effects of the bombings and prohibited any public criticism of U.S. nuclear strategy, and the atomic bomb victims (*hibakusha*) themselves were often ostracized or sequestered by their families, so the peace movement was severely restricted until the end of the Occupation. However, by the time of the Bravo test blast, numerous publications about Hiroshima and Nagasaki had built up a strong public awareness of the issue. When the H-bomb was detonated, a Japanese tuna fishing boat, the *Daigo Fukuryū Maru,* had wandered into the blast perimeter, and a short time later radioactive fallout rained down on the crew and cargo. The crew suffered the effects of radiation sickness and were hospitalized when the boat returned to Japan, but the tuna it brought back found its way into the markets of Tokyo, Osaka, and other cities, and had to be recalled. Worries over irradiated fish and the six test blasts that the United States carried out over the next two and a half months prompted several housewives' organizations to issue statements and begin petition drives calling for an end to nuclear weapons testing. Con-

sumer concerns thus became a means for women to become politically engaged.

The middle-class housewives of Suginami Ward are often credited with starting the petition drive that led to the creation of the
Council Against the A- and H-Bombs, and the start of annual
August commemorations of Hiroshima and Nagasaki from 1955.
In fact, movements had sprung up independently throughout different regions of the country, and the Suginami women's role was
to help link these groups together into a nationwide movement.[30]
Many of the women who later joined the protests to oppose Anpo
had come out of the peace movement, and at the time the Japanese government made it clear that because of the "special relationship" it had with the United States through the Mutual Security
Treaty, it would not object to the nuclear testing.[31]

Another major avenue for women's political participation was
related to educational issues. Overseeing children's education was
(and still is) considered to be primarily the mother's rather than
the father's responsibility, and so women greatly outnumbered
men in groups like the Parent-Teacher Association. These groups
became venues for debating current issues relevant to their children's education, such as the government's efforts to reassert centralized control over the educational system by curtailing the
autonomy of local school boards and demanding state certifica-
tion and approval of all teachers, textbooks, and curricula. Many
women were especially troubled by the government's attempts to
reintroduce ethics (*shūshin*) classes, which had been used during
the war to preach the ideology of the Imperial Way. Therefore,
what spurred women's political activism was a desire not only to
protect the gains they had made in the postwar political system
but to ensure that such gains would be passed on to their children.

A New Citizen Ethos

A FOURTH factor in citizen participation in the Anpo protests
was the continuing development of the notion of the citizen subject and a political ethos in which an enlightened citizenry en-

gaged in civic action for the public welfare. At the time of the protests, the term "citizen" (*shimin*) still sounded vaguely foreign and bourgeois, and its exact connotations were not clear to everyone. The Japanese term is usually considered to be a translation of the French word *"citoyen"* or the German *"bürger."* The two characters of the word literally mean "people of the city or market," so the word *"shimin"* implied an urban modernism that ran counter to the prewar agrarianism touted by the state. However, self-proclaimed citizens' movements were still debating the characteristics of their political subjectivity even as they called on others to join the Anpo demonstrations as citizens.

Terms such as "the masses" (*taishū*) or "the people" (*jinmin*) were much more familiar because of their use in both Marxist discourse and mass society theory. Within the Marxist framework, both words connoted the proletarian working class as the agent of social transformation. The working masses thus held ontological priority as the subjects of the inevitable socialist revolution, but the idea of "the masses" also carried the nuance of being an uncultured group that had to be enlightened if they were to become politically engaged subjects. The Japan Communist and Socialist parties therefore saw themselves as the political vanguard that would raise the workers' political consciousness and lead organized labor to assume its proper historical role.

However, the debates over subjectivity throughout the 1950s show that many progressive writers and intellectuals were dissatisfied with the constraints of Marxist orthodoxy, both as far as their own cultural production was concerned and in terms of social actions needed to produce a democratic revolution.[32] The subjectivity theorists wanted to move away from a notion of class as absolutely determinate and to give more weight to the individual as the agent of history. They also focused on instilling the heart or spirit of democracy in people's lives, because Japan had already gained the superficial external forms, the formal institutions of democracy, while retaining prewar figures and prewar lines of authority within those forms.[33]

Citizen movement theorists also found mass society theory to be inadequate because of its portrayal of the masses and its focus on external forms. The theory characterized mass society as shaped by economic and technological forces, which broke apart and leveled old social classes that previously had mediated between mass and elite. Thus, the theory tended to downplay the role of human agency, except by elite rulers, and citizen masses were portrayed as irrational and prone to manipulation by demagogues. This portrayal may have been more persuasive when analyzing the prewar masses' lack of resistance to the state. In the postwar period, however, the task was to transform the alienated imperial subject into an autonomous citizen and to convert mass society into a democratic one. Therefore, citizen movement thinkers defined democracy as a continual activity or process that required a conscious, engaged citizenry, rather than by the presence of institutional forms. For them, democracy was not a condition that resulted when society attained a particular threshold of urbanization and industrialization.

By positing the citizen rather than the proletariat or external forces as the agent of historical change, movement theorists were also forced to reconsider the idea of the public sphere as the proper field for political engagement. They drew a distinction between actions serving only private interests and those taken for the sake of the common good, and they tried to uncouple the idea of the public sphere from identification with the state. Citizens' movements and their ideologues encouraged people to become politically active by saying that regardless of class or social standing everyone held equivalent status as citizens, and the government's actions threatened everyone alike.

Although they made their appeals as ordinary citizens, intellectuals probably enjoyed some of their greatest postwar influence at the time of the Anpo protests. Their ideas found a wide audience, because several avenues existed for disseminating their views to the general public. General-interest monthly magazines (*sōgō zasshi*) featured articles by prominent intellectuals and critics as well as regular roundtable discussions between them. Weekly magazines, which began to proliferate in the latter half of the 1950s, often asked for short pieces from well-known thinkers, and even daily newspapers solicited articles from them. Ironically, citizen movement theorists gained a wide audience because of their higher social status at the same time that they, in effect, sought to demote their own elite authority by advocating everyone's equivalence as citizens.

This notion of equivalence meant that citizens' groups tended toward egalitarian organization and consensus decision making. And because these groups saw democracy as an active process, they constantly adapted their theory to actual political praxis. Some of the key citizen movement theorists were influenced by John Dewey's pragmatism and would revamp their ideas according to what happened when they engaged in actions such as the Anpo protests. Thus, the notion of the citizen was always indeterminate to a certain degree, because it was continually being rearticulated through political praxis. It was, however, this indeterminacy that made the citizens' movements a viable alternative for those protesters who could not identify with the industrial working class or Marxist ideology.

Catalysts

STUDENTS AND youth represented a catalytic fifth element to the protests, the "Anpo generation." They were crucial because of the direct radical actions they took in the protests and because of their resistance to the leadership of the established opposition. The Anpo generation acutely felt the traumas of Japan's defeat in World War II and were incensed by the instantaneous "conversion" to democracy of teachers and community elders who had been the most rabid advocates of wartime ideology just before the surrender.[34] However, the new postwar educational system also brought some welcome changes. The decentralized system allowed for a freer curriculum than later generations would experience, because teachers were not limited solely to textbooks approved by the Ministry of Education. Some teachers made their students' courses more relevant by having them do research in local communities and places of work. This type of social engagement later influenced student movements to go to rural areas to educate the farmers (*kikyō undō*) or to the factories to raise the consciousness of the workers. These movements were guided by an elitist notion of going out to enlighten the masses, but many of the students changed their attitudes when they encountered contradictions in their situations.

A second major trauma the Anpo generation student activists suffered was their disillusionment with the Japan Communist Party over its ideological flip-flops and suppression of dissent. As the party leadership moved to a more parliamentarian approach in line with Comintern directives, the students and youth butted heads more and more with the central committee. For example, the students heavily criticized the party in 1956 when it refused to send people out to help the farmers at Sunagawa who were protesting the expropriation of their land for the expansion of the U.S. airbase there. Then, at the end of 1958, the student organization Bund (Kyōsanshugisha Dōmei, or the Communist League) formed after an ideological clash with the Japan Communist Party leadership resulted in mass expulsions and resignations of students. By the time of the Anpo protests, Bund had taken over the leadership of Zengakuren (Zen Nihon Gakusei Jichikai Sōrengo, the All Japan Federation of Self-Governing Student Bodies), the national federation that brought together all the student councils at Japan's universities. The mainstream faction of the student movement, therefore, was Marxist but frequently acted independently in defiance of the party's authority. The antimainstream faction of Zengakuren consisted of students who retained their party membership, but they too were often critical of the party's leadership. Thus, by March of 1960, the antimainstream student groups were often conducting their own separate but parallel actions from the mainstream.

This is not to say that all the students who participated in the Anpo protests came out because of their Marxist ideals or communist affiliations. Even though the leaders of both the mainstream and antimainstream factions of Zengakuren were communist, the bulk of the students were not ideological. Most of them did not really comprehend or care about the minute differences in Marxist interpretation that defined the various leadership groups. They were unconcerned with the factional battles for control of the student organs. Many of them held a vague notion that Japan ought to take a position of unarmed neutrality, but there was a wide range of opinions about how that ought to be accomplished. Again it was the forcible ratification of Anpo that brought a marked increase in the numbers of students who went out to protest. What united the students was the sense that direct radical action was needed to resolve this crisis of democracy. The idea of direct democracy linked the students to the citizens' movements, and many student activists became involved in such movements after they graduated and helped foster others in the late 1960s. During the 1960 Anpo movement the wall between the students and citizens was a highly permeable barrier.

Snapshots of June 15

IN ORDER to examine these aspects of the citizen's movements that were so crucial to the Anpo protests, this book traces the development of four different groups—one that originally organized around the issue of war responsibility, a workers' poetry circle, a women's network, and a citizen's group that formed in the midst of the 1960 Anpo protests. These groups exemplify the transitions social movements made in the late 1950s and early 1960s in the ways they organized themselves, the political philosophies they adopted, and the new modes of expression they explored. They looked for alternatives to the prewar hierarchic elements that existed in the workplace, their local communities, and the political system. They also rejected the hierarchic relations inherent in the democratic centrist organization of the Japan Communist Party, which was more efficient at handing down orders from the central leadership than at incorporating feedback from the masses into new policies.[35] And they all were present at the Diet on June 15.

June 15 was a day that had a profound impact on the entire movement against Anpo. It was planned as a "second May Day," and the protest march around the Diet was intended to feature private company unions as a complement to the June 4 general strike that had focused on unions in public sector industries such as the Japan National Railways. June 15 was also the day when eighty citizens suffered injuries in attacks by right-wing youths and when, in a bloody skirmish between riot police and students, a young coed from Tokyo University named Kanba Michiko became the first fatality of the protests. Close to two hundred students were arrested and nearly six hundred were injured severely enough to require medical treatment, mostly for head and facial wounds. More than fifty students from Tokyo University alone were hospitalized for over three weeks.[36] In addition, sixty professors who were attacked while trying to mediate between the police and students had to be hospitalized for more than five days.[37]

Tensions were already high after the June 10 Hagerty incident, where demonstrators had come to protest the arrival of Eisenhower's press secretary, who was doing advance work for Ike's scheduled state visit. The protesters hemmed in Hagerty's car and harangued him for an hour before a helicopter swept him off to the embassy. Although it was Japan Communist Party–affiliated, antimainstream students who had blockaded Hagerty's car, the incident seemed to revitalize the Zengakuren mainstream faction as well. The Kishi administration, however, was deeply embarrassed by the incident and placed the police on high alert. On June 13 and 14, police raided various labor offices and university campuses to arrest labor and student leaders and place them under preventive detention.[38] The government also mobilized over ten thousand police for the demonstration, dispatching nearly 3,500 of them to the Diet compound.[39]

The demonstration was not scheduled to begin until late afternoon, allowing more people to come, but since it was a Thursday, the participants only numbered about sixty thousand. The authorities did not allow the marchers to gather at Shimizudani Park as originally planned, but they finally received permission to assemble at the band shell in Hibiya Park. The attending groups were divided into four major blocs, with the laborers leading out in bloc A at around 4:00 PM.

Inaba Yoshikazu was one of those marching in the lead bloc. He worked at the Japan National Railways repair facility at Ōi and had been mobilized by his labor union to take part in the march. He was living at a company dormitory near the Takadanobaba station, and it was a short ride by train or trolley to the demonstrations downtown. After the forcible ratification on May 19, Inaba found himself going to the protests almost daily, but initially he was driven to participate less by his own inner desire than by his union's commitment to provide a certain number of workers from the plant for the united actions. For half a year, he had listened to the Sōhyō representatives who came to the factory to explain to the workers how the Anpo struggle related to them. The Japan Socialist Party and Japan Communist Party ideologues and union leaders cast the protests as a proletarian uprising with laborers as the agents of change, but like many, Inaba had difficulty identifying with their supposed role or feeling that the treaty had a large influence on his work situation.

He was more concerned with the workers' poetry circle that he had organized together with Nakamura Kiyoshi, calling it The Poets of Ōi [Factory] (Ōi Shijin). Although many of the circle movements that were formed in the 1950s were highly politicized, the Poets of Ōi were not organized by a cell leader, nor did they engage in ideological proselytizing. Inaba and Nakamura formed the group to give themselves and others an outlet for expressing their feelings about work and life. Thus, the union local rather than the poetry circle was the channel used to mobilize workers at the factory. Since going to the demonstrations took workers away from their means of livelihood, many of the united actions were scheduled for the weekends. For weekday demonstrations, the unions had to rotate volunteers and provide travel expenses for the workers and a small allowance for food. Inaba was glad to get out of the factory, but he went to the protests more out of intense curiosity than out of a fervent desire to express opposition to the treaty. His attitude was the same as that of the writer Oda Makoto in *Nan demo mite yarō* (I'm Gonna Look at It All), which described his travels through America, Europe, and Asia.⁴⁰ He wanted to see for himself what was going on and to experience it directly.

Since the unionists were placed in the lead, Inaba did not see the attacks that club-wielding right-wing youths from the Restoration Action Corps (Ishin Kōdōtai) made on the citizen marchers behind them. The attackers avoided the tightly organized blocks of unionists and students, choosing some small bands of Christians and theater actors instead. Witnesses claimed that the Action Corps had targeted women marchers in particular, and although the men in the groups tried to protect them, twenty-nine of the eighty injured in the incident were women.⁴¹ Inaba had already finished marching and had gone to eat some noodles before he heard on the radio that students had broken into the Diet compound and that someone had been killed. Ironically, Kanba's father, Toshio, was also at a small restaurant when he heard the same radio announcement, which sent him rushing off to the Diet with the awful premonition that it was his daughter who had been killed.⁴²

In contrast to Inaba, several members of the women's group the Grass Seeds (Kusa no Mi Kai) felt compelled to go to the Diet that day to voice their objections to the ratification of the treaty. The women who went to the demonstration did not reach their decision easily. They were not a political action group but had come together to study and discuss problems that women faced in everyday life. They called their group a new type of *idobata kaigi* that served to exchange community information and enforce social sanctions and mores.⁴³ The Grass Seeds started in 1954, when contributors to a readers' column in the *Asahi* newspaper wanted to meet face-to-face and delve more deeply into the issues they had raised in the column, such as children's education and care of the elderly. Since the column and the readers' contributions varied from region to region, the groups that developed out of the column each had a slightly different character, and a number of them took different names. Thus, they adopted the principle that each of the local groups was an independent body, and in order to protect this autonomy, the Grass Seeds felt that they should avoid committing themselves to any particular political body or platform. The model of informal, egalitarian gatherings that also had a public character suited the Grass Seeds and other such citizen movements that organized themselves on the principles of local autonomy and voluntary, individual participation.

The Grass Seeds' usual tendency was to engage in extended research on specific issues. They conducted studies on the family system, the Parent-Teacher Association, and "moral education" that the government wanted to reinstitute in schools. They also formed liaisons with groups such as the Japan Mothers Conference (Nihon Hahaoya Taikai) and the Council Against the A- and H-Bombs. When Kishi introduced the Police Duties Bill in the last months of 1958, the Grass Seeds began to research and debate the issue, and articles in their magazine *The Grass Seeds* indicate that members generally shared the same feelings about the bill. They also issued a very short declaration that directly reflected their concerns about the revival of wartime structures, but they could not reach a clear consensus about participating in demonstrations or issuing lengthier statements.[44] Therefore, they said, they aimed at sharing a process more than a final decision and emphasized unity of direction rather than unity of action.

Anpo proved to be a more divisive issue, especially prior to May 19. Some members, especially the younger ones, pushed heavily for the group to declare its opposition to the Security Treaty system and to engage actively in protests with other citizen organizations. Others felt, however, that making public declarations in the group's name and committing it to marching in the demonstrations would take it beyond their framework of gathering for informal discussions. Since the Grass Seeds were unable to resolve this difference of opinion, they let local branches decide their own course of action. Members were torn between their desire for consensus of opinion and the need to express their individual conscience and go to the protests. However, the forcible ratification of Anpo shifted the focus of the problem. As their brief statement on May 30 declared, "The ruling party has trampled on democratic politics by ratifying the treaty unilaterally through violent means. Whether one approves or disapproves of the treaty, we must protect democratic parliamentary politics."[45]

Nakanishi Masako felt compelled to go to the protest march on June 15 even though it was her son's birthday. Members of the group assembled for the march behind a group of high school students, and Imai Yaeko was particularly moved by the words of one boy who spoke from the top of a truck when they reached the gates of the Diet. He said, "Anpo has caused us grave concern about our future, since we don't know whether or not we might have to go to war because of it."[46] This made Saitō Tsuruko think of her own boy, who had just started high school and who had no awareness of the issue at all despite her activities with the Grass Seeds and the ban-the-bomb group the Children of the Cedars (Sugi no Ko). When university students at the main gate appealed to the Grass Seeds to join their sit-in, they were sympathetic, but the action seemed too radical and caused those like Nakanishi to think about the responsibilities they had for their own children at home.

Unlike marchers in the earlier blocs, the members of the Voiceless Voices (Koe Naki Koe no Kai) were keenly aware of the violence that took place against the protesters. They were marching in the last bloc behind those attacked by the Restoration Action Corps, and they heard reports of the bloodshed. The right-wing youths attacked the theater troupe, Christians, and other citizen groups at around 5:30 PM, clubbing the protesters with roughly one-meter-long sticks and trying to run them over with their truck. The Voiceless Voices saw the wounded as they marched past and heard reports that the police had turned a blind eye and did not intervene to stop the attacks.

The protest organizers had been anxious about the possibility of such attacks from the beginning. They were especially concerned about the women—some of whom had brought their children—who had little or no previous experience at demonstrations. As people waited at Hibiya Park to begin their march, the organizers made continual announcements warning the marchers to take care. As they stood there waiting, the Voiceless Voices tried to boost their spirits with the song that Nakada Yoshinao had composed from the text of a flyer they had passed around at the June 4 general strike. The words "Citizens all, be brave! Walk with us and show them how we feel" proved especially poignant for them that day.

Their group had formed on the streets in the midst of the Anpo demonstrations. Their name was a sarcastic response to Kishi's assertion that he would only listen to the "voiceless voices," the "silent majority," not to the protesters demanding his resignation and the dissolution of the Diet. Kishi made this statement May 28 during his first press conference after the forcible ratification. Reaction to the events of May 19 were so intense that he had sequestered himself in the prime minister's residence for a week, but he emerged unrepentant and attacked the press for criticizing him.[47] Thus, at the next major protest, the June 4 general strike, two people appeared toward the back of the march carrying a placard that identified themselves as "voiceless voices" and encouraged onlookers to join them.

Kobayashi Tomi, an art teacher, and Fuha Mitsuo, an assistant film director, belonged to a life histories circle. They had heard one of their group tell of how bystanders lining the streets at the demonstrations seemed anxious to join in but held back for some reason. They surmised that many like themselves had never taken part in a demonstration and were not members of an established opposition group, so they found it difficult to join the march even though they had taken the trouble to come watch. However, the placard that Kobayashi and Fuha carried reassured the onlookers, and by the time they had circled the Diet, three hundred people had joined them. Kobayashi found it so exciting that she went back to the starting point and marched around again gathering hundreds more citizens. They began to exchange names and telephone numbers so that they could meet at the next demonstration, and by the time they reached Shinbashi Station, Kobayashi had collected two hundred names. When a reporter asked whom the group comprised, Kobayashi replied that anyone who did not belong to a particular group was a member. Their only criterion was whether or not one was willing to walk together with them for a while, so their numbers continued to grow although the personnel fluctuated considerably.

The Voiceless Voices acted as individual citizens and had no headquarters or executive leadership. The group only maintained contact persons for information, and a sympathetic owner of a coffee shop downtown offered them the use of her place on Saturday afternoons if people wanted to get together. They also started a newsletter so that they could communicate and debate with each other. They felt this was especially important, because they did not hold to any one ideological position or affiliate themselves with any particular party. Their occupations and class positions varied widely, so eventually the Voiceless Voices grouped themselves by place of residence, with each of the local groups making their own decisions. What brought and kept them together was their feeling that Kishi had created a crisis of democracy and somehow they had to show their will (*ishi hyōji*) by getting politically involved.

Many of the Voiceless Voices saw the effects of the violence that took place on June 15 at the South Gate of the Diet. Some ten thousand students from the mainstream faction of Zengakuren had gathered there at around 4:00 PM and made a series of speeches. At 5:15, as citizen marchers were being attacked by the Restoration Action Corps, the students began prying open the gate, finally succeeding in doing so at around 6:00. They then tried to drag out the trucks that had been placed to block the entrance. The riot police countered by using water cannons to knock the students away. The students threw rocks at the police, and the police picked them up and hurled them back, catching them in a net set up between the trucks. Shortly before 7:00, the police pulled back some seventy or eighty meters, and the students once more poured into the compound. When they did, the riot police attacked them, using their nightsticks to club the students and administer choke holds while dragging them off to detention.[48] Kanba's body was discovered by one of the trucks sometime around 7:30 PM. The police would claim that she had died from internal injuries after being trampled to death by other students, while the opposition insisted that the riot police had strangled her.[49]

During the melee, some of the students ran toward the terminal point of the march to appeal to others to lend their support. The Voiceless Voices had seen some of the injured students as they marched down the road toward the prime minister's residence, and on hearing the call, some of the women rushed back to the site, driven by a basic human impulse to care for the victims of violence. Tsurumi Shunsuke found their actions symbolic of the whole citizen participation in the Anpo protests. The demonstrators were driven not by ideology but by a basic need to fix the democratic process that Kishi had so blatantly violated.[50]

However, when they arrived back at the scene, they found Japan Communist Party officials warning people away and blocking the road to the area. Poet and critic Yoshimoto Takaaki (or Ryūmei) would later call this moment at the South Gate "an end to fictions," when the Japan Communist Party lost any legitimate claim to being the vanguard of the movement. He claimed that the location and actions of the students, party officials, and citizen protesters directly reflected their political positions.[51] He saw Bund as the true vanguard, because they were doing what the proletariat could not afford to, that is, directly confronting the reactionary state's power. He vilified the Japan Communist Party leaders for their slavish devotion to the Comintern's outdated ideological line and their attempts to suppress those who challenged their authority. Since Bund was formed by students who had resigned or were expelled from the party, they developed their own theoretical analysis and action program for the Anpo struggle and openly defied party directives throughout the protests. The Japan Communist Party was unable to control Bund, so all it could do was condemn the students for ideological deviations and try to prevent them from getting outside support. Party officials not only blocked citizens from coming to the aid of the students; they then tried to dissuade people from contributing to or attending the memorial service that Bund arranged for Kanba on the eighteenth.

This was in fact the second time that Bund students had stormed the gates of the Diet. The first was November 27, nearly seven months earlier, during a demonstration that was supposed to culminate with Japan Socialist Party officials presenting petitions against the treaty to representatives of the Kishi administration. The Liberal Democratic Party had locked up the Diet compound and suspended parliamentary debate on the treaty, so the students sought to reopen the political process, stating their intent to reclaim the Diet on behalf of the people.[52] Communist and Socialist party leaders were concerned about this rhetoric and had carefully positioned the Bund students so that they would be far away from the front gate when the petitions were formally presented. The students, however, relocated themselves so that when the front gate was unlocked to receive the petitions, they pushed their way into the compound. The police were greatly outnumbered and powerless to stop them, but the students were not intent on occupying the Diet building or vandalizing it. Instead, they held rallies, staged zigzag marches, made speeches, and sang songs late into the evening, enacting their notions of direct democracy.

The Liberal Democratic Party condemned the students for

having violated "sacred ground" (*seichi*), invoking an image of politics that wed religion to state administration (*matsurigoto*) and cast the Diet as a shrine administered by the Liberal Democratic Party priests. Japan Communist Party and Japan Socialist Party leaders also vehemently denounced the Bund students as "Trotskyist left-wing adventurists" and apologized for their behavior when the Liberal Democratic Party proposed a bill to outlaw demonstrations anywhere near the Diet. Despite their ideological opposition to the Security Treaty, opposition party politicians also considered themselves, in effect, lesser priests at the national shrine.[53] They insisted on being the sole conduit through which the anti-Anpo petitions were presented to the ruling party, so when the students charged into the Diet compound, it threatened the political privileges that Communist and Socialist party politicians held as a "loyal opposition" that posed no real threat to Liberal Democratic Party dominance.

In the following months, Bund would increasingly dismiss the united actions as ineffectual "funeral processions," and the students would look back to November 27 as a model. A few minutes after 7:30 PM, the Zengakuren speaker car announced that Kanba had been killed and that over two hundred other students were being transported to the hospital. When the students found out about Kanba's death, they began to reenter the compound, where they staged a rally surrounded by riot police. At 9:00 PM, the speaker car announced the possibility that two other students had been killed. The rumor proved inaccurate, but it enraged the students, who screamed at the police to doff their helmets and observe a moment of silence. The riot police did not comply, and the students rose up, and they began talking about going to the front of the Diet to hold a rally just like they did on November 27. A group of Japan Socialist Party representatives tried to dissuade them, saying it would provoke another police attack, which did in fact come just after 10:00 PM. This attack forced the students outside, so they moved around to the front of the Diet, finally regrouping in front of the heavily barricaded gate at midnight. This time, the police used tear gas to disperse the students, and they inflicted more injuries by clubbing fleeing students. The police also attacked members of the media that night, as the famous live broadcast from Radio Tokyo showed. The reporter continued to broadcast even as the police first swore at him and then grabbed him by the throat to drag him off. He cried out, "There's no law here, no order or anything. Only suffering. Only the rampage of the police and the suffering of the students."[54]

During the long, bloody evening, there were not enough medical personnel to take care of the injured. Doctors and nurses had to run from one site to another trying to give what little treatment they could manage. One of the nurses dispatched from the Tokyo Police Hospital, Shiba Aiko, also belonged to a citizens' group called the Mountain Range (Yamanami no Kai) and ended up having to tend to injured students as well as the police. Even though her hospital was designed to handle emergency cases, they could only dispatch two doctors, two nurses, and two aides to the Diet that day, and Shiba went back and forth around the compound. When an old worker in one of the compound buildings asked her what she thought about the scene before her eyes, she replied that "if I was standing out there in the middle of that crowd, somehow I would probably be drawn into taking part."[55]

Shiba felt like one of the battlefield nurses she had seen in the movies. At one point some female students ran up to her to get some help and told her that someone had been killed. She and her nurse companion were unable to resist their cries for help, and they went off to the gate surrounded by professors who protected them as they went through the crowd. Then Shiba was sent back to the compound to tend to police who were injured by rocks the students had thrown. Shortly after, she was sent to the basement, where injured police filled the hallway while injured students lay inside the room. Most of the injured were even younger than she was, and she wondered how the energy of youthful dreams could result in such blood and sweat. Both sides were young and claimed to want peace.

It was ironic that someone from a group originally formed to talk about the issue of war responsibility and deal with the problem of survivors' guilt had the task of tending to the wounded and the dead in the aftermath of the violence. The Mountain Range was started in 1947 by a schoolteacher up in Akita together with his old high school friends. They had all been at military training school, but after the war they felt deceived and that everything they were taught had been lies. As one of the group noted, they had only been taught how to die, not how to live.[56] However, it seemed to them that people did not want to deal with the issue of war responsibility, and so they started up their own magazine to take up the question. Although they went on hiatus for six years, they reformed in 1956 and began to expand the scope of their writings to become a kind of life histories circle with particular focus on rural concerns. Shiba and Mibu Fumi had joined the group a few months before the June 15 demonstration after getting to know one of their patients who was a member. Now they found themselves working in what seemed like battlefield conditions.

There were not enough ambulances that night to take all of the wounded to the hospitals, and Shiba worked through the night in the basement. Kanba Michiko did not make it as far as that room. The police took her body back to the Tokyo Police Hospital where Mibu was on duty. Mibu was given the task of applying the makeup to Kanba's corpse, but she could not keep from weeping as she wiped the grime from Kanba's face.

Kanba's death was deeply shocking to all who were involved in the protests. First of all it was shocking because the nature of the protest was legalistic. The protesters were exercising their right to petition the government, and their demands were for the restoration of the democratic process, not armed revolution. The fact that Kanba was a student at Tokyo University, Japan's premier institution of higher learning, reinforced the shock. Tokyo University students stood at the head of an already elite group, and their graduates would fill the top positions in business and government. But the most shocking thing was that it was a woman who had been killed. Women accounted for only 15 percent of the student population at Tokyo University, and there were not even any women's toilets on campus.[57] Going to demonstrations was considered improper or dangerous for educated, middle-class women, and parents often tried to prevent their daughters from participating. It was even more unusual for Kanba to have been an officer in Zengakuren. The student movement leadership was virtually all male, and even when women were represented at student rallies, they were usually relegated to giving the greetings and leading songs. Kanba's death was also unexpected because women students were generally placed at the rear of demonstrations and surrounded by male students, preferably from a sports club, for protection. One of Kanba's female friends who saw her shortly before her death urged her to pull back from the front, but Kanba insisted that as a student leader she had to remain where she was.[58]

Aftermath

THE FIRST effect of the bloody June 15 protests was that Kishi immediately canceled the state visit of President Eisenhower, who was in the midst of a Far East tour through the Philippines, Taiwan, Okinawa, and South Korea. The prime minister made his announcement after an emergency meeting of the Cabinet held early on the morning of June 16. Kishi was unwilling to risk the embarrassment that massive protests would bring, so he issued a statement that "under Japan's present conditions this is not an appropriate time for welcoming an important state guest" and that he would invite the president again when the emperor asked him to do so.[59] He blamed the "violent acts of a minority" for the "postponement" and again claimed that "international communism" was trying "to destroy democratic order through planned, mass violence."[60] Eisenhower quickly agreed to the cancellation, expressing his "full and sympathetic understanding of the decision," but any reaffirmations of American support for Kishi's administration were already too late. Other Liberal Democratic Party leaders knew that they had to replace Kishi if the party was to survive, and even as the treaty went into effect, "it was taken for granted generally that Mr. Kishi would retire as Premier soon."[61] Any satisfaction that the protesters might have felt at the cancellation of Eisenhower's state visit, however, was offset by the death of Kanba, the imminent "automatic" approval of the treaty, and the mass media's turn against the movement.

In the wake of the incident, seven major daily newspapers— the *Sankei*, *Tōkyō shinbun*, *Tokyo Times*, *Nihon keizai*, *Mainichi*, *Yomiuri*, and *Asahi*—published a joint editorial on June 16. The joint declaration was unprecedented, and its appearance implied that the mass media had reached a consensus on the issue. Moreover, the day after it came out, the editorial was picked up by forty-one other newspapers around the country, and television networks such as Fuji TV also broadcast its contents.[62] The declaration read:

WIPE OUT VIOLENCE, PRESERVE PARLIAMENTARY DEMOCRACY

Quite apart from whatever may have been the causes, the bloody incidents on the night of June 15 inside and outside the Diet were utterly deplorable and threw parliamentary democracy into a crisis. Never before have we been so deeply disturbed as we are now about the future of Japan.

In a democracy, differences should be contested with words. Whatever the causes and whatever the political difficulties may be, the use of violence to settle matters cannot be permitted under any circumstances. If a social trend permitting violence should once become general, we believe that democracy will die and a grave situation will arise which will endanger Japan's national existence.

Consequently, the Government, which bears the grave responsibility for the present situation, must speedily exert every effort to resolve the current situation. In this connection the Government must make it clear that it will respond to the sound judgement of the people. At the same time, since the suspension of the Diet's function is one of the reasons for the current confusion, the Socialist and Democratic Socialist Parties should, at this time, lay aside their disputes for the time being and return to the Diet. We sincerely believe that it is the wish of the people that they return to the Diet and cooperate in resolving the situation by restoring Diet procedures to normal.

We therefore sincerely appeal to the Government and Opposition parties to respond to the fervent wishes of the people by agreeing to protect parliamentary democracy and by dispelling the unusual anxiety now troubling the people.

The *Sankei Newspapers, Tokyo Shinbun, Tokyo Times Shinbun, Nihon Keizai Shinbun,* the *Mainichi Newspapers,* the *Yomiuri Newspapers,* the *Asahi Newspapers*[63]

Although the editor primarily responsible for the contents of the declaration, Aikawa Shigeyoshi, claimed that the newspapers had not reversed their critical stance toward the government for forcibly ratifying the treaty, the import was clear to both sides. Members of the Liberal Democratic Party and state bureaucrats welcomed the statement, and Nakasone Yasuhiro, then head of the Science and Technology Agency, called it a formal apology to their party.[64] Citizen protesters, for their part, were outraged by the implication that the violence of June 15 was due to their continuing demonstrations rather than to police repression. They found it especially galling that the editorial claimed to speak for the people of the nation (*kokumin*) in urging the opposition to stop its protests in order to "normalize" politics instead of censuring the Kishi administration for violating the democratic process.

Some were aware that the newspaper editors had, in fact, been planning such a piece for weeks. Maruyama Masao had intimate contacts with many newspeople and was already admonishing the press to remember their former commitment to independent "newspaperism" three days *before* the June 15 incident.[65]

Citizens' movements felt the newspapers had betrayed them, turning away from *representing* public opinion to trying to *manipulate* it for the benefit of the state.[66] They began to keep vigils at the Diet press club and to carry placards demanding that journalists heed their consciences and tell the truth. Other banners implored editors not to cave in to the authorities.[67]

The Kishi administration had in fact tried to control the mass media through the Mass Media Counter-Measures Committee, comprising communications and enterprise owners. Ever since the defeat of the Police Duties Bill in 1958, administration officials had claimed that the newspapers were biased in favor of the opposition, so they wooed editors with luncheons and gave those who were friendly to the government's viewpoint access to Cabinet officials. They also succeeded in canceling certain newspaper columns and radio programs and getting editors to blacklist certain figures from appearing on television.[68] The Grass Seeds were directly affected by the Counter-Measures Committee's campaign when the *Asahi* altered the thrust of the "Hitotoki" column to shun discussions of social issues. These types of actions only confirmed the need for citizen movements to rely on their own communication media to discuss and debate issues.[69]

After the incidents of June 15, the student leadership of Bund quickly organized a memorial service for Kanba, setting it for Saturday in conjunction with the nineteenth united action against the treaty. Despite the outpouring of sentiment for Kanba, the Japan Communist Party and Japan Socialist Party leadership still branded her a Trotskyist because of her Bund affiliation and spread rumors that Zengakuren was plotting violence for June 18. Furthermore, the parties excluded Bund students from the planning of a second, nationwide memorial service for Kanba on the twenty-fourth. The parties were still concerned with a loss of authority but did not see that they continued to forfeit support by such actions. In spite of such obstruction, Tokyo University students held a memorial on June 18, starting with a 12:30 PM service at Yasuda Tower on campus and then marching to the front gate for some speeches. Afterward, six or seven thousand students began their procession to the Diet, joined by some three thousand citizens along the way, and finally reached the South Gate at 2:00 PM for another service.[70] So while the Bund students had criticized the Communist and Socialist parties for organizing "funeral procession"–style demonstrations, they now found themselves leading an actual funeral march.

The united action that day was one of the single largest demonstrations Japan had ever seen. Students, laborers, and citizens had poured into Tokyo from around the country, and an estimated 330,000 people marched around the Diet that day in a last-ditch attempt to get the government to rescind the treaty. However, people knew that at midnight the Anpo treaty would "automatically" came into force without being ratified in the Upper House. Therefore, in spite of the numbers, the mood was relatively somber and quiet. Those present felt as if they were mourning for both Kanba and democracy. Bund had staked everything on the Anpo issue, rather than focusing on labor issues such as the rationalization of the industrial workforce, and when the treaty came into force at midnight, the students were distraught. One of the Bund leaders looked out on the crowd and bitterly declared, "This has all been just a great big zero."[71]

This assessment was overly dramatic and premature. Once the treaty went into force, Kishi finally submitted to the inevitable. The Liberal Democratic Party could no longer support a prime minister who had sparked such a high level of dissent and, moreover, had caused a third of his own party to declare their opposition to the treaty. On June 23, Kishi declared that he was resigning from office. Despite his announcement, demonstrations and limited strikes continued to be held around the country. Another national memorial for Kanba Michiko was held the day after Kishi announced his resignation and drew roughly ten thousand participants. Over one hundred thousand demonstrators gathered in Tokyo on July 2 for the twentieth united action to protest the "automatic" ratification of Anpo, and the twenty-first united action twelve days later attracted similar numbers. There was still considerable fallout from the Anpo protests that kept the participating organizations active. As for the students, many of them traveled down to Kyushu in July to lend their support to the Miike coal miners' strike.

Beyond these activities, the citizens' movements of the Anpo protests imparted important legacies to later social and political movements, such as the anti–Vietnam War movement of the late 1960s, the resident-based environmental movements (*jūmin undō*) of the 1970s, and the new social movements of the 1980s. These movements adopted organizational structures and political philosophies similar to those of the Anpo era groups, so while the currents that surfaced in the Anpo protests seemed to disperse in the summer of 1960, they continued to flow underground and feed new streams as well.

3

THE MOUNTAIN RANGE
AND WAR RESPONSIBILITY

Japan's widespread devastation from World War II forced the Japanese to reexamine the beliefs that they had held before their defeat. They had been taught that they were engaged in a "sacred war" that did not admit the possibility of defeat; there would only be victory or else annihilation and communal unity in death. But Japan had lost decisively, and the emperor had surrendered—without ever using the word "surrender." When his recorded speech was broadcast, he proclaimed "according to the dictates of time and fate that We have resolved to pave the way for a grand peace for all the generations to come by enduring the unendurable and suffering what is insufferable."[1]

The euphemism for surrender has been widely quoted, but what is striking about the phrase concerns the question of agency. The emperor did not ask the Japanese people "to bear the unbearable."[2] He declared that he himself would suffer what cannot be borne.[3] But despite the identification that the Japanese people were presumed to feel with the emperor, was the unendurable the same for both? For the Japanese state, the one absolute, nonnegotiable condition in seeking an end to the war had been the continued existence of the emperor's status as sovereign ruler.

Above all, the emperor had to survive as the sacred and inviolable personification of Japan, according to the prewar ideology, but now he was about to make himself subject to other powers that might depose him or try him as a war criminal. The emperor, however, was hopeful that the Allies would not do either of these things and so turned to the question of having a country left to represent. Directly after declaring that he would "endure the unendurable," the emperor proclaimed, "Having been able to save and maintain the structure of the Imperial State, We are always with you, our good and loyal subjects,"[4] calling on them, in effect, not to put up further resistance and bring retaliation from the enemy. For the emperor, the unendurable was losing the symbolic import of his position, his "death" as sovereign.

For the Japanese subjects, however, death was not unendurable. They were taught that dying together for the sake of the emperor was a glorious communion with all the ancestral spirits watching over the land. Death was also cast in aesthetic terms. Committing suicide rather than surrendering to the enemy was beautified as *gyokusai*, the shattering of a jewel into a myriad pieces.[5] The one thing that would be unendurable for a good Japanese subject would be to survive, shamefully ostracized from the community of death.[6] The good soldier, the patriotic subject, had only been trained to die; such subjects were not prepared to live on after the war.

This spiritual devastation was just as important as the physical destruction that Japan had suffered. What was one to do once "things fall apart" and "the center cannot hold," as W. B. Yeats said in "The Second Coming"? How could people assess what had brought them to this point? What had gone wrong, and who or what should be held accountable? What should one believe in now that everything one knew before had been proven wrong? These questions were all bound together under the rubric of war responsibility, the key issue that the Japanese had to grapple with if they were to construct a new society that avoided the mistakes of the old.

The Victim Mentality

Two WEEKS after the emperor announced Japan's surrender, Prince Higashikuni Naruhiko, the first postwar prime minster, urged "general penitence of the entire population" (*zen kokumin sōzange* or *ichioku sōzange*), calling for all Japanese to apologize to the emperor for, in essence, losing the war.[7] The call was a self-serving attempt to diffuse the wartime leaders' specific responsibility by spreading the blame throughout the entire populace, so SCAP quickly removed him. However, Higashikuni's statement was telling as an indication of the absolute inviolability the emperor would continue to have in the postwar period. If blame for the path that Japan had taken could not be laid on the emperor, then it would have to be placed on his subjects. The question was which subjects had to shoulder the responsibility.

The prominent Tokyo University professor Maruyama Masao has asserted that in the immediate postwar period intellectuals took it upon themselves to atone for the war and create a "community of contrition" (*kaikon kyōdōtai*) based on an idea of subjectivity and individual responsibility.[8] These intellectuals felt that a new start was needed to convert the "rationed freedom" of wartime Japan into something spontaneous and liberating. Feelings of hope and joy for the future mingled with an abhorrence of the past. Therefore, these intellectuals felt they had to be self-critical and to make some fundamental critique of their past. The crux of the problem they felt was in ridding Japan of its feudal remnants and creating a new subjectivity, a modern ego. Early in 1946, the intellectual journal *Modern Literature (Kindai bungaku)* carried a roundtable discussion on Japan's inability to deal with the question of war responsibility and to overcome its feudal remnants. The participants agreed that this inability was due to their failure to establish a modern, presumably Western-style ego, but they could not agree as to the remedy.[9]

However, despite these pronouncements of self-criticism, Maruyama like others saw the military as the main culprit in carrying out the disastrous war. His 1947 lectures on the rise of fascism depicted how civilian right-wing groups from below joined with military officers to create a movement that culminated in an attempted military coup on February 26, 1936. After putting down the rebellion, the state then coopted their movements to create a pervasive system that displaced any personal realm of values by which people could resist the state.[10] The ideology of the imperial order filled private as well as public space and suppressed expressions of autonomous subjectivity.[11] Thus, even though Maruyama claims that intellectuals did not by and large support the war, he describes them as having to hide their misgivings carefully.[12]

Ordinary people could similarly separate themselves psychologically from the military leaders by emphasizing how they were coerced to comply and by enumerating the sacrifices they had to make for the authorities. Moreover, those at the home front had few images of themselves as assailants and aggressors to conflict with this sense of victimization. State control of the press during the war meant that those on the home front had scant information about what went on at the battlefront, so people were not necessarily aware of the conduct of the soldiers there. Although widely rumored, it was only during the Tokyo War Crimes Trials that "the massacre of Nanking [Nanjing] in 1937 and other atrocities committed by the Japanese, well-known to the soldiers who had carried them out, were for the first time revealed to the people at large."[13] Those who returned from the front might also feel constrained in what they could describe, given the atmosphere of total mobilization that the state had created. There was little room for public displays of doubt or dissent from the "sacred war." The operative ideology was that of self-sacrifice for the good of the nation (*messhi hōkō*).

Certainly not everyone believed in this ideology or adhered to the dictates of the state during the war, but even those who did understood that by 1945 things were not going well, even if they were not told of the battle defeats. When the mainland was being bombed from the spring of 1945 and urban dwellers were being evacuated to the countryside and the ration system was falling apart,[14] people knew that the war was unwinnable, but at least publicly there could be no discussion of defeat and what might come afterwards.

The surrender, then, only reinforced whatever latent resentment might have existed during the war owing to the privation that the civilian population had to endure for the sake of the military campaign. The sudden facile conversion of wartime authority figures, especially teachers, into postwar "democrats" had a profound effect on the younger generation in particular. As good subjects, they had followed their orders and sacrificed for the state, and now even after the Americans came in and set up their Occupation forces, many of these same people retained their elite status. Such latent resentment fueled people's sense of victimization, and the main focus of this resentment was turned toward the military.

The composition of the defendants at the Tokyo War Crimes Trials was indicative of where the United States wanted to direct the blame for the war. SCAP believed that what had gone wrong in the 1930s and 1940s was that military leaders had usurped civilian authority, and so their task was to purge the government of the military's baleful influence. The International Military Tribunal for the Far East lasted from May 1946 until April 1948, and the preponderance of high-ranking military officers among the twenty-eight Class A defendants showed that the top echelon of the military was to be the primary target of the trials. SCAP's purge of wartime authorities in the first few months of the Occupation had been quite circumscribed as it tried to maintain political stability while transforming the society.[15] So despite the pervasive participation in the war effort by most people, the blame for the war was set on a highly select group. The indictment described a "criminal, militaristic clique" dominating the government from 1928 to the end of the war that "intended to and did plan, prepare, initiate, or wage aggressive war" against the Allies "and other peaceful nations, in violation of international law,"[16] so the Tokyo trials helped fix the blame for the people's victimization on military leaders such as Tōjō Hideki. Maruyama Masao's widely read essays on the trials also focused blame on the military. His pieces brutally dissected the psychology of the military leaders on trial and analyzed how the military produced the prewar fascist state.[17]

The focus on military leaders was partly dictated by the Occupation's decision to shield the emperor from any of the proceedings. MacArthur had determined not to prosecute or depose the emperor for fear of sparking an uprising among the Japanese as the Occupation set up camp. The most that was demanded of the emperor was that he renounce his divinity, but the postwar constitution still legitimated his position as a "symbol of the State and of the unity of people."

The trial made scapegoats of the defendants, but the "victor's justice" was generally acceptable in at least two ways. On the one hand, it could purge the victors of their pent-up hostilities and stave off broader, more random retaliation.[18] On the other hand, it allowed the Japanese to absolve themselves of involvement in the war effort. It also helped to displace the anger they felt about the U.S. fire bombing campaigns and atomic bombings, shifting it away from their occupiers onto their leaders. The focus that the trials brought to the top echelons of the military meant that civilians and even low-ranking soldiers could see themselves mainly as victims of the wartime system and defer the question of an individual's war responsibility.

As critic Oda Makoto put it in 1966 in the context of the Vietnam War, "Countless records of wartime experiences have appeared in the twenty-one years since the war, but all are reconstructed from the point of view of the victim. The accounts of students, soldiers from rural areas, evacuated schoolchildren, and repatriates from overseas are all filled with tragic victimization. Together they have contributed to a situation in which the term 'wartime experience' is synonymous with 'experience as victim.' "[19] Oda overstates the case, but he points to the problem of historical amnesia that is required to maintain the stance of victimization. The postwar recovery, especially after the Korean War, made it easier to gloss over memories that forced one to confront at least the latent capacity for being a victimizer if not the actual fact of it.

This problem of historical amnesia in the victim mentality is also the key issue in Hara Kazuo's documentary film *The Emperor's Naked Army Marches On*.[20] The director follows around a former soldier, Okuzaki Kenzō, who like the Greek Furies takes it upon himself to pursue the surviving members of his wartime military unit, force them to admit their part in cannibalizing their troops, and make them apologize for it. The usual defense that these officers present is that everyone suffered, so what was the point of dwelling on such horrors of the past? But Okuzaki insists that if everyone suffered, then everyone must atone for their past sins. The question is how to make amends. Although dredging up past traumas disrupts these men's families now that the war is over, it does not necessarily transform them personally. When the former officers he relentlessly chases down are reluctant to admit their guilt or apologize, Okuzaki is willing to dispense justice himself by beating up the culprits. He feels that he has divine dispensation to mete out justice, even using coercive means that are analogous to what the wartime military used. Okuzaki's extreme measures, however, point to the depth of Japan's willful erasure of memory and its connection to the victim mentality.

Another indication of this erasure of memory is the controversy over the Ministry of Education's attempts to revise the history textbooks in order to tone down the portrayal of Japan as an aggressor in World War II and to elide descriptions of major atrocities it committed.[21] Right-wing civilian groups have also become more vocal in the past few years, claiming that they wish to "restore" a proper history of Japan by erasing the portrayals of Japan's actions in the colonial period and the war. They tendentiously stand language on its head by asserting that it is the current textbooks that are "revisionist" rather than their own efforts. The psychological impetus behind this movement is a sense of continuing victimization at the hands of the West. These "restorationists" insist that the Nanjing Massacre, for example, was a fabrication of the foreign press and that Japan was justified in trying to combat Western imperialism, for which it should not have to apologize.[22] A further subtext is that the West continues to use Japan's conduct during the war to thwart it from attaining a position of equality (or even dominance) on the world stage. How long, they wonder, must Japan continue to apologize for the war? Therefore, in their eyes, historical memory must be "restored" to a "pristine" state in which Japan is only a victim, not a victimizer.

Their position, however, ignores the fact that the government never officially acknowledged any responsibility for the war until fifty years after the surrender.[23] Statements by the Shōwa and Heisei emperors were always couched in language that obviated agency, using passive constructions that stop at the point of noting that something regrettable happened between, for example, Japan and Korea during the war. Syntactically those statements, which were few and far between, were indistinguishable from the usage in the announcement of Japan's surrender in which the emperor expressed regret to its Asian colonies for not winning. "We cannot but express the deepest sense of regret to Our Allied nations of East Asia, who have consistently cooperated with the Empire towards the emancipation of East Asia."[24] The Japanese government's handling of the "comfort women" controversy is also consistent with public denial of historical memory.[25] In responding to the comfort women's demands for an official apology for the military's system of forced prostitution and compensation for the victims of that system, the Japanese government has refused to acknowledge that any such system existed (despite the evidence from the victims, witnesses, participants, and even official records). The government denies culpability while, at the same time, setting up a fund supplied by *private* contributors to offer limited compensation to the women.

Despite the state's attempts to either evade or erase any memory of Japan as anything other than a victim, however, there has been dialogue at the level of ordinary people about the question of war responsibility. Oda's claim notwithstanding, some people did look to themselves and critique their own willing participation in the war effort.[26]

New Mountain Ranges

ONE OF the key instruments that prompted a reassessment of people's war responsibility was a book published in 1949 called *Listen to the Voices of Wadatsumi: Writings of Japanese Students Killed in the War (Kike wadatsumi no koe: Nihon senbotsu gakusei no shuki).*[27] It was a compilation of letters, diary entries, and poetry that kamikaze pilots and other suicide squads had left for their families and loved ones just before being dispatched overseas on their missions. Many of these "volunteers" were university students, and after the war, students at Tokyo University began to collect the letters. These student soldiers were identified with the sea god, Wadatsumi, because they had to cross the ocean on their missions and because they would be enshrined as gods in the Yasukuni Shrine for defending the nation. So the god's "voices" in the book title refer to the soldiers' letters.

Numerous reading groups formed around the country that used the book to reassess their experiences of the war through the thoughts of these soldiers. Surprisingly, these writings were not all paeans to the emperor full of patriotic bluster but rather showed that the soldiers were concerned with much more human relations. Throughout the 1950s, people continued to grapple with the issues of survivors' guilt, accountability, and war responsibility, and the *wadatsumi* groups helped maintain an ongoing dialogue about the war. People seemed to derive three main points from the readings: first, an anti-authoritarian bent; second, a perspective of history that focuses on the lives of ordinary people rather than the elite; and, third, a profound concern with the task of reeducation.

One of the people who was influenced by these reading groups was the founder of the Mountain Range, Shiratori Kunio. Shiratori had been in the naval academy learning accounting during the war, and after the defeat he got together with middle school friends who also entered military schools during the war to form their own circle to reassess their experiences. One of his friends had been in the navy, training to become a kamikaze pilot; another had been in the air force academy, and another had been a marine. As Shiratori put it, they had all been young fascists convinced that they would die before they turned twenty.[28] But then with the sudden changes that resulted from the surrender, he realized that everything up to that point had been a lie. The wartime ideology, like the plains around Nagano, had been burned to the ground. He was angry with himself rather than depressed or enervated (like the characters in Dazai Osamu's famous novel *The Setting Sun*), but he also began to have doubts about possibly being deceived once more. Therefore, he felt that they had to excavate their wartime experiences fully to prevent that from happening.[29]

In 1947, Shiratori and his friends started a magazine called *Nameless Flower (Na mo naki hana)* after Hani Gorō came to talk at a local gathering. They changed the name to *Mountain Range (Yamanami)* in 1950 after a friend of his saw a play by that name and was taken with the image of a whole range of mountains standing together rather than a tall mountain like Fuji standing alone. Many of those who belonged to another one of the local *wadatsumi* groups also joined the Mountain Range, and they began to produce writings about the war. They published their magazine once every four months, but when Shiratori began to study for his university entrance exam, he was forced to suspend his work on it. So from the fall of 1950 to 1956, the *Mountain Range* went on hiatus.

While the group was against war, it differed from other antiwar groups in that the Mountain Range approached the question from the position of having survived their former belief in the wartime ideology. In the September 1950 issue of their magazine, the members discussed their reactions to the movie *Listen to the Voice of Wadatsumi* and complained that such antiwar movies always deal with antiwar students when they should be describing the experiences and war responsibility of the nation's people.[30] Shiratori says he would like to see a movie made from the viewpoint of those who were left behind (*ikinokotta*). The term *"ikinokoru"* is usually translated as "to survive," but for the group the point was that they believed at the time that they should join their comrades in death. They had been taught that it was shameful to be left behind, so their survivors' guilt had an added dimension that a movie about students who were against the war in the first place could not provide.

As they wrote in the July 1950 issue, they had grown up in an era in which cries of "hooray for the soldiers!" filled the air, and as schoolchildren they were taught only how to die proudly for the country and the emperor. They were not taught how to live. Surviving meant betraying those who had died, because they had been taught that dying together and being with the community of dead heroes was the highest value. They had no pride at all in surviving the war, so when it ended, all they could feel was despondence.[31] When they finally reassessed what they had believed in, they also had to grapple with the problem of having to deny the value of their friends' and relatives' deaths.

As those who had been left behind, the Mountain Range considered it their responsibility to pursue the issue of war responsibility. This role meant that they could not assume the position of victim, and they had to acknowledge responsibility at the level of the individual. The members took self-critique as the foundation for their gathering and were not content to shift the blame for the war onto the military leaders. They had, in Maruyama's words, established the group as a community of contrition. They stood in stark contrast to the way the victim mentality appeared to be manifesting itself in the rest of society.

While the group's magazine was on hiatus, Shiratori went to

Tokyo University, graduating in 1954. He disliked it and thought that it was like serving in the military. When he graduated, he sent off applications to Aomori and Nagasaki to become a high school teacher. Although both places accepted his application, he ended up going to Noshiro High School in Akita Prefecture, which had sent him a special invitation, even though he had no idea of where it was.[32]

Shiratori had trouble picking up the local dialect in Akita, but he got to know the students well because he lived in the dormitory. As it turned out, even in this faraway locale, the students were quite active politically. One group formed to oppose the testing of nuclear weapons, and another *wadatsumi* group had formed there as a literary club because the school would not permit it as a school club. Since they could not meet in the school building, Shiratori offered them his room for their gatherings. In the winter of 1955, he formed a reading group of people who wanted to study the general-interest monthly *Women's Forum (Fujin kōron)*.

One might note that Shiratori was carrying out these activities in the context of a less tightly controlled educational system than would later prevail. In the 1950s, the Ministry of Education had not yet reasserted fully centralized control, and some local school boards still retained a degree of autonomy. Teaching materials were scarce, so many teachers were quite creative with their texts and curricula. They often made their classes more relevant by conducting research on the areas surrounding the schools, so there was greater interaction between students and the local community in this period.

When Shiratori went home to Nagano for summer break in 1956, he and his friends decided to revive their magazine. This time the people associated with it were spread out in three locations. One-third of the group were from Nagano, one-third were from Noshiro and had been in the *wadatsumi* group there, and one-third were people Shiratori had "wasted" time with in Tokyo while he was at school.[33] All of his friends from Tokyo had gone to the countryside afterwards, and so the group was unique in being so spread out. Eventually this geographic dispersion would lead the group to formulate the principle that any place where three or more people gathered, they could use the Mountain Range name and decide on their own activities. They would have no central headquarters, and they would use the *Mountain Range* magazine to communicate with each other. By 1960, the group consisted of some two hundred people in twelve small circles from Aomori to Shikoku.[34] Each group mimeographed its own members' writings, which Shiratori then collated into the magazine. In addition, various individuals and regional branches produced eight of their own related magazines whose contents reflected the membership's differences in class, employment, region, thought, ideals, and so on. An indication of the emphasis they placed on a decentralized structure is that all of the branches, with the exception of the Tokyo group, were located in rural areas.

When the circle was re-formed, the group had to rethink its organization. A disjuncture had already developed between the wartime generation that founded the group and the postwar generation to whom they wanted to convey their experiences. In issue 17, one of the younger members criticized the founders for dwelling on the past and not writing more about the present. In response, those from Shiratori's generation had to reconsider the problem of creating a sense of solidarity with those who had been too young to take part in the war effort. Ochiai Hiroshi put it in these terms: the legacy that his generation, which had been drawn into fully participating in the war, could offer to the postwar generation would be to make them realize the latent potential they had for doing the same thing. Shiratori felt that memories had to be replaced with prophecy, but war experiences themselves could not be transformed. Instead, he asserted that his generation had to join their memories of the war experiences with an assessment of situations they faced with the so-called reverse course and state leaders who were trying to revive prewar systems. Memory could increase their prophetic powers with regard to events unfolding right before their eyes.[35]

Therefore, the Mountain Range wrote both about their war experiences and about present-day realities. They continued to record wartime experiences at the level of the people, digging deeper into them in order to give voice to what had previously been silenced, and to reeducate themselves and others as a step toward creating an alternative society.[36] But in addition to war experiences, the group also dedicated themselves to recording the thoughts of ordinary people at their jobs or local communities. Writers consciously injected themselves into these records, so the magazine featured numerous pieces that contained the words "and me" attached to particular occupations or events, such as "Anpo and me." The group, then, ought to be situated alongside other life histories movements that sprang up during the 1950s.

The notion of getting ordinary people to record their own lives had prewar antecedents in the "How to Write Your Daily Life" movement (*seikatsu tsuzurikata undō*), which was directed at working-class children in the 1920s and 1930s.[37] This movement was revived by progressive educators, who shifted the efforts from children to adults, especially female laborers;[38] by Japan Communist Party organizers who sought to raise the consciousness of the proletariat; and by local activists who sought to create a counterweight to a society overly concentrated on the urban center of Tokyo. That is, there were many such movements across Japan that sought to use the freedom of expression that was guaranteed by the postwar constitution to secure themselves more egalitarian positions in society.

The Mountain Range, however, differed somewhat from these other movements to make records of ordinary people's lives in that it was more heterogeneous, including both men and women coming from a variety of different occupations and locales.[39] They also differed from other movements in specifically opposing attempts to "enlighten" the masses and direct the content of people's writings. For example, they cite the attitude of organizers of *Life Magazine (Jinsei zasshi)* who said: "You should understand how hard it was for us. When you talk to farmers and young people, they don't understand regular words, so you have to stoop to their level in order to talk with them. We want you to understand how sad that makes us."[40] This arrogance made these organizers untrustworthy in the eyes of the Mountain Range members.

Shiratori saw the movement to make records of ordinary life as an opportunity to look, feel, and write about the way things are rather than to shape the records to fit an ideological framework. However, he was not naive about difficulties in interpreting what "the way things are" actually means. There is an epistemological problem of being sure of the actuality of what one sees and in relating feelings (*jikkan*) that spark the initial awareness of existence. He contends that the last stage of recording "the way things are" leads to the logical, theoretical problem of abstraction. Strict adherence to "the way things are" means that one stops with the recognition of emotion and a monotonous repetition of detail. Furthermore, for the experience to have any significance beyond a purely individual expression, one has to be able to combine it with other people's experiences. The group therefore grappled not only with the question of writing their histories, but also with rewriting themselves.

"Ways to Drink and Methodologies of Circles"

IN A SENSE, when the Mountain Range re-formed in 1956, it was really like starting a new circle. Since they communicated primarily in writing and since the groups were so spread out, they finally began to make plans to get everyone together. The parents of one of the members ran an inn for travelers on pilgrimages to the Togakushi Shrine in Shinshu, and the member convinced them to let the group use the facilities for four days. So the first face-to-face gathering of the Mountain Range took place in August 1959 in the midst of typhoon weather. A look at the "agenda" for the conference is illuminating for its open structure.

August 8 (Thursday)

7:00 PM	Opening, toast
7:00–9:00 PM	Introductions—things about oneself
9:00–10:00 PM	Things up to this point—this and that
10:00–11:00 PM	Play and folksongs
11:00 to whenever one likes	Whatever one wants

August 9 (Friday)

From whenever one likes to 8:00 AM	Whatever one wants
9:00–11:00 AM	Go back over what was said yesterday Jointly contribute topics
Noon–2:00 PM	Lunch, whatever one wants
2:00–6:00 PM	Ways of making records Ways of organizing
7:00–10:00 PM	Conversing with everyone

August 10 (Saturday)

9:00–11:00 AM	Discussion of the Mountain Range's pledge
11:00–4:00 PM	Hiking at Takahara, go to campsite
4:00–10:00 PM	Camping (no talking about difficult things)

August 11 (Sunday)

7:00 AM	Breakfast
8:00 AM	Climb Togakushi Mountain
3:30 PM	In front of the Togakushi Shrine, "until we meet again!"[41]

The group had not established any principles for their organization or come to any agreement about what they should be doing, so the informal conversation of day one was crucial to gaining some mutual understanding of who they were. The first conference set the pattern for all the others in having the children there open the gatherings with a toast. The "rules" that Chair Kishida Ryōji declared at the beginning of the gathering have continued to the present: "Those who want to drink can drink and those who want to skip out can do so as well. Do things freely. You can talk while lying down. We'll be concerned if you drunkenly ramble on, but it's up to you to control yourself. You can't think straight if you're drunk. But the worst, most troubling thing is if you are stubbornly serious."[42]

In other words, the atmosphere they wanted to create was that of a free-flowing symposium or drinking party in the tradition of ancient Greece. Members sometimes even referred to their group as a drinking circle.[43] They also brought along their husbands or wives and children, something that typically would not occur at a "serious" conference. People roamed about freely and took breaks when they wanted, but everyone was given a turn to speak. The conditions were designed to encourage people to say whatever they wanted and to feel free to disagree with others. If people became too serious, the group felt it would stifle any creativity in the discussion. As Shiratori put it, "A dialogue of the spirit can only be creative when undertaken in free conditions."[44]

The group had only one major piece of "business" to discuss, and that was the pledge (*yakusoku*) that had been proposed. The pledge was not an organizational chart but rather an outline of a few minimal conditions. After their discussion at Togakushi, the group finally wrote up the pledge in the May 1960 issue of their magazine. It contained just four brief points: "In order to excavate (*horiokoshi*) the lives and thoughts at the base of Japan (*Nihon no teihen*) and to make a record of them, we will (1) regularly publish a magazine and (2) collect monthly dues of fifty yen from members. (3) Any place where more than three people gather can form a Mountain Range group. (4) Editing care of Shiratori Kunio, Noshiro High School, Hatakemachi, Noshiro City, Akita Prefecture.[45]

The short phrase prefacing the terms of the pledge imply that they saw themselves mainly as a research and writing circle, but the imagery of digging into ordinary people's lives implies a number of things. On the one hand, it indicates that they sought to give their subjects their own voice. They were not producing academic studies or novelistic treatments, although they would make in-depth investigations. On the other hand, the image of unearthing ordinary people's lives and thoughts implied that they intended to go beyond mere description and assess their significance as well.

However, the phrase that was most contentious was "the base of Japan," sparking considerable debate over what it really meant. "The base" clearly excluded the elite and those in positions of authority, but it was more difficult to articulate exactly what this category included. Using the term "base" distinguished the group from Marxists who used words carrying ideological connotations, such as the "proletariat," "the people" (*jinmin*), or "the masses" (*taishū*). The members of the Mountain Range, however, did not have a fixed conception of people's class consciousness or historical roles. Nor did they presume that particular individuals necessarily represented their ostensible class or category.

Given the rural background of the circle, one might assume that "the base" meant the peasantry. One of their big debates was over the lack of farmers in the group. Most of the members came from rural backgrounds, but they themselves were not farmers, so some of the group felt that they could not represent "the base" without farmers and workers in small and mid-sized businesses. One Mountain Range member wanted to use the magazine to communicate with village groups and rural youth organizations that had their own magazines. But Shiratori also warned about the danger of being overly concerned with numbers rather than thinking about how to connect with farmers. He worried that people might end up trying to "enlighten" the peasants, as certain elite progressives and Japan Communist Party organizers tried to do.

While they continued to debate the definition of "the base," the group chose to leave it to the individual how to interpret the idea. This result is indicative of some of their key notions about organizational theory. They did not insist on coming to a consensus on the term, nor did they decide on the meaning of this mission statement through majority rule. Each person was free to create his or her own meaning. They considered it essential to respect and embrace all the differences of opinion within the group and demanded that people give voice to their disagreements.

While the first minimal condition they established for the group was publishing a magazine on a "regular" basis, they were in fact quite flexible in their definition of the word "regular." They did not actually mean that they had a strict obligation to publish on a fixed schedule or even a strong conviction that they would be able to do so. They usually put out three or four issues a year, but sometimes the number dropped to only one or two issues per year.

They were similarly lax about membership dues. Actually, dues were never considered a condition of membership, and most people did not in fact pay them. Even though the price of paper tripled over the next fifteen years, they never bothered to change the amount for dues. Shiratori's philosophy was that they should put out the magazine even if they went into debt, so they always lost money. The group did not even bother to maintain a membership list. They did not establish any principles for distinguishing a member from a nonmember, so if one sent a piece in to the magazine or came to one of the gatherings, one was considered part of the group.[46] In other words, they were not concerned with establishing strict criteria for participation or amassing sizable numbers of people.

The stipulation that a Mountain Range group could be formed wherever more than three people gather meant that the group was fluid and decentered. After the Togakushi gathering, numerous affiliates popped up in several different locations because of the freedom in this pledge. Many of these small groups disappeared shortly afterwards, but they all set up their own magazines and activities. Some groups like the Tokyo Mountain Range broke up only to re-form later on with new people. In the case of the Tokyo group, its personality changed as student members graduated from their schools and went to different locales. Groups also developed within the Mountain Range based on shared occupations, status, or social concerns, such as the Teen Club (Jūdai no

Kai) or the Wadatsumi Mountain Range. Over time, the energy within the Mountain Range circle shifted around from place to place as some groups grew very active while others became more restive.[47] Again the group's loose structure enabled it to continue despite these shifts.

The first three stipulations of the pledge are remarkable for their indeterminacy. It would be difficult to deduce the character of the Mountain Range from them. The members are fond of saying that their philosophy of organization was not to have any organizational principles. But in fact, the loose nature of the group implied certain principles of group formation that were key to many circles and citizens' movements both then and in the decades to follow. The Mountain Range had a powerful anti-authoritarian streak and consequently emphasized the periphery over the center. They chose to chronicle the provinces (*chihō*), the countryside (*inaka*), the tip (*mattan*), and the backside (*ura*) from which they originated and maintained no center except their individual selves. As Suzuki Motohiko put it, "You should dig underneath your own feet and I'm going to dig under mine."[48] They criticized centralized organizations such as the government or the mass media for imposing standardized, colorless, one-way communication from the center outward.[49]

Their rejection of ideological consensus as a principle of formation was also a way to avoid centralized hierarchic domination. They encouraged rather than suppressed differences of opinion and took a slow, deliberative approach to everything. They kept one step removed from the political or cultural fashions of the day and took what they referred to as a "three-time approach" (*sankai hōshiki*), that is, they would thoroughly discuss something three times before deciding on anything as a group. The idea was that the first time a subject was brought up, whether by someone within the group or by those from another organization, the group first needed to get to know that person and his or her perspective. The initial encounter functioned like the self-introductions at the Togakushi gathering and might even involve some joking or teasing as part of the process. The second encounter, however, allowed for a slightly deeper discussion and exchange of experiences, and by the third time the group might be able to circumscribe the issue fully.

The "three-time approach" was not a literal model but rather a general philosophy. Shiratori said that what was most important was getting to know all the points at which people agreed and disagreed, and being clear about what points people did not fully understand.[50] Members rarely expressed complete agreement with what others said, nor did they totally reject other people's opinions. This approach made it difficult to compromise, but by going back and forth on the same topic from many different angles, the group was able to reach a more profound comprehension. Opposite to the mass media, which never looked back on the same thing, extended conversations often started in the local magazines of the Mountain Range and were then also incorporated into the version Shiratori edited. With the feedback from other local groups, the dialogue could then be refined and broadened.[51]

The slow, deliberate approach that the Mountain Range adopted was indicative of the long view they took and has helped the group continue for so many decades. This approach applied to the way people became involved in the group as well. Although the Mountain Range was very inclusive, it also sometimes took a long time for people to identify fully with it. Generally speaking, people came into the group in one of three ways. Some came because they knew Shiratori and were drawn by his personal appeal. Others came because they had read some of his writings or those of other members. Still others came because they knew a friend or relative who belonged to the group. They might come to one of the general gatherings that the group continues to hold every other year and begin to get acquainted but still not think of themselves as belonging to the group. Conversely, some members might not come to the gatherings for several years but are still considered fully part of the group when they reappear.

Since membership in the Mountain Range is not contingent on attending the assemblies and since there are no real criteria for membership other than contact with people in the group, the process is much more like one of becoming friends with the group. What seems to hold the Mountain Range together are bonds of friendship created by sharing experiences and discussing their significance.

The Mountain Range and Anpo

THE TOGAKUSHI conference took place as protests against the Security Treaty had just begun to gather steam. However, over the ensuing months, the Mountain Range did not make any resolutions about Anpo or issue any public statements as a group. Even when the treaty was forcibly ratified on May 19 or when Kanba Michiko was killed on June 15, they refrained from any emergency declarations. This did not mean, however, that most members favored Anpo or supported the Kishi administration. Most were concerned with the heightened possibility of Japan being drawn into a war because of the treaty, and like other citizens' movements, they feared that Kishi's use of force to ratify the treaty foretold the resurgence of fascism. Many of them took part in demonstrations, especially those who were students at the time, and more than sixty members responded to an appeal for contributions to help those injured on June 15.

However, in order to guarantee the autonomy of each member and local group, the group as a whole did not take any official actions. In keeping with their idea of personal responsibility, they held that each individual should decide what he or she wanted to do.[52] They then published reports in their magazine, which not surprisingly focused heavily on their experiences at demonstrations rather than on diplomatic issues or political strategy and ideology. The variety of locations that sent in reports serves as an important reminder that the protests were not confined to Tokyo but were spread out across the country.

Members' descriptions of the Anpo protests tended to emphasize their heterogeneity in the forms of action, the different locations in which they took place, and the type of groups involved. One housewife from Tsugaru told of how she had joined the Tsugaru Mountain Range group after seeing their sign at a demonstration that encouraged ordinary citizens to march together with them. An Akita member told of how her fellow workers on strike at the hospital had joined with the Anpo protesters to voice both groups' demands together.[53]

Demonstrations in Kyoto were dominated by students to a greater degree than those in Tokyo, and the local population nurtured them more. So despite the students' tendency to be more radical than the workers and to do things like stage sit-ins in the middle of the busiest thoroughfare or block the trolleys that ran down the middle of the street, bystanders did not get mad at them. As in Tokyo, bystanders generally waved and shouted encouragement. Since there was no real equivalent of the Diet building in Kyoto and Osaka on which to focus the demonstrations, they also tended to meander more than in Tokyo. Different groups would take different routes on their marches.[54]

The number of articles and reports on the Anpo protests in the various magazines the Mountain Range put out attests to the importance the issue had for the group. Their deliberate "three-time approach" also meant that they continued to raise the Anpo issue long after other groups and individuals had forgotten about it. One member estimated that one would not hear anything about Anpo in the mass media four months afterwards, so they consciously put out a special issue on the protests an entire year after they were over. They also continued to debate the ramifications in their groups and at the nationwide assemblies into the 1970s.[55]

The Mountain Range has continued to meet as a whole group once every two years, always in a different location. One reason for rotating the locations is to avoid any centralization of the group, but the practice also gives people an opportunity to see places that they might not otherwise visit. It provides an occasion for members to become acquainted with the particular issues that are most important to the local groups and also to do some sightseeing. Some participants go on side trips afterwards to take advantage of the travel opportunity. Typically about one hundred people come to any given meeting, although the composition varies somewhat each time.

The basic format of the gatherings has stayed the same since Togakushi except that the membership now often breaks up into smaller groups on the second day to discuss particular themes of interest. Participants still float in and out of the meetings or change groups if they want. The discussions are still conducted in egalitarian fashion, so everyone speaks in turn and one is allowed to say whatever he or she wants. In line with the three-time approach, the meetings have often continued a theme from one gathering to the next despite the two-year break. As they moved into the 1970s, the group began to discuss the rising ideology surrounding private life. At the same time, they reconsidered the significance of Hiroshima, its relationship to Anpo and to Okinawa, which in turn led to a discussion of issues in the broader expanse of Asia. That is, their themes shifted to more contemporary issues while maintaining the experience of war as the base from which these considerations began.

The group's mission of chronicling people from various walks of life and spreading their works through small-scale communications networks has spawned several publishing ventures. The Tokyo group in particular has many members connected with the publishing world, and as a consequence their magazine appears more often and more regularly than others. They have also produced a series of small hand-bound booklets on "anonymous" Japanese and their lives, featuring a falconer in Akita, the wife of a kamikaze pilot, and fishers in a northern village, for example. Members of the Tokyo group felt that being part of the Mountain Range, therefore, widened their horizons and made them feel closer to people all over the country from all walks of life.[56] They emphasized the very personal, concrete contact they had with the people whose lives they recorded, noting that they had learned a lot through those people and that their home regions came alive through their conversations.

Members of the Mountain Range attribute the longevity of the group to its indeterminate structure and commitment to on-going dialogue. Their composition is not uniform in terms of class, gender, occupation, or geographic locale. However, because the group is radically egalitarian, the members feel that it serves as an alternative community to the highly restrictive hierarchies of work, school, neighborhood, or government. Without the Mountain Range, their lives would be unbalanced.

Their descriptions find an analogy with the famous folklorist Yanagida Kunio's anthropological analysis of the world of *jōmin*, the ordinary people at the base of society whose constancy provides the foundation for Japanese culture. The secular workaday world (*ke*) with its normative social rules needs to be punctuated by regular festive occasions (*hare*) in which the usual social relationships are suspended. These festivities serve as a corrective to the everyday work world. The members of the Mountain Range, for their part, try to carry over the nonserious, egalitarian, multivocal atmosphere of the group to the other parts of their social framework.

The Mountain Range also implemented absolute local autonomy in order to avoid the tendency of all types of organizations—political parties, religious sects, companies, schools of literary and artistic traditions, to name a few—to recapitulate the hierarchic structure of the state and rally around powerful leaders who become little emperors. Even though Shiratori is one of the main figures of the group, the group does not depend on him for their existence. They specifically reject centralized structures and their insistence on harmony and unitary thought imposed by the powers at the center. Instead, the Mountain Range is devoted to debate and disagreement, or, in the words of Tsurumi Kazuko, the group "emphasizes the function of discommunication rather than communication among its members."[57]

However, one wonders how long the group can continue once

the generation of those with direct experience of the war has passed away. For most of this early generation, the day of Japan's surrender was the beginning of their lives, and they speak of having been reborn through it. August 15, 1945, for them is Year Zero, although probably in a different way than for most.[58] It afforded the chance to construct a new system on top of the old one razed in the bombings, but it was also a chance for them to dig carefully through the ruins in order to see precisely what they used to be. For them, rebirth took place in radically personal terms and was not just an allegory for society. The surrender created an existential crisis by positing their continued existence. To survive, they had to take personal responsibility for the way they were in order to effect changes under their new circumstances. Almost every issue of their magazine has had a piece on their experiences related to war. Young people today, however, have only known affluence and have seen their country only as an economic superpower. Thus, the group itself may eventually dwindle, although its organizing principles had become commonplace among citizens' movements by the 1970s and in that way provides a legacy for the future.

4

THE POETS OF ŌI FACTORY
AND WORK CULTURE

IN THE PROCESS of reconstructing Japan, labor was a major focus for both the Occupation and the established opposition parties. SCAP hoped that a vibrant labor movement would be a counterweight to the power of the industrial conglomerates, which it saw as a major contributor to Japanese fascism, making labor-management relations more equitable and less prone to authoritarian control. SCAP immediately ordered a series of labor laws that established workers' rights to organize, engage in collective bargaining, and strike, and prohibited management's obstruction of any of these rights. These laws helped foster an explosive growth in the number of unionists from a mere five thousand in October 1945 to nearly five million by December 1946.[1] However, soon after this initial encouragement, SCAP began to curtail the labor movement, reversing course as the cold war reset the Occupation's priorities. SCAP concentrated on purging the influence of the Japan Communist Party on organized labor in 1950, firing over twelve thousand suspected communists from their jobs.

SCAP was especially worried about communists in the union leadership. The Japan Communist Party gained a certain amount of credibility in the immediate postwar years because it had openly

opposed the fascist state during the war and suffered severe repression for it. SCAP had set free political prisoners after the
defeat, and the Japan Communist Party for its part termed the
Occupation a "liberation" and initially adopted an accommodationist stance toward it. Because Marxist theory gives ontological
priority to the working class, the party made a concerted effort to
organize the workers, and many activists took up leadership positions in the unions. SCAP began to undermine their leadership
from 1947, when, at the last minute, MacArthur blocked the general strike scheduled for February 1. SCAP's antagonism toward
the party's attempts to foster a militant labor movement culminated in the Red Purge of 1950. The Occupation also encouraged
the formation of a more mainstream, anticommunist labor federation, and Sōhyō, the General Council of Trade Unions of Japan,
was established in 1950 with this role in mind. However, the left
wing of Sōhyō soon gained control of the organization, and the
federation became closely engaged with the political program of
the Japan Socialist Party.

The leadership of both the Japan Communist Party and the
Japan Socialist Party sought to strengthen the labor movement to
bring about a bourgeois democratic revolution that they hoped
would set the stage for the eventual social revolution. In order to
accomplish this objective, party ideologues felt that they needed
to enlighten rank-and-file workers regarding their historical role
and raise their political consciousness. Thus, despite the proletariat's ontological priority, in practice the leaders tried to exert
organizational and ideological control over the labor movement.
The unions were a major instrument of control, but the parties
also sought to extend this control to the workplace culture circles
that sprang up in the mid- to late 1950s. These circles were small
groups of laborers who engaged in some kind of cultural activity
after work hours, such as singing in choral or folksong groups,
writing and performing drama, dancing, creating visual arts, or
writing poetry or other literary pieces. The left political parties
promoted their own circles and set out to incorporate all of these

various circles into a centralized mass organ that could be mobilized for political activities. That is, the Japan Communist and Socialist parties looked to integrate the circles into their political hierarchies as part of their united front strategy.

However, the leadership of the two parties did not comprehend well the mentality of the workers who joined these circles; their elitism and instrumentalist appropriation of these movements made this fact clear. Workers did not consider circle activities to be merely a means to political activism, but pursued them because the activities suited their own ways of expressing themselves. The circles were an extension of their workplace community rather than leisure time separate from work, and so the circles added value to their jobs and forged a different type of labor culture from the war years. Circles like the Poets of Ōi Factory saw their activities as a vehicle for autonomous expression that emphasized the positive value of labor and not just their exploitation or alienation.

When circles engaged political issues, they also approached them from a different perspective than the Japan Communist Party and Japan Socialist Party theorists did. When party ideologues mobilized workers in the Anpo protests, they emphasized that the treaty was a form of American imperialism and that the proletarian working masses had to rise up together to oppose it. Workers themselves, however, did not necessarily comprehend all the nuances of the treaty or care about the cold war machinations of the American leaders. Instead, they saw how Kishi's naked wielding of power could affect the democratic rights they had recently acquired. They had suffered violent suppression of those rights by the police and right-wing thugs, so their political consciousness arose out of physical experience rather than intellectual theories. Therefore, the hierarchic authority that the Japan Communist Party in particular tried to impose over laborers and their movements contradicted the workers' desire for egalitarian, participatory forms of labor culture and politics. This essential contradiction meant that the mainstream labor movement gradually lost its vitality and was slowly supplanted by other kinds of social movements in the 1970s.

Factory and Union

THE POETS of Ōi Factory was a small poetry circle that Inaba Yoshikazu and Nakamura Kiyoshi helped start in 1954. The two were working at the Japan National Railways repair facilities at Ōimachi, located one stop south of Shinagawa station in Tokyo along the Keihin Tōhoku line. Their small circle of ten people was only one of many poetry circles that sprang up at the factory, and the poetry circles were only one type of culture circle that was popular at the time. Such circles flourished in the mid-1950s and constituted an important alternative to hierarchic forms of community found in corporate management, the government, and even the union. So although the Poets of Ōi was small in number, it illustrates certain salient characteristics of circles associated with the workplace and reveals the type of labor culture that workers sought to create.

Jobs at the Ōi repair complex had low status within Japan National Railways because they were, to use the modern parlance, the "3Ds," that is, dirty, dangerous, and difficult.[2] When Inaba and Nakamura came to work for the railways shortly after Japan's defeat, the railroad was still using a large number of steam engines, which got especially grimy. The factory complex they worked at was massive, servicing train cars from all of Japan National Railways' Tokyo lines, the Tōkaidō line running from Tokyo to Kyoto and Osaka, the Yokosuka line running out to Kamakura and a major U.S. naval base, and others. By the late 1950s, the repair yards were a hodgepodge of old red-brick buildings with rusty exposed pipes alongside new steel and concrete factories.

At the time, nearly 2,900 workers were employed at Ōi, and it was one of the major strongholds of the National Railway Workers Union (Kokutetsu Rōdō Kumiai, or Kokurō for short). The Ōi factory was a closed shop, and since even the middle-level managers and supervisors had to join, over 95 percent of the people working there were union members. Work life at Ōi was therefore synonymous with the union. As was typical of closed shops, workers were automatically inducted on being hired, and union dues were automatically deducted at a rate of between one-and-a-half and two percent of one's wages.[3]

Kokurō formed at the end of February 1946 just before the new Labor Law went into effect, and by July it was already locked in a battle to oppose management's attempts to fire 75,000 railway employees. Since this incident occurred before the Yoshida administration rescinded the right of public employees to strike in 1949, the union used the threat of a nationwide strike to force the company to back down from its rationalization plan.[4] Workers right after World War II often challenged the very way that businesses operated, because business leaders were in disarray and workers were suffering severe economic hardships. In hundreds of cases, workers took control of production when management denied their demands for better wages and more say in the workplace. In May of 1946, MacArthur issued a condemnation of production control strikes, and their numbers quickly fell off. However, family wages, job security, and greater control of the workplace continued to be the focus of the labor movement into the 1950s.[5]

By the fall of 1946, the union movement had gathered strength, and the Congress of Industrial Labor Unions of Japan (Zen Nihon Sangyōbetsu Rōdō Kumiai Kaigi, or Sanbetsu Kaigi for short), with strong ties to the Japan Communist Party, pushed an initiative for a general strike scheduled for February 1, 1947. Some 2.6 million government workers were ready to strike, and millions more from private sector unions had pledged to join later. Their demands were both economic, such as the establishment of a minimum wage, and political, such as the dissolution of the Yoshida government.[6] However, shortly before midnight on January 31, MacArthur banned the strike, forcing strike leaders to call it off tearfully at the last minute.

This act marked the beginning of the Occupation's attempts to rein in the labor movement, leading finally to the expulsion of suspected communists from leadership positions in the unions in 1950. The expulsions were a major component of the Red Purge carried out from May to December of that year. SCAP also encouraged and actively supported the formation of the General Council of Trade Unions (Nihon Rōdō Kumiai Sō Hyōgikai, or Sōhyō, as it is better known) as an anticommunist alternative for labor. Sōhyō was formed from a faction that had split off from Sanbetsu and the left and neutral factions of the presurrender General Federation of Japan Trade Unions (Nihon Rōdō Sōdōmei). From its inception, Sōhyō was the largest federation of labor unions in Japan, encompassing nearly all unionized public sector employees from municipal workers in prefectural offices to teachers to telecommunications workers to Kokurō, the fourth largest affiliate.

Sōhyō's formation was partly a reaction against the "conspiratorial 'transmission belt' unionism" in which Japanese Communist Party cells and fractions worked to subordinate union organs to the party's agenda.[7] Many of the labor organizers were Communist, but the bulk of the workers were not, or, as labor researcher Sumiya Mikiyo put it, the labor movement was like a crane—the crest of its head was red, but the rest of its body was white.[8] Rank-and-file workers responded when organizers tried to meet their needs rather than the demands of the party ideologues, but conflicts arose when organizers were overly directive.

The founding of Sōhyō was also driven by a younger generation of activists who wanted to replace the old guard union leaders. These younger activists wanted to change union organization, which was based on personal ties between paternalistic bosses and their followers, and the use of outside union professionals. They favored instead greater union autonomy from political parties and the promotion of economist interests and demands.[9]

Nonetheless, the left-wing elements of Sōhyō soon took charge, and the group became very active politically in opposing the efforts of the Yoshida government to reimpose wartime institutions. Moreover, given what was perceived of as tight integration between the state and big business, Sōhyō leaders reasoned that economic struggle had to be integrated with political struggles. They thought they had to "guide" the workers to prevent them from being "swallowed up by the establishment." So despite its anticommunist origins, the leaders and activists in Sōhyō ended up operating in a similar fashion to the Japan Communist Party cadres.[10]

With the 1949 restriction against public employees' right to strike, Kokurō had to resort to tactics such as work-to-rule slowdowns in the 1950s to oppose the company's rationalization plans and gain more of "a voice in calculating pay raises, restricting efficiency-based wages, and controlling the authority of supervisors."[11] The union's emphasis on job security was well founded as the company focused on replacing and modernizing its equipment, converting to diesel and electrification. The company's drive meant that 160,000 Japan National Railways employees lost their jobs from 1948 to 1951, many of them because their work of supplying coal for the trains was eliminated.[12]

Kokurō responded with militant shop-floor struggles to win a voice in determining the standards for pay and promotion and the way work was assigned. It was joined by another militant union, the National Railways Locomotive Engineers Union (Kokutetsu Dōryokusha Rōdō Kumiai, or Dōrō), which was established in 1951. Since the Japan National Railways always ran considerably over its capacity, work-to-rule protests (in which workers slowed down to the contractual minimum pace) and refusals to take overtime work proved to be effective actions even when the public sector unions were deprived of the right to strike. The Ōi factory was considered one of the three staunchest locals of Kokurō nationwide, and Inaba and Nakamura remember that in the confrontational atmosphere of the time they were always protesting something.

The strength of Kokurō and Dōrō enabled Japan National

Railways workers to resist the kind of productivity drives that management led in the private sector following the industrial revival from the Korean War. American officials encouraged and helped fund these drives by which management sought to regain control of the shop floor and rationalize the work force to increase productivity and profits.[13] One of the key tactics in this effort was to foster the establishment of "second" unions that were pro-management and to emphasize harmonious relations between labor and management. These "second" unions generally supported the productivity drives provided they led to higher wages and better work conditions for the workers who remained.

Another manifestation of the growing labor-management accommodation in the private sector was the advent of quality control circles, which started in the early 1950s after W. Edward Deming came to Japan to introduce the concept. In quality control circles, workers "participated" in raising the efficiency and safety of the work group as well as the quality of a product by discussing the production process and making suggestions for improvements. This participation, however, was not the same thing as workers' production control. Suggestions were directed at management goals rather than objectives determined by labor. Furthermore, part of the workers' "merit" pay was tied to standards of ability or safety set in the circles or to the number of suggestions that the management incorporated into production. Thus, quality control circles could be used to punish monetarily or rationalize workers who appeared less productive and to increase competition among workers for management favors.[14] Although quality control circles have been touted as a means to facilitate better teamwork on the line and to increase workers' voices in production, they could in fact serve to break down earlier worker solidarity and reduce workers' autonomy.

It was within this context of management's attempt to displace worker culture with managerial control that the workplace culture circles blossomed in the mid to late 1950s. These workplace circles were the opposite of quality control circles in that they arose out of worker initiative.

A Small Circle of Friends

INABA CAME to work at the Ōi facility about a year after Japan's defeat in the war, following brief stints at cutting lumber and fixing roads. During the war, he had attended what would be middle school today, and after graduating he went to work at an airplane factory that was also experimenting with rockets. Nakamura had wanted to work on steam locomotives and found work first at the Hamamatsu factory in Shizuoka Prefecture. He transferred up to the Ōi factory in 1957 in part because he had literary aspirations and Tokyo was where most other major poets were located. But at the time, Nakamura asserts, it was almost unimaginable for manual laborers from the countryside to pick up a pen and write poetry, and those who studied intellectual works ran the risk of being labeled "red."[15] This was because, during the war, workers had no social or political space in which they could express themselves, he says.

While he was at Hamamatsu, Nakamura organized a poetry circle called the "Flock" (Mure), and when he transferred to Ōi, he and Inaba and others formed the Poets of Ōi. At Ōi as in countless other workplaces across the country, a wide variety of circles devoted to cultural activities had begun to pop up like bamboo shoots from around 1954. Choral groups were extremely popular, and Inaba also joined a circle that sang Russian folk songs. Some workers formed drama troupes. Writing circles were quite popular, with names that reflected both the natural and industrial worlds. Group names such as the Acorns (Donguri), the Bamboo Shoots, (Takenoko), and Fresh Leaves (Wakaba) contrasted with those such as the Gears (Haguruma) and the Torches (Tomoshibi). Other names such as Clanging Bug (Kankanmushi) suggested both worlds at once, as did the name Mole Cricket (Okera), which is also an idiom for being broke. The circles were not exclusive, and workers floated freely from one to the other, sometimes belonging to more than one at a time.

The Poets of Ōi were typical of circles that people formed on their own rather than under the guidance of Japan Communist

Party organizers. Circles formed under party guidance used cultural activities as a way to politicize their members and were intended to function as cells of the party. For example, the afterword to a 1952 volume of workers' "liberation poetry" said these poems about the Keihin industrial corridor around Tokyo revealed the crises of present-day society and gave people the courage to overcome them. It went on to exhort: "Workers with a rich poetic spirit, glory! Wave the conscience of the nation! Glory to all your comrades!"[16] By contrast, the Poets of Ōi had no fixed ideas about how or what they should write. They did not feel compelled to write in a social realist style or to create works that raised the political consciousness of the proletariat. They had no set political agenda and debated whether or not political activities would dilute their creative output. The group also differed from Japan Communist Party–organized circles, on the one hand, and literary circles that taught particular schools of writing, on the other, in that the Poets of Ōi were not under the tutelage of an ideologue or acknowledged teacher who set standards of writing for them. Instead, they gathered as equals out of a shared interest in poetry.

Precedents for the Poets of Ōi already existed within the Japan National Railways a decade prior to their formation. In February 1946, a group of rail workers created a poetry circle called the Eastern Railways Poetry Group (Tōtetsu Shiwa Kai) and began to publish a magazine called *JNR Poets (Kokutetsu shijin)*. Over time, however, the circle evolved into the League of JNR Poets (Kokutetsu Shijin Renmei), and their publication virtually became an official union organ. By the time the Poets of Ōi organized themselves, it was an established venue for aspiring rail worker–poets to build their reputations. The Poets of Ōi disliked the kind of lofty literary critiques that the editors of *JNR Poets* or the union leadership gave to people's creative works. As rail workers, they tried to guard their amateur status and resisted pressures to conform to particular styles of writing. Therefore, they did not hold formal meetings to present and critique each other's work, which they felt would stifle their creativity; instead their meetings were more like informal chats.

The physical layout of the factory at Ōi facilitated the informality of the group. The repair facilities were completely open without walls to block off the work sections. Workers could walk around freely from one area to another if they wanted to talk to each other during slack periods. They could even yell over to another area if they wanted to arrange to talk. Inaba and Nakamura pointed out that before the productivity drives of the 1960s and 1970s, the work itself was not as tightly regulated as it would be toward the end of their careers.[17] The repair work was episodic with fluctuating rhythms and waves. After the morning rush, there would be a lull until about lunchtime. There were busy periods in the afternoon and early evening, but the workers were not heavily pressed all the time. The lulls in work allowed them moments to reflect and converse, and they could conduct the business of the circle in the middle of work.

Thus, the culture movement for the Poets of Ōi was part and parcel of their workaday lives. They did not consider the circle as a separate leisure-time activity that provided an escape from the drudgery of their jobs. They did not draw a clear line of demarcation between the sphere of work life and private life. The bulk of their poetry concerned reflections on their work, although not in a political form delineating the workers' exploitation by the capitalists. Inaba cites a poem from a collection called "Songs of the Railroad" as an example.

Gatan!
Oh my. Something's wrong with that bridge.
Watching the iron bridge as it recedes into the distance,
I take a notepad out of my pocket
And, swaying back and forth, jot down a memo.
Wordlessly I raise my hand
To the track worker who gets smaller and smaller.
I can hear the echoes
of the picks beginning to hammer away.
"To-ko-shien-tei, to-ko-shien-tei"
Watching the tracks flowing past,

Tracks that I just can't get away from,
Suddenly an intense notion
Rose up in my heart—
My whole life is protecting these tracks.[18]

Even though the worker is riding as a passenger, the sound of a bump on the tracks brings him right back to his job. He knows that the thump means the bridge needs a particular type of repair. The particular skills he has developed for his work make it impossible for him to go anywhere without thinking about the job. The Poets of Ōi, then, saw their poetry as a way to reflect on their experiences of current conditions both at work and in the larger society. Their circles were a means of expressing that labor culture as a positive value, not merely as exploitation or alienation. It was also crucial that these circles constituted a collective, egalitarian vision of their lives as workers. Since the workplace was their community, circle activities were like neighborhood gatherings of people who shared some common interest or who met to solve community problems.

In 1959 the group finally began to put out an irregularly published monthly called *The Poets of Ōi,* which they continued until 1970. Anyone in the group could contribute poems and essays, and they would print some seventy or eighty copies to pass around to other poetry circles and individual workers. Unlike *JNR Poets,* which was professionally typeset, *The Poets of Ōi* was produced as handwritten mimeographed copies, which was an affordable way for their small group to publish their work. Their distribution method once again emphasized their amateur status. Without a member's help in cutting the mimeos, they could not have continued. The mimeos also visually reinforced the image of manual skill associated with their work rather than the mechanical perfection of a typeset magazine.

As Nakamura asserted: "Once you turn pro, the strength of your writing gets weak. The first time you get money for a manuscript, then it's not a circle anymore; so of course it's no good to get money for your writing."[19] Since the group's prime motivation for writing was not dreams of literary success, they also experimented with other ways of generating dialogue about their poetry. Some members occasionally solicited responses from other workers by putting up flyers with unascribed poems in the bathrooms and listening to comments. They felt that fellow workers were more likely than literary critics to be able to comprehend and assess their raw reflections of work.

Although most of the Ōi factory circles developed spontaneously, the union also began to offer modest monetary support and tried to incorporate them into larger mass organs associated with Sōhyō and the Japan Socialist Party. One of these national-level bodies was the National Congress of Culture (Kokumin Bunka Kaigi), which was officially established on July 17, 1955. The congress was created by artists, critics, intellectuals, and union members, especially those with connections to Sōhyō, to build on the proliferation of workplace circles springing up around the country. The mindset of the founders was, however, at odds with that of workers like the Poets of Ōi. The congress was intended to facilitate exchanges between workers and "men of culture" (*bunkajin*), who would help the workers improve their arts. As the *Asahi* reported, the congress had lined up specialists to work with workers' circles in eleven different areas including film, drama, dance, music, education, literature, art, and so on. In other words, the congress' leaders sought to "enlighten" the masses in creating a broad cultural movement with political implications.

The other problem the congress faced was that of creating a centralized body that still allowed for local autonomy. The leadership's attempts to direct the movement seemed to diminish the vitality of the circles, and by 1958 the congress had already begun to lose impetus and to stagnate. Kyushu poet and activist and congress member Tanigawa Gan claimed that the political direction that the Japan Socialist Party and Sōhyō tried to impose on circle activities was stifling the creativity of circle members by limiting their freedom of expression. The more tightly these circles were integrated into the party's united front, the more the gap widened between mass and elite, and the more the feedback loop of communication between the two groups broke down. According to Tanigawa, when congress director Uehara Senroku addressed the 1958 national assembly, he had the "desperate air of a beloved commander trying to encourage his starving troops" as he called on members to create active regional subgroups as a way to revitalize the movement.[20] However, Uehara's call encouraged Tanigawa to form an autonomous regional movement with a new organizational philosophy, and he and coal miner Ueno Eishin spent the year traveling around Kyushu and the neighboring Yamaguchi Prefecture on Honshu to discuss the possibility with hundreds of local circles.

The regional group that Tanigawa founded, Circle Village, differed from the National Congress of Culture in trying to ensure local autonomy for each circle and encouraging rather than suppressing structural diversity as a way to generate creative energy. Circle Village itself was to facilitate exchanges between participating groups rather than to direct activities as a central committee or headquarters. Tanigawa also felt that organizers had to change their relationship to the masses by learning from their experiences with them rather than trying to make them conform to the directives of elite party leaders. Organizers should help circles develop their own philosophies and forms of leadership, he believed, and use those to modify the theory and praxis of the elite. This was, in fact, what happened to a sociology student at Tokyo University, Ōsawa Shinichirō, who like many other students had gone out to the factories to raise the workers' political consciousness. Ōsawa had a connection with the National Congress of Culture through his teacher and went out to the Ōi factory in 1959 at a time when the congress was trying to create awareness of the Anpo issue. He eventually joined the Poets of Ōi, helping them read intellectual works such as Sartre's writings on existentialism, but he also became critical of trying to subsume such circles into mass organs: "If unmediated totalization were pursued, it would result in homogenization and stagnation and lead to terrorism or mannerism. . . . Even if these small circles are not yet able to solve the problems of large organizations, they can offer a clue as to whether or not the community we seek should possess the kind of human relations found in these smallest social units and whether they will be creative communal relations or stagnant human relations."[21]

Talks with Ōsawa piqued an interest in the Anpo protests and politics in general, and the group began to write about their experiences. Interestingly, one member of the League of JNR Poets was critical of the turn that the Poets of Ōi were taking toward political subjects. While the critic did not object in principle to their raising political issues, he felt that the group should focus more on art and not dilute their creative activities.

Inaba answered that going to the demonstrations had opened him up to a broader spectrum of things to think about, and that this variety would stimulate rather than stifle his poetry.[22] He claimed that the group needed to pursue new activities and that over the next few years it should try to go beyond being just a club of friends. The Anpo protests were a formative experience for Inaba, and even though he had written poetry before this time, he claimed that 1960 was "year one" for his writing. That is to say, he began to see himself in relation to areas beyond work, so from that time he began to write with more conscious awareness of himself.[23] In a sense, Inaba's line of reasoning is the opposite of the logic of the proletarian literature movement that Japan Communist Party theorist Kurahara Korehito had revived in the early postwar. Kurahara held that literature had to mirror objective conditions of the proletariat's exploitation and raise their political consciousness, thereby becoming an instrument of revolution. Art existed for the sake of politics. For Inaba, politics existed for the sake of free artistic expression by which workers could develop their autonomy.

The Poets of Ōi were unusual in that they continued their activities for over a decade. Many of the workplace circles that had been popular in the late 1950s withered away after just a few years, owing in part to the changing nature of industrial work and labor-management relations. The Poets of Ōi considered this loss a dire problem. As they wrote in their inaugural issue: "When the labor movement lost its circle activities, it became a gathering that had lost itself."[24] The circle maintained the same basic membership. Their numbers did not swell during the 1960 and 1970 protests against the Anpo Treaty, nor did they drop after the flurry of political activity died down. They engaged in a variety of outside activities as well, such as doing joint exhibitions with photographers, helping proofread other people's plays, or doing the layout for the union magazine. But eventually, as people transferred or retired or took ill, the group only came together at weddings or hospitals or retirement parties. Their raison d'être arose from their work, and without it there could be no circle.

Work Life: Thinking with the Body

WHEN INABA and Nakamura first came to the Japan National Railways, steam locomotives were still in heavy use, and the work that they did in that era made them so grimy that people called them "pitch black papas" (*makkuro papa*). They were often mistaken for coal miners, and in fact the Japan National Railways had employed a large number of miners prior to 1950 to supply coal for the trains. Like the miners, the repair personnel were at the very bottom of the social hierarchy in the Japan National Railways family. In the immediate postwar period, they were also always tired because of the scarcity of food, and during lunch break they would take naps inside the cars. But despite these conditions, Inaba and Nakamura felt that they also had more freedom in their lives both inside and outside the workplace than they would have later. This was the reason they ended up writing poetry. They felt freer to express themselves and to use a form that was not typically associated with blue-collar workers. They considered poetry their salvation, even though women laughed at them for it.[25]

Another contrast to the 1970s and 1980s was that the work in the 1950s was based more on manual technical skills (*ude ga mono iu*), and this labor depended on a closer relationship between people and machines. The era of the steam locomotive was vastly different from the later high-tech trains in that workers treated the steam engine almost as if it was a living creature. In order to determine whether or not the train was running well, workers had to be finely attuned to the pulse of the sounds it would make. Songs and chants were also integral to keeping the rhythm and pace of the work, and in discussing the nature of railroad work, Inaba cites a poem that consists entirely of calls and onomatopoetic sounds that suggest a train set in motion.[26] He also quotes another poem about workers trying to clear the tracks after a terrible snowstorm in which the workers' chant as they dig out a path is identified with the sound of the locomotive trying to chug forward.[27] The worker trusted the machine, which in turn responded to the worker. The worker felt as if the locomotive were a part of him. Furthermore, the work was more communal, and the rail workers had to cooperate with and trust each other, as when the workers wave at each other in the poem in the previous section. The communal aspect of the work and the strength of the unions, then, made the slogan of company unity, "the Japan National Railways as one family" (*Kokutetsu ikka*), more effective in the early postwar period.

There was, however, one notable case in which the worker was not allowed to feel that the locomotive was a part of him. Since the Japan National Railways was a nationalized industry, it was an arm of the state and as such was obligated to provide the emperor with his own train. When Nakamura was in Hamamatsu, he helped build the emperor's special locomotive, and he wrote a poem in 1952 about the experience.

OVERTIME FOR THE EMPEROR'S LOCOMOTIVE

Today once more,
An electric light casts long piled up shadows
Across the darkened workplace.
It has nothing to do with the sunset outside the factory.

Overtime for the emperor's locomotive
Has gone on for months.
The craftsmen, like ants,
Like dolls
Fix each place marked in red.

The light of the nickel-plated handrail
The light of the glossy amber copper pipe
The light of the paint like a piano's black skin.
The light of the craftsmen's stained eyes
Gently protected by a gigantic shadow
Building a fairyland locomotive
For you
Centered on you
For the people and Japan.
I will paint it like a picture book.

No flags
No paper lanterns
No shouts of banzai
No one moved to tears
Dragging along his thin shadow
The craftsman's face thinks of you
As he carefully prepares the locomotive
Work clothes get soiled
Hands get dirty
Faces get dirty.

This is a factory of tired craftsmen
Far from Nijūbashi and the Ise Shrine
A place where roars leak out.
Even if we make this "toy" locomotive
Grander than the old days,
The best of the postwar,
You aren't reflected
In the eyes of the craftsmen going home after work.[28]

The workers here feel only a tenuous connection to the locomotive, which is described as a fantasy vehicle rather than a "real" train. Part of this alienation has to do with the work process. Workers were strictly controlled whenever work was done on this locomotive. Supervisors watched them constantly and carefully noted the hour and minute that workers entered and came out of the locomotive. They were also constantly giving orders to the workers forbidding them to do this and that.[29] The workers were unable to control the process of building the train, and they would rarely if ever see the locomotive or anything similar, so they were unable to feel any identification with it.

Nakamura's poem took first place in the annual Japan National Railways arts competition for 1952. However, the content of the poem prompted an investigation of the union's main office, and his poem was pulled from publication in their arts magazine. Nothing in the poem is overtly critical of the emperor himself, so according to Nakamura, it was the mere fact that he had written it at all that prompted the ban.[30] The association of manual labor with the emperor and the portrayal of the workers as indifferent to the majesty of the emperor's train were enough to get the poem censored. Since the poem and the story of its suppression were never made public, Nakamura did not suffer any right-wing reprisals at the time. The piece was eventually carried in a 1989 anthology of poetry about the emperor.

The contrast between the grime of the work and the gleam of the emperor's train is a key element to the poem. However, the use of the term "craftsman" (gikō) rather than a generic word like "laborer" (rōdōsha) is also crucial here. The term indicates the pride that Nakamura felt in his work. Workers in the repair facility saw themselves as artisans with a skill that took more than a decade as a modern journeyman to master. It took a trained ear and eye to know exactly where to hammer a warped chassis or an unbalanced door, since striking one spot would cause another area to bend in a different direction. In the case of locomotives, the variety of materials and tools used and the complexity of fuel, hydraulic, mechanical, and later on electrical systems involved meant that one had to acquire a broad range of knowledge to be able to do repairs. Workers had to gain this knowledge through experience, through the repetition of the physical activity until the correct motion became second nature. Once this level of ability was attained, physical sensations, such as the thump that prompts the railworker passenger to jot down a note on fixing the bridge, were enough to put this knowledge into operation.

Inaba therefore says that while the students who came to make ties with the factory workers had one kind of intellectual knowledge, they were ignorant of the type of knowledge the workers had. Laborers also gained their knowledge in an entirely different way than the students, a process that Inaba described as thinking with one's body, not just one's head. It was this experiential basis for knowledge that elite Socialist and Communist party theorists, who were locked into a scientific rationalist mode of thought, did not comprehend about the workers. Workers had a completely different idea about the determinism of material conditions than Marxist theorists, and thus their view of labor itself diverged from that of intellectuals.

In contrast to Marxist ideologues in the Japan Communist Party, who tended to view work in negative terms, workers like Inaba and Nakamura saw some intrinsic value in their labor despite being well aware of their exploitation as industrial workers. The physical exertion of their work was not mere suffering; it also activated their knowledge. Tragically, their work at the Ōi factory continued to affect the bodies of these repairmen years after their retirement. In addition to the dangers of the heavy equipment and the problems of dust and grime, workers suffered from the use of asbestos at the plant. Many who went to work in the early postwar period later died from the exposure. Nakamura himself underwent cancer treatments, and even though he retired in 1984, his lungs still cannot sever their connection to the railroad, as he puts it. He worries about the possibility of a recurrence and notes that the work he did at the beginning of his career still tugs at his body.[31] At the same time, he was also a bit sad to retire. The value or meaning of the railworkers' labor was not so much in the product, such as the emperor's locomotive, but rather in the process of doing the work well.

Inaba's notion of thinking through the body was part of the reason he became involved in the poetry circle, and it was also the reason he went to the Anpo demonstrations so often. He was not motivated by the ideological line of the established opposition parties. Like countless other workers, he had listened for months to Sōhyō organizers who had come out to the factory to explain the dangers of the Security Treaty to them and to encourage them to take part in the protests. Japan Communist Party and Japan Socialist Party ideologues had cast the protests as a proletarian uprising against American imperialism and strained to get workers to connect their shop-floor struggles for better wages and more say in the work process to Western imperialism. However, most workers were bored by the union meetings and did not see any direct connection between their local struggles and the Anpo controversy, at least before June 15. Rather, because workers acknowledged that the union for the most part made efforts on their behalf, they felt some obligation to go to the demonstrations when the union demanded it.

Unions committed themselves to quotas at demonstrations, so local branches sent a certain number of workers to the protests and strikes. Ordinarily the union would require a few workers from any particular work group to take part in these actions, and workers would take turns fulfilling the obligation. Those who were mobilized might volunteer or they might be chosen by drawing straws, by games of paper, rock, scissors, or by other methods.

However, during the Anpo protests the scale of the demonstrations grew much larger and protests often continued for days, so these methods were not sufficient to fill the quotas. Group leaders had to make special appeals, and workers who volunteered to go exerted peer pressure on the more reluctant workers, stressing the need for solidarity. Yet, there were some workers who enjoyed going to the protests or found them interesting and wanted to be there. The Ōi factory sent 20 percent more workers than their quota during the Anpo protests and 10 percent more than the quota in the protests against the Bill on Political Violence introduced in 1961.[32] So one cannot say that workers did not display any autonomy in their actions. After their part of the march was over, many individual workers stayed on the scene, as was the case with Inaba on June 15.

Nakamura remembers going to the demonstrations about ten times during May and June; he was mobilized through the union quotas. By contrast, Inaba remembers going there almost every day, in part because he lived in an area he considered relatively close to the Diet. He also had previous experience going to protests from two years earlier with the actions against Kishi's proposed Police Duties Bill. However, the most important motivation for Inaba was that he wanted to see and experience the protests for himself. This determination was an extension of his idea of "thinking through his body." Although he constantly referred to himself as an onlooker or bystander (*yajiuma*), he meant that he had to observe by taking part in the actions. The only way to witness the events accurately was to do the same thing as other participants and see things through their eyes.

The rhythm of the demonstrations with the scrums and zigzag marches and chants of *"washoi, washoi"* evoked the atmosphere of carrying a portable shrine around the neighborhood at a local festival. He preferred joining the students, who were more active and willing to take radical action. He was extremely put off by the attitude of the progressive "men of culture" (*bunkajin*) when they attempted to use their elite social status to ward off attacks by rightists and the police. He recalls seeing these men shout at their right-wing attackers, "What are you doing? We're men of culture!" in order to separate themselves from the others who were being beaten. Their elitist attitude outraged him and made him aware of the gulf in consciousness they had with the workers.

Students were similarly outraged when they saw their professors stand to the side and yell at the police not to hit them because they were teachers while the students absorbed the brunt of the attacks. Some of this antielitist sentiment carried over to the workers' and students' feelings about opposition party leaders who tried to make themselves the sole channel for registering dissent and the sole conduit for presenting petitions and talking with the conservative administration.

Inaba's poems about the Anpo protests are a raw reflection of the experiences he had starting from the forcible ratification of the treaty on May 19. He castigates the riot police and paramilitary right-wing groups as puppets, tax bandits, and bloodthirsty watchdogs for Kishi, but on the other side he gives a more complex picture of the protesters.[33] The protesters were not necessarily motivated to go to the demonstrations out of ideological commitment to the revolution. They were not fearless, heroic figures standing firm against the agents of repression. On the fateful evening of June 15, Inaba went back to the Diet after dinner, having heard of the battles taking place between the students and riot police. He stayed late into the night and made his own record of what happened.

THE RECORD

[1]
Since I lost the game of paper-rock-scissors,
I had to go to the mobilization that night.

I had no rain gear.
My body should have been toughened by work,
but the May rain made me shiver.
But that's okay.
Look at that girl's hips.
They're so big.
They're soaked to the skin.
They shed the water.

And so
That girl demonstrating and shouting "down with the treaty"
had surprising sex appeal.

"Hey girl! You do that and you won't be able to have kids!"
I bantered as I strolled along
That girl's round hips crossed my mind.

[2]
In the scrum
I clung to a red flag.
Spotlights were swarming and
I was bathed in flashes of light.
The night was broken into pieces.
Shards of light carved into our cheeks
and scattered.
I couldn't stop my knees from shaking.

June 15—evening
under the armored truck's headlights
iron helmets gleam
They wield clubs and get ready to charge
While taking that stance,
some guy is smirking
the distorted reflection of my face
on his wet helmet.

> *The guy glared at me*
> *I glared back at him fiercely.*
> *but then I—*
> *an utter coward—*
> *dropped my gaze, flustered.*
> *To cover my embarrassment I grinned.*
> *The guy seemed to be sneering beneath his helmet.*

Someone threw a stone.
It bounced off a helmet, making a dull thud.
In an instant
The strained atmosphere shot sharply through my pupils.

The armored truck's loudspeakers
raised a high-pitched sound, signaling the charge.

Flares popped off.
My guts blanched and turned inside out.
When the tear gas canisters exploded, my vision became hazy.
Through the haze off in the distance
Riot police helmets wriggled back and forth pressing closer.

They raced in shouting and swinging their clubs.
Clumsily I tried to cover the back of the student's uniform next to me.
I heard a dull sound over my head.
The student squatted down holding his head.
Dark blood gushed out from between his slender fingers.
I winced, a sharp blow
easily smashed my shoulder blade.
We had nowhere to run
Unless we could escape to a dark cellar the size of our own pupils.

The terrorists shouted,
"We want machine guns!"
The terrorist inside me cried out
"I'll blow their brains out!"
I shouted out as I twisted my body.

I had no feeling in my body for a while.
"I might get killed."
With this awareness
I suddenly thought of the round breasts of that girl to whom
I couldn't say "I love you" yet.

"Hey student! We can't die yet! What a waste!"
I was holding a student
while the wet asphalt made me slip
we crawled away as billy clubs rained down.

Anyway
We've got to get away where there are no clubs.

But
We can't stray far from the Diet.
So we put our arms around each other's shoulders
like old, old friends
and hung around the Diet.

[3]
The crane thrust straight up into the June sky.

The treaty was ratified.

I went underneath the train
like I had so many times for so many years.
I scraped off the sticky mud.
My nostrils readily sucked in the dust.
Unconsciously I frowned
So
why am I so light-hearted?
Humming as I tightened the bolts
my heart was overflowing.
What on earth was happening?

Fifty tons was lightly carried up to the sky.

Next time I'll tell her,
I'll tell that girl straight out, "I love you."[34]

As the last stanza indicates, Inaba found taking part in the dem-onstrations to be exhilarating, because they seemed to open up new possibilities for action. However, he had also experienced the repression of the state and was deeply angered by the Joint Dec-laration of the Seven Newspapers, which implied that the pro-testers were responsible for the violence of the demonstrations. The events of the Anpo protests began to crystallize his dissatis-faction with both the state and the progressive camp that opposed Kishi's government. He felt that the mass media, which had for-merly been sympathetic to the protesters, had betrayed the move-

ment. He despised the "men of culture" for their elitism and un-
willingness to stand with the workers and students. He criticized
the Japan Communist Party for trying to control the protests and
force the demonstrators to conform to their ideology. He was also
disappointed with the widening gap between union leaders and
the rank and file.[35]

This dissatisfaction only mounted as time went on. In the
1960s, the labor movement became increasingly unable to cope
with the increasing pressures to rationalize the work force, the
erosion of skilled labor and its replacement with new technologies, and the growing dominance of management control of work
culture. "Workers lost the solidarity arising from common treatment in terms of seniority and age. They further lost solidarity as
newly introduced technologies transformed the experience of production by deemphasizing group work and requiring less skill.
Their status became less secure and more dependent on individual
effort and ability than ever before."[36] The new automated technologies both displaced skilled workers and curtailed their ability
to set the pace and direction of their work. By reducing the degree
of cooperation workers needed to carry out their jobs and weakening their attachment to the work group, automation effectively
placed more and more authority in the hands of management.[37]
Inaba and Nakamura use the term "computerization" to describe
how their skills were made irrelevant. They mean that machines
ran the workers instead of workers running the machines.
Workers became caretakers of equipment that controlled production so that their skill with machines and cooperation with other
workers was devalued. The increased productivity and efficiency
that corporate management desired came at the cost of worker
autonomy.

Militant unionism was further sapped by the formation of
a pro-management union, the Japan Railway Workers Union
(Tetsudō Rōdō Kumiai, or Tetsurō), in 1969. Tetsurō was established to compete with Kokurō and Dōrō, and Japan National
Railways management encouraged workers to leave the militant

unions for Tetsurō. The management also tried to implement a restructuring plan throughout the 1970s that would, among other things, reduce the labor force by 74,000 workers.[38] Kokurō and Dōrō fought the plan, but the effects in the 1970s became palpable. Throughout the 1950s and 1960s, the work force had stayed consistently at around 460,000 workers, but from 1971 to 1981, the number dropped to 401,000, and it continued to fall by 20,000 to 30,000 workers each year after that, reaching 276,000 employees by the time the Japan National Railways was privatized.[39] Faced with these pressures, Kokurō and Dōrō were gradually forced to sacrifice shop-floor control and to allow management to implement a "merit" wage system. The unions grew unwilling to challenge the management over workers who were punished for political activities, as in the case of some young antiwar workers who were fired in the late 1960s. Inaba did some support work for them but confessed that there was little he could do to help.[40]

As Inaba saw the decline in workplace culture from the mid 1960s, he began to rethink the nature of work. In 1980, he wrote a poem called "Possessed by Work" (Rōdō o yamu), which takes a different perspective on the unconscious compulsion to do one's job from the poem about the worker who cannot stop thinking about the railroad tracks.

I shoulder a brush and set out
Scraping the mud and dirt off the train machinery
That's my job.

The main resistor—MR for short—speed regulator
Its size is
750 mm tall, 850 mm wide, and 2,000 mm long
Under the center of the floor, two pieces set left and right
Cling to the car
Clinging to a total weight of 1.5 tons
Preserving one's existence by
Clinging to it

I cling to the main resistor
Scraping off the mud and sweeping off the dirt
Each time I sweep it off it dances up and falls down
There are iron filings and human feces
There are various different kinds of dirt depending on the line it
    travels
Particles invisible in the darkness of the train repair shop
Sparkle in the light that shines in
And get sucked into my lungs

Once
I even found
a severed wrist that was mummified.
Yes, a story from long ago.
Now. What I can't remove
Is black hair, probably some woman's, wrapped up in an accident
Hardened in blood.

Single-minded for thirty years
Is that too cool?
In other words,
Somehow it just turned out that way while I've been here
Firmly bound and tossed around by
The office and relatives,
By friends and organizations, by feelings and obligations and rules
My soul gets knotted
Sometimes it cramps up a bit

I brush away.
The iron texture appears from underneath the mud and rust.
The one sure thing in this job
Is our bodies
That get contaminated by those microscopic substances
In the mud and dust that falls off

Get rid of your job!
Don't let your hands or body
Make you do something out of habit!

But
In day-to-day life
I am quietly possessed by work
And the repaired train cars leave as always.[41]

The poem sparked an ongoing debate in the magazine *JNR Poets* over the image of labor that Inaba depicted, starting with the title of the poem. The verb *"yamu"* implies being afflicted by work, like a sickness, and some critics took it to mean that labor necessarily meant suffering. Inaba, however, claimed that he meant something like being possessed (*toritsukareru*) by work.[42] He did not mean that he could not enjoy work or that it was totally negative. However, the poem seems to focus on work as a kind of malaise that permeates and contaminates the workers' bodies. It seems as if the pride and craftsmanship that Nakamura talked about in "Overtime for the Emperor's Locomotive" has been lost.

His advice is to throw away one's job and free oneself of the work habits that the body maintains, but then he keeps right on fixing the trains as always. He does not in fact repudiate "thinking through one's body," but he seems to realize that times have changed and he will have to adapt. Like many others, Inaba ascribes some of his compulsion to keep working to generational factors, saying that those born in the first decade of the Shōwa emperor's reign tend to be wedded to their jobs.[43] The typical image of this generation is that they are workaholics who never take a vacation and always stay later than everyone else. This personality type has given rise in Japan to the recent phenomenon of death from overwork (*karōshi*).

Skilled workers from this generation whose talents were increasingly rendered irrelevant often had severe difficulties when they retired. Inaba points to the example of a friend who always made work his life, even though he had told himself for years that he should take more time off with his family and do some things for himself. However, he could never bring himself to do this, and once he retired he ended up getting sick and collapsing.[44]

Nakamura and Inaba realized that proposals in the 1980s to privatize the Japan National Railways spelled an end to the union and the work culture they had known and signified the "triumph of management culture."[45] The Liberal Democratic Party Committee on National Railway Reconstruction complained in 1982 that union control over raises and promotions was "totally out of step with social common sense,"[46] so it became clear that the state was attempting to break the public sector unions affiliated with Sōhyō. Both Nakamura and Inaba began to make plans to retire. Nakamura did so in 1984, and Inaba retired two years after that, just before the privatization of the Japan National Railways, which officially took effect on April 1, 1987.[47] Their tenure at the railway coincided with the rise of the postwar labor unions and their shop-floor struggles, the gradual erosion of union strength, and finally the dissolution of the "legs of the people" into six separate companies. As such, their lives reflect the changes in work culture that occurred in the course of the railway's transformation.

While the workplace culture circles in the very male domain of industrial labor basically died out in the 1960s and 1970s with the changes in the nature of labor, other circles in different sectors continued to be viable. Women's circles and citizens' movements grew stronger and more significant in comparison to the labor movement. The next chapter turns to these social movements.

5

THE GRASS SEEDS AND WOMEN'S ROLES

Over the past three years, the voices of housewives carried each day in the *Asahi shinbun's* "Hitotoki" column have reverberated in our hearts with countless hopes arising in our lives for society, politics, economics, education, culture, and various other areas we habitually consider. Being moved by this, we seek to organize the "Grass Seeds" to lend whatever strength we can to enhancing people's lives, bringing happiness to the home, and making society a better place to live.

We desire to create a reliable group by sowing seeds along some shady path and having them take firm root in the soil, not by competing with others in flamboyant activities. Instead, our hope is that groups in each region could gather to discuss collectively things that cannot be decided individually.

The Grass Seeds, June 12, 1955

THE POPULAR CATCH phrase of the early postwar period that "women and nylons had gotten stronger" was in part a rueful male observation that women had become more vocal and assertive, as if clothes made the woman. Certainly women were accorded legal rights that they did not have before Japan's defeat in the war, but women also became stronger because they had to struggle to retain those rights. The defeat in the war had shown the bankruptcy of the political system, but deep connections between the emperor system and the family-state ideology also led women to critique the implications of the official "good wife, wise mother" doctrine and to reconsider their social roles in the household system. Many of them explored new means of self-expression and new forms of community through circle movements. Circle activities often served to socialize their members in politics and promoted a more public presence for women. Exposure in the mass media gave women engaged in social protest more visibility, but newspapers and magazines also provided forums for discussing women's concerns.

Two major areas of concern around which women organized, beyond that of their own status within postwar society, were education and nuclear disarmament. These concerns were tied to a continuing identification of women with the domestic sphere and motherhood, but the peace movement was sparked by consumer concerns as well. Consumerism had been key to the formation of some early postwar women's movements because of problems with the black market, rampant inflation, and a scarcity of goods. However, the social and economic contexts for the peace movement and later environmentalist movements were radically different. These later movements arose in the midst of Japan's "postwar miracle," as people began to question the direction of its rapid economic growth and the social costs it was exacting. The philosophies and organizational strategies of women's groups such as the Grass Seeds that developed in the late 1950s and early 1960s had such a profound impact on later citizens' movements that they were often thought of in gendered terms.

A New House

THE IMPLEMENTATION of universal adult suffrage under Article 15 of Japan's new constitution in 1946 widened the imagined postwar community and legitimated women's participatory demands. Article 24 further declared that marriage was to be based on the consent of both individuals and that laws regarding

choice of spouse, property rights, inheritance, choice of domi-
cile, divorce, and other matters related to marriage and family
must uphold the equality of the sexes. Thus, the revision of the
Civil Code in 1947 abolished the old household (*ie*) system and
accorded women legal rights within the household. Wives gained
the right to retain their own financial assets and to inherit a portion of the household property on the death of their husbands.
In the event of divorce, mothers could now seek custody of their
children. Interestingly, the 1947 revisions implemented many of
the changes that had been proposed for the old Meiji Civil Code
back in 1933 to better suit the shift toward nuclear families.[1]

However, women had to struggle to retain the rights that were
instituted in the immediate postwar period. In 1951, as the occupation of Japan drew to a close, the Japanese government geared
up to reverse the changes that had been instituted by forming a
committee to investigate ways to rescind both articles 9 and 24 of
the constitution. Despite disavowals that the committee sought to
revive the prewar household system and family-state ideology,
committee chair Kishi Nobusuke declared in 1954 that "it was
absolutely necessary that the form of the household be suited to
Japanese traditions and customs and social conditions because the
nation [*kokka*, which combines the characters for "country" and
"family"] was shaped by the spirit of the household."[2] In response
to these moves, a movement to oppose the revival of the family
system (Kazoku Seido Fukkatsu Hantai Renraku Kyōgikai) was
formed. This movement brought in many women who previously
had not imagined getting involved in politics. The more that conservatives pushed the "beautiful tradition" of the family system,
the more that protesters were able to shed the silent suffering they
had endured in the prewar period and demonstrate, often with
child and placard in hand.[3] Thus, while the Occupation had given
women formal political representation, they still had to win the
rights they were granted on paper and make them their own.

The starting point for women's postwar social movements
was their experience during the war years. For countless women,

wartime had produced, as Tsurumi Kazuko puts it, an acute mismatch between their affective postures and their ideological roles.[4] They were torn by the conflict between their duty as "good wives, wise mothers" raising patriotic soldiers for the war and their sorrow at having to sacrifice their husbands and sons. Mothers also felt regret when they realized that evacuating their children to the countryside during the Allied bombing campaigns late in the war often resulted in mistreatment or neglect because of the added burden their children imposed on the rural areas.[5] Moreover, mothers and widows of soldiers killed in battle did not always receive the honor they expected from their neighbors, and, unable to remarry, they were often placed in the position of becoming the sole breadwinner for their in-laws as well as their children.[6] However, the "good wife, wise mother" ideology also admonished women to suffer their tribulations silently and to be acquiescent to those in positions of authority. Tsurumi claims that the first step women had to take in redefining their social roles was to express their feelings about what they had suffered during the war. Given the intensity of the contradictions women felt in the subordinate roles they were expected to perform, the examination of their feelings produced much stronger opposition to war and more impetus for social change than seen among men.

The trend of forming writing circles to record women's experiences of the war was thus a significant aspect to the general life histories movement in which ordinary people made records of their lives.[7] While much of the writing focused on their victimization, the process of sharing the results also prompted some women to see themselves as partly responsible for their situation. As Makise Kikue, a Tokyo journalist, wrote of her own life histories circle, children who had been in elementary school during the war would shed tears on reading the accounts of their mothers' experiences during the war. However, children who did not have any memories of those times sometimes scolded their mothers, saying, "Why didn't you do something before the war actually started? You looked like fools who knew nothing about the coming of the war."[8] Such criticisms led many women to look at themselves more critically and to conclude that their suffering was partially the result of their own "ignorance" in accepting the jingoistic wartime ideology. As one member of a women's writing circle wrote, "We are responsible for the making of the war because we were ignorant enough to obey our leaders blindly and to be induced to cooperate wholeheartedly with them."[9] Another woman from this circle asserted that the prewar educational system inculcated chauvinistic values that produced their ignorance, and since their children did not have any idea about the content of such ethics classes, they did not comprehend "why their mothers were blindly driven into the last war."[10]

Despite the critique of their own complicity in the family-state ideology, women's early postwar movements still retained a very strong identification with the roles of wife and mother.[11] Alternative images for women analogous to Rosie the Riveter in the United States had not developed in Japan during the war. Rather, women's patriotic duty was cast in terms of bearing children. Prime Minister Tōjō Hideki's wife, Katsuko, for example, exhorted women to eschew luxury and raise large families because "having babies is fun."[12] Despite heavy conscription of males, the percentage of women in the work force rose very little during the war compared to the United States, Britain, Russia, or even Germany, one indication of the strength of Japan's family-state ideology.[13]

Thus, women's groups in the postwar period continued to emphasize their roles as wives and mothers, even those affiliated with the Japan Socialist Party (such as the Japan Women's Council, or Nihon Fujin Kaigi) and the Japan Communist Party (such as the New Japan Women's Association, or Shin Nihon Fujin no Kai). The prevalence of the term *"fujin,"* which implies a *married* woman, in the names of the groups is one indication of this continuing identification. However, "the activist housewife reinterpreted 'good wife, wise mother' to justify her involvement in larger public issues that affected home life."[14] It was their position as housewives in charge of expenses for the domestic sphere that enabled women to organize around consumer issues. Groups such as the Japan Housewives Alliance (Shufu Rengō Kai, or Shufuren for short) would demonstrate in the streets wearing kitchen aprons and wielding placards in the shape of rice ladles (*shamoji*, a symbol of women's household authority) to emphasize that the kitchen was their springboard to political activity. Their members embraced women's traditional roles, as evidenced by the kimono some of them wore to the protests, but they sought a political presence to carry out their roles more effectively.

The Housewives Alliance was founded in 1948 by Oku Mumeo, a member of the House of Councilors who believed that housewives needed their own organization to exert direct pressure on the government to alleviate the problems they faced with a lack of goods in an inflationary, black market economy. Oku had a long history of progressive activism from the 1920s. She helped found the women's rights group New Women's Association (Shin Fujin Kyōkai) in 1920 together with Ichikawa Fusae and Hiratsuka Raichō and became its leader two years later. The group pushed for equal opportunity, and its major achievement was to convince the Diet to rescind the law that forbade women from attending public meetings. Oku later turned to labor and consumer issues, starting a magazine called *Working Women (Shokugyō Fujin)* and setting up child care centers and a lecture series for working women.

Thus, when Oku stood for election in 1947 under the new postwar constitution, she was already well known as a reformer, and this exposure helped her get elected for three consecutive terms. Shortly after the 1947 election, she established the alliance, which focused on the problems of harmful products such as lead in chinaware, additives in baby food, and the use of pesticides. The alliance set up testing centers for goods and staged protests against such things as shoddy safety matches and textiles and a rise in prices at the public baths. The group also sought to enlighten ordinary housewives about these problems through lectures and traveling seminars, and then to mobilize them in mass actions. The alliance also stressed direct negotiations with politicians and industrialists to effect change, a form of engagement that was possible only because of Oku's access to elite channels. It was her visibility and leadership that carried the group.

Protecting the Peace

WOMEN'S DOMESTIC roles also served as a main impetus for the disarmament movement in Japan. The Liaison Group for the Japan Mothers' Assembly (Nihon no Hahaoya Taikai Renraku Kai, or Hahaoya Taikai for short) explicitly drew a connection between women's wartime experiences as mothers and their involvement in the peace movement. The assembly was formed in June 1955 as an umbrella for constituent organizations ranging from family-oriented groups such as the Setagaya Family Association (Setagaya Kateikai) and the Association to Protect the Children (Kodomo o Mamoru Kai) to the Women's Democratic Club and Federation of Japanese Women's Associations (Nihon Fujin Dantai Rengōkai, or Fudanren), to the women's sections of national teachers' and public railway unions. The assembly therefore embraced a variety of resolutions regarding women's rights, responsibilities toward the family, children's education, health and welfare concerns, and work conditions. However, these concerns all stemmed from women's position as mothers. As their manifesto said:

> We mothers in Japan have come together from north and south with children on our backs . . . and we have spoken our words of prayer for world peace in our sincere desire to safeguard the happiness of our children. . . . [In the past] mothers were forbidden even to mention this very natural feeling they had: that they neither liked nor wanted war. We mothers were not even allowed to shed tears as we sent our sons away to war; we had to bear this sadness only by gritting our teeth. . . . [And our war dragged] countless other youths of foreign coun-

tries into the war, causing their mothers to experience the same thing.

We are confident that fathers and children will support and encourage . . . this great march begun by mothers.

And only through their cooperation will we be able to participate in movements such as the Movement to Prohibit Nuclear Testing and the Movement for World Peace.

We are no longer isolated individuals, scattered and weak.[15]

The peace movement had been slow to develop in Japan owing to Occupation era restrictions on publicizing information about the bombings in Hiroshima and Nagasaki and the social ostracism that the atomic bomb victims (*hibakusha*) had to endure. The Occupation policy of censoring the media began to ease in late 1948 and formally ended in mid-1949, allowing for the publication of memoirs and literature about the bombings, provided that they were not deemed politically inflammatory. However, actual photographs of the effects of the bombings were not published until after the Occupation ended,[16] and medical academies were not allowed to investigate or discuss publicly the effects of the bombings until 1952. Up to that time, survivors were not allowed to grieve publicly or to receive any public support or counseling, and they were also stigmatized and ostracized from Japanese society. The Japanese government did not establish a council to survey the victims until November 1953.[17]

The bomb victims were also often discriminated against and ostracized from their own communities even as their experiences were appropriated as part of the Japanese people's collective memory of victimization. Many of those who suffered disfigurement felt compelled to sequester themselves from ordinary society, and even victims who did not bear visible marks of their exposure often kept silent about their condition to avoid rejection by others. Women, for example, found it difficult to get married if they were known to be atomic bomb victims.[18] Therefore, many of the victims were reluctant to become involved in political movements and to put themselves in the public eye. Thus, it was difficult to develop a peace movement that put the actual victims at the forefront during the Occupation period.[19] Instead, the peace movement arose from other quarters.

Ironically, the nuclear disarmament movement in Japan was sparked by the Bravo hydrogen bomb test that the United States conducted at Bikini atoll on March 1, 1954. The Bravo test triggered this movement because a 140-ton Japanese fishing boat, the *Daigo Fukuryū Maru,* was showered with radioactive fallout from the blast while trolling for tuna 150 kilometers to the northeast. The ship returned to its home port of Yaezu in Shizuoka Prefecture two weeks later, by which time the twenty-three-member crew had developed symptoms of radiation poisoning. The captain of the ship, Yamamoto Tadashi, and another crew member, Masuda Sanjirō, were immediately taken up to Tokyo for treatment, and the radio operator, Kuboyama Aikichi, eventually died on September 23.

Japanese felt the incident represented their continued nuclear victimization at the hands of America, and the Yaezu City Council passed a resolution on March 27 calling for an end to the production, testing, and use of nuclear weapons and for international management of the peaceful uses of nuclear power. Thirty-six other city and prefectural councils immediately followed suit, and eventually all but four of the country's prefectural councils passed resolutions condemning the tests and calling for their end. The Yoshida government, however, was reluctant to press any demands on the United States to end the testing or compensate the victims, because Foreign Minister Okazaki Katsuo had told the Diet, "Since our country bears a special relationship with America in being bound by the U.S.-Japan Security Treaty, we would like to cooperate with American testing and maintaining secrecy about nuclear weapons."[20]

In the face of government inaction, housewives pushed forward the growth of the peace movement. They reacted sharply when reports came out that the *Fukuryū Maru*'s 9,400-kilogram cargo of tuna and mackerel had been distributed to markets in Tokyo, Osaka, Hokkaido, and Hokuriku. The radioactive fish was quickly impounded, but tuna sales plummeted because of widespread fears that marketers had been unable to retrieve all of the contaminated cargo. Fish sellers put up signs to reassure their customers that the fish they sold was safe, but the six nuclear tests that the United States conducted over the next two and a half months kept concerns over the quality of the fish in the public eye. These concerns prompted women around the country, especially those from the urban middle class, to organize groups and begin petition drives calling for an end to nuclear weapons testing.[21] These activities grew into a national campaign headquartered in Tokyo's Suginami Ward that led to the founding of the Japan Council Against the A- and H-Bombs (Gensuibaku Kinshi Nihon Kyōgikai, or Gensuikyō) and the first annual Hiroshima commemoration in the summer of 1955.[22]

The women's reading circle Children of the Cedars (Sugi no Ko Kai) and its leader Yasui Kaoru are often credited with originating the peace movement in Japan, although the group was just one element in a broad, dynamic trend. The legend surrounding them, however, is an important indication of the role that women played in the peace movement. The Children of the Cedars was a small group of educated middle-class housewives from Suginami Ward who had gathered to read works in sociology under the guidance of Yasui Kaoru, a professor at Hosei University. The group was organized in November 1953, when some housewives heard a lecture by Yasui and were inspired to ask him if he would lead a study group.[23] Yasui had been active in the area, helping to establish the Parent-Teacher Association branch for one of the ward's grade schools and also serving as director of the public meeting hall in the district. Because of these ties, the small group of twenty-four soon grew to one hundred members. They were mostly housewives in their forties, who because of their wartime experiences fervently desired peace and felt that the readings would give them ideas on reshaping Japan's society. Yasui selected works for the group to read that ranged from E. H. Carr to C. Wright Mills to Mao Zedong, and he lectured on them to the group. However, as they were working through E. H. Carr's *New Society*, the H-bomb test at Bikini atoll caused Yasui to shift his attention to the issue of disarmament.

Yasui called on the Children of the Cedars to make practical application of the social theory they were reading, and on May 9, 1954, they established the Suginami Petition Drive to Ban the H-Bomb together with forty-two other organizations in the ward, including cultural groups, a union of fish merchants, the social welfare council, Parent-Teacher Association and board of education members, labor groups, and students. Yasui was chosen to head the organization, which explicitly claimed nonpartisanship. Their goal was to collect 100,000 signatures within a month, but they vastly exceeded this mark, gathering 270,000 signatures in that period, or more than two-thirds of the ward's population. One key strategy was to send women volunteers to the local market areas. This put women in high-traffic public places where they could meet people in their communities. The Suginami group also made an appeal to form a nationwide petition drive, and in August the Suginami Council set itself up as a clearinghouse for the petitions. By October, they had collected 1.1 million signatures, and by January 1955 the number had doubled.[24] However, this figure paled in comparison to the dramatic increase in the number of signatories by August of 1955. Other groups around the country had taken similar initiatives in the wake of the Bravo test, and nearly 32.4 million signatures were collected by then.

The speed with which the petition drive took off indicates that the Suginami group was in fact just another effect of the peace movement rather than its cause, and certainly the groundwork had been laid by the amount of information and literature on the Hiroshima and Nagasaki bombings that was finally appearing at the beginning of the decade. Yasui and the Suginami contingent rode the crest of this wave and proposed a mass gathering in Hiroshima on the tenth anniversary of the bombing, making appeals for participation at several international conferences. On August 6, some two thousand citizen group representatives and private individuals together with fifty representatives from thirteen foreign countries held the first annual Hiroshima commemoration, where they established Gensuikyō and chose Yasui as its representative.

The Children of the Cedars continued to work in the peace movement during Yasui's tenure as the head of Gensuikyō. However, as the commemorations became larger, the opposition parties took more interest in Gensuikyō, and by 1962 they had leadership positions in the group. However, the Japan Socialist Party and the Japan Communist Party had contending interests, the Socialists wanting the group to call for opposition to all nuclear weapons (and later to nuclear power plants as well), while the Communists wanted Gensuikyō to oppose nuclear proliferation by the Western bloc. Yasui was unable to reconcile their positions or to return leadership initiative to the local citizens' and atomic bomb victims' movements, and the group acrimoniously split apart at the 1963 Hiroshima gathering. The Japan Communist Party formed the Japan Congress Against the A- and H-Bombs (Gensuikin), while the Japan Socialist Party sponsored the Japan Council Against the A- and H-Bombs (Gensuikyō). Yasui resigned his position and told the Children of the Cedars that he would not lead their reading group sessions any longer. He advised them to engage in other activities, but the circle had been organized around the personality of Yasui and depended so heavily on his leadership that when he withdrew from the disarmament movement in 1963, the circle fell apart.

Groups such as the Japan Housewives Alliance and Children of the Cedars exhibited some of the same organizational and philosophical problems as other groups centered on elite intellectuals. The rank-and-file membership depended heavily on the personality of the group's leaders for their ideas and activities, and often sacrificed their own initiative. Organization tended to be hierarchic, with the leaders viewing their task as one of enlightening

or advancing the consciousness of the group. Such vertically organized groups floundered without strong leadership, leading to factional splits or the disintegration of the group.[25]

The Children of the Cedars and the Suginami petition drive
were emblematic of women's political engagement in the latter
half of the 1950s, especially those from the urban middle class.
Consumer issues were a comfortable, socially acceptable avenue
for women to become politically involved, and Suginami was an
uptown residential area of Tokyo dominated by middle-class families of businessmen and government employees.[26] Japan was in
the midst of a massive migration to urban areas and stood at the
cusp of an era of rapid economic growth. The economy and its
infrastructure had received a major boost through U.S. procure-
ment orders during the Korean War, and the government's 1956
Economic White Paper proclaimed that the postwar was now
over (*mohaya sengo de wa nai*) with production levels finally sur-
passing the highest prewar levels. Unlike the years immediately
following the defeat when the Housewives Alliance was formed,
families now felt that they had a small, rather fragile, margin of
prosperity to protect. Moreover, they felt that this margin was
possible only because the militarized economy of the prewar period
had been transformed into one based on "peace and democracy."
Therefore, the ties between nuclear proliferation and the reverse
course of Japan's conservative government became concerns for
the middle class. Those concerns turned into direct confrontation
four years later with the 1960 Anpo protests, and in order to re-
direct the political activism that they generated, the new prime
minister, Ikeda Hayato, would announce the government's plan
to double people's income by the end of the decade. The Liberal
Democratic Party hoped that greater economic satisfaction would
translate into political quiescence.

The mid-1950s was a period of massive urbanization and
fluctuating social formations. From 1950 to 1955, migration to
the major cities of Japan led to marked increases in their population. Tokyo grew by 29.4 percent during this period and Osaka

by 26.2 percent.[27] Thus, the first major subsidized, suburban apartment complexes, or *danchi*, began to sprout up in 1956 to alleviate the severe housing shortage that developed in urban centers owing to the heavy in-migration.[28] These complexes tended to be built in outlying areas, often in places that had very few neighborhood shops close by. They were new communities and mostly enclaves of middle-class businessmen and their families. The new apartment complexes also had a higher percentage of nonworking wives than in other places, so women had the time and opportunity to form study circles and culture groups in their neighborhoods. Such activities sometimes led to political activism, as was seen during the Anpo protests.[29]

However, their economic composition also made these complexes a major target for the consumer sales market. The postwar economic recovery that fostered the massive migration to urban areas also created the burgeoning consumer ethic that developed in the late 1950s. This ethic was reflected in the catch phrase "three sacred treasures," which parodied the imperial regalia of the mirror, the sword, and the jewel by elevating the value placed on the electrical appliances that marked the acquisition of middle-class status: an electric washing machine, a refrigerator, and a television.[30] Another phrase, the "three C's," was similarly coined by advertisers to characterize consumer desires, although the 1950s list of car, cash, and camera gave way to that of car, color TV, and cooler (i.e., air conditioner) in the 1960s.[31] The "sacred treasures" were highly symbolic of Japan's rapid economic growth, because in spite of Japan's seeming focus on overseas trade, it was domestic consumption that drove the economic miracle in the 1960s.[32] And in order to spur domestic consumption, advertisers had to aim their pitch at women, who had control over the family budget. However, such consumerism in the late 1950s was actually quite dear for the new middle class, which had to be frugal to afford these symbols of affluence.[33] They could see but not quite reach the "bright life" that would have been unimaginable just a decade earlier.

This consumerism was confined geographically to urban-suburban locales, and a palpable material gap existed with rural areas. A comparison of urban and rural diffusion rates for consumer goods in the late 1950s shows that only radios and sewing machines were widespread in both areas. Items such as washing machines, refrigerators, rice cookers, vacuum cleaners, cameras, record players, and TVs, while still limited, were all much more heavily concentrated in the cities.[34] When the economy took off in the 1960s, the diffusion rates for these products skyrocketed in the urban areas rather than the rural.

Consumerism was not limited to electrical products, and the consumption of culture, especially urban intellectual culture, was another important component of the economy. Mass education played a role in the selling of this culture, and items such as Iwanami Shinsho's inexpensive pocketbook series of intellectual texts and translations, both domestic and foreign, found their market with the great numbers of university students. General-interest monthly magazines (sōgō zasshi), which ran to book length, were also at their height, giving intellectuals a major forum for presenting their views. Thus, the formation of the Children of the Cedars as a reading group and its heavy reliance on an intellectual like Yasui was symptomatic of the age. However, the growing mass consumption of culture began a shift toward shorter, less difficult weeklies (shūkanshi), which proliferated by leaps and bounds in the late 1950s and early 1960s. The weeklies provided another forum for intellectuals as well, but they and the mass media in general also experimented with more popular writings and approaches that incorporated the opinions of ordinary people.

The Grass Seeds formed against this backdrop of urbanization, a developing consumer society, wariness about the government's political retrenchment, and women's involvement in the peace movement. The group looked to the future in an effort to make a "brighter world" (akarui shakai) while finding motivation in memories of their past lives under the military.

Pausing to Reflect

THE GRASS Seeds developed from a column that appeared in the "Homelife" (*katei*) section of the *Asahi shinbun*. Kageyama Saburō, who was put in charge of this section when it started up after the war, wondered how he could use it to show the trend toward the liberation of housewives. He had the idea of starting a column aimed at women, but he was unsure of what to call it. He thought that words such as "chat room" (*kondanshitsu*) or "tea room" (*ochashitsu*) would be too closely identified with the kitchen, and he wanted something more general. Eventually, he came up with the title "Hitotoki," a word that implied pausing for a moment, presumably to reflect on and discuss matters. Kageyama conceived of this column as a forum for women's voices. He lined up twenty-five well-known authors, critics, and artists to write short pieces for the weekly feature, which debuted on October 2, 1951. "Hitotoki" generated an overwhelming response, and Kageyama was so impressed by the letters he received that he proposed the column be taken from reader contributions rather than essays by professional writers. Some of the editorial staff objected to this change in format, but as the number of reader contributions continued to mount, the staff began to think the format might become an interesting selling point for them. Thus, "Hitotoki" became the first newspaper column in Japan devoted to reader contributions.

The shift represented a fundamentally different way of conceiving the media's function in society. Newspapers often cast themselves as the voice of the people. Editorials often asserted this position and the very title of the *Asahi*'s "Vox Populi, Vox Dei" (Tensei jingo) column literally made this claim, but editors in fact often saw their role as one of educating and enlightening the public. They hesitated to let the people (*kokumin*) speak for themselves. Kageyama, by contrast, said he was not aiming at "enlightening" women through "Hitotoki."[35] He wanted to hear from thousands and tens of thousands of readers in order to understand them. He also hoped that they would take a critical stance and not simply write in as fans or treat the column as an advice column in which readers passively accept the word of the writers.

By the spring of 1952, "Hitotoki" turned entirely to its precedent-setting format, and it proved so popular that its readership was said to far outstrip that of the newspaper's editorials. As one commentator noted, "Almost nobody reads the editorials. . . . The reason people don't read the editorials is that they do not reflect any of the people's (minshū) difficulties or troubles or their anger at inequities. People feel the chill in the words of those looking down on the world below from the windows of the company offices high above." By contrast, people avidly read the "Hitotoki" column because it "became a shared public space (kyōtsū no hiroba) for people to think and talk with each other." It reflected a "warmth oozing out from their lives" that the editorials lacked.[36] They loved the column because it functioned as a place where ordinary "nameless" (mumei) housewives could converse as equals rather than be lectured at by "experts."

"Hitotoki" first appeared in the Tokyo edition of the Asahi, and the contributions reflected an urban base. From January 1952 to June 1953, just barely over half of the letters came from people within the city limits. Kageyama noted that the contributions started with women living in the middle-class Yamanote area, but soon women began to write in from the working-class downtown (shitamachi) area and then the factory belt around Tokyo. Later contributions came in from the countryside and mountain and fishing villages. The average age of the contributors was thirty-six but they ranged from eighteen to sixty-three years of age, attesting to the column's broad appeal. The range of contributors continued to widen from June 1953 to June 1954, with nearly two-thirds of those writing in to the column living outside of Tokyo. The average age also dipped slightly to thirty-four.[37]

During this initial period, the Asahi also experimented with new editorial procedures and presented surveys on issues raised in the column such as "trends in kindergartens" (January 11, 1952), summaries of various responses to ideas presented by individuals such as "women's happiness" (August 12), various opinions on readers' inquiries about such things as elections (September 19), and reportage by contributors from the perspective of housewives.[38]

The popularity of "Hitotoki" led to the creation of other readers' columns such as "Voices" (Koe) and "Dimples" (Kataekubo) in the *Asahi* and "Contributions" (Tōsho), "Swapping Lies" (Usokurabu), and "Women's Feelings" (Onna no kimochi) in the *Mainichi shinbun*. The phrase "women contributors" (*tōsho fujin*) became one of the buzzwords of the day, although sometimes it was used disparagingly by men who claimed either that the columns were leading to a decline in the level of writing and should be left to professionals like editors and culture critics or that women who wrote in were exceptionally gifted and could not represent ordinary citizens. Many of the women who wrote to these columns were exceptional, but not in the way that such critics imagined. Those in rural areas, for example, sometimes had to deal with social approbation just for writing letters to the newspapers. As one woman wrote to Kageyama, "On the one hand, it's encouraging to see women writing things, but on the other hand, people make fun of those who do this by calling them '*tōsho fujin*' and such."[39] It took courage to be identified as one of these persons if no other like-minded women lived in the area, and the need to talk with other such women became a major impetus for the formation of the Grass Seeds.

The problem with "Hitotoki" was that while it allowed some voices to be heard that would not ordinarily appear in a newspaper, it was necessarily selective because of the limited space allotted. In the first three years that "Hitotoki" ran, Kageyama received letters from nearly twenty thousand different individuals, so many of them were left out even after the column became a daily feature. Moreover, the women were dependent on the newspaper for their "conversation." They were one step removed from talking with each other, and since the editorial board of the newspaper controlled the column, they could lose their forum if the editors decided to change the format or drop the feature altogether. In addition, newspaper reporters and editors were overwhelmingly male and did not share the interests of these women.[40] Therefore, a group of enthusiastic participants finally suggested face-to-face gatherings so they could carry on more extended, in-depth discussions with each other. In February of 1955, just as the column went national, readers in wards throughout Tokyo began to organize themselves into six different groups and to hold meetings. By June, the groups had held their first general assembly and started their own magazine called the *Grass Seeds*. They then issued a general call in "Hitotoki" for others to join them, and women in outlying prefectures responded by forming their own regional branches from Hokkaido to Kyushu, a process that continued for several years.

The Grass Seeds were not the only group to develop out of the column. Like the other major dailies in Japan, the *Asahi* had a nationwide distribution with branch offices in larger cities around the country. Since each local edition had its own regional distribution, the "Hitotoki" column presented the contributions of readers within that particular area. Thus, the column had its own local character wherever it ran, and distinct albeit like-minded groups developed from it. While Grass Seeds groups sprang up in Tokyo and Kokura in northern Kyushu, the Wellspring (Izumi no Kai) developed its own organization in Nagoya, and the Hitotoki group, which was basically a reading circle, formed in Osaka.[41] The previous summer, another group composed of domestic servants called the Kikōkai (a neologism signifying a mingling of their hopes) formed after a young woman from rural Gunma prefecture contributed a piece in "Hitotoki" reflecting on the differences between city and country after having migrated from her rural home to work in Tokyo for a merchant family.[42] Rather than attempt to consolidate all of these groups into one centralized organization, the Grass Seeds decided to adopt the principle of local autonomy for themselves. Thus, while the Wellspring and the Osaka Hitotoki groups maintained sisterly relations with the Grass Seeds over the coming decades, they remained functionally independent of each other. The Grass Seeds frequently cooperated with the Mothers' Assembly and Gensuikyō, both of which were also established in the summer of 1955, but they did not consider themselves obligated to follow all the decisions of these larger bodies. When members of the Grass Seeds became involved in other groups, they participated as individuals rather than as official representatives of the group. Internally, regional branches of the Grass Seeds held their own meetings and developed their own activities so that each constituent branch tended to develop its own personality according to the interests of its members.

Although the structure of the Grass Seeds was attributable partly to the peculiarities of the way the press was organized in Japan and although the mass media facilitated its inception, the group also sought to overcome the media's limitations. They desired a more direct, unmediated form of engagement, and they started up their own small-scale magazine (*mini komi*) to facilitate greater freedom of expression and autonomy than the mass media (*masu komi*) could provide. The call to join the group consciously rejected hierarchic organization and invoked the model of traditional women's gossip sessions around the village well (*idobata kaigi*) in a new form.[43] The image of women gathered around the well implies an informal circle without any centralized management where people could freely discuss community concerns and thus derives from the postwar circle movements rather than the formal hierarchies of political parties and government or big business. Unlike movements affiliated with the Old Left parties, the Grass Seeds did not espouse any set ideological line and felt all the more acutely the need to debate social and political issues at length before deciding on any course of action. However, since member groups were spread out across the country, they used their magazine to keep the outlying groups involved and to raise and discuss issues when they were unable to meet face-to-face.

The magazine also presented reports from various research groups that the Grass Seeds had formed to investigate social issues. For these reasons, they considered the magazine an essential part of their democratic praxis.[44]

Parasol Protests

THE GRASS Seeds saw their group as part of the same current of women's groups including the Women's Democratic Club, the Association to Protect the Children, and the Mothers' Assembly that tried to redefine their wartime role as "good wives, wise mothers" and forge a new path for themselves and their children. The avowed purpose of the group was to construct a "brighter world," and their impetus came primarily from what these women suffered during the war. The war and the defeat fundamentally altered their attitudes, especially with regard to acquiescing to authority,[45] but they did not attempt to discard their social roles entirely, and they did not have a fixed notion of how the "brighter world" would look. Instead, they started with different ideas on how to organize themselves.

At the time of their first general assembly, the Grass Seeds had roughly one thousand members, but in keeping with the communal gossip session model, the group did not create a central executive committee. Instead, it maintained a liaison committee (*renrakukai*) comprising representatives from all of the local branches. The liaison committee could itself be thought of as another gossip session where local branches could learn how everyone else was thinking. It met every month and also chose people to manage the office, take care of the group's accounts, and edit the group's magazine. However, the committee could not make decisions that were binding on all of the local groups, and the regional branches all had their own area gatherings at which they raised their own topics for discussion. The Grass Seeds also held an annual general assembly, and they chose a representative for the group at each assembly, but this representative did not have executive powers, and the position usually rotated after a year or two at most.

Because the group did not form around any particular ideology or arise in response to a specific political issue, the Grass Seeds sought to create a flexible organization and initially focused their energies on studying and debating current issues, and writing about them. They tended to be very deliberate about taking any action, as their research groups show. These study groups were considered to be so essential to the character of the organization that they were all represented on the liaison committee. The oldest and largest of these was the group established to investigate the problems of the elderly. This research group formed in 1955 and drew a large number of people, because growing old was a situation they would all face themselves one day. Their continued interest in the issue over the years also reflects the reality that, with scarcely any public care facilities, most housewives end up having to take care of their in-laws.[46] Therefore, they need to know about things such as the availability of government pension funds and provisions for medical care.

Some seventy members eventually worked on the group, which unlike many of the other study circles cut across different regions. The type of research they carried out was not merely academic, although they did consult with "experts" on the issue at times. Much of their investigation consisted of conducting their own interviews and surveys or working together with groups such as the Women's Feelings (Onna no Kimochi) group in Osaka. The study group on the elderly looked at the effects of aging on family relations, problems finding housing and nursing homes, health concerns, and economic issues. They used the results of their research to make policy recommendations to city officials, the Health Ministry, Diet members, and the national pension agency. This particular group engaged the government directly as did the Housewives Alliance, but they also used their research to find out how other women were coping with the same problems. Most of the other study groups produced materials for the Grass Seeds' own internal consumption, as, for example, the one that recorded people's lives or the one devoted to poetry writing.

Another small but important study group was the one researching the history of the Parent-Teacher Association. Like the research group on the elderly, this group was formed immediately after the Grass Seeds were established. Its formation reflected the concern and responsibility members had as mothers for the education of their children and the fact that the Parent-Teacher Association was one of the few educational bodies in which women had a significant presence. Also, as a direct descendant of the Parent-Teacher Association in America, the association represented the whole process of democratization under the Occupation, which tried to curb the role of the Ministry of Education and give more authority to the local school boards. The members of the Grass Seeds research group were mostly local Parent-Teacher Association officers, and they were key in raising the association's awareness of government attempts to reassert centralized control over the educational system and reinstitute elements of the prewar curriculum.

The struggle over education was particularly vociferous, because it conjured up images of the highly coercive prewar school system. The 1956 Law Concerning the Organization and Management of Local Educational Administration marked a major shift toward structural centralization. The law changed elected school board positions into appointed positions, took decision-making powers over budgets and teachers out of local hands, and forbade board members from having political affiliations, which in practice meant ties with left-wing parties or the teachers' union.[47] When Kishi assumed power in 1957, he declared his intent to enforce a nationwide rating system for teachers to be administered by school principals, who were appointed by the Ministry of Education rather than the local school boards.

These moves, in conjunction with the August 1958 bill to standardize school curricula under Ministry guidelines and reintroduce ethics courses, were perceived as a drive to remove "left-wing influences" from the classroom and return to prewar conventions.[48] The teachers' union adopted the tactic of waging a unified struggle on a national scale, engaging regional units simultaneously. Such general strikes cost the union dearly, and over the course of the rating struggle, more than 200 teachers were arrested, 400 dismissed or suspended, 1,000 demoted and 3,000 reprimanded, and over 52,000 suffered pay cuts.[49]

The Grass Seeds were deeply troubled by the proposed legislation for the teacher evaluation system, and when the Liberal Democratic Party introduced the bill in the Diet in 1958, the Parent-Teacher Association research group was instrumental in eventually rousing the Grass Seeds as a whole to oppose the bill and join the protests against it. Ultimately, the members wanted to ensure that their children would not be victimized by the educational system as they were during the war.

The Grass Seeds had been ambivalent about engaging in political activities, but this position began to change in 1958 with the crises surrounding the new teacher evaluation system and the Police Duties Bill. The Tokyo groups in particular felt the need to join these protests and the demonstrations against Anpo later on in order to stop the reverse course that the Liberal Democratic Party was promoting. The basis for their increasing activism in the face of these prewar revivals was their experience of the war. The war had permeated all aspects of everyday life, and the Grass Seeds felt that the wives and mothers who had gone through it had to root out its vestiges.[50]

Therefore, they also undertook a major project to record their wartime experiences and pass them on to the younger generation. Fifty women from seven Tokyo branches began to collect members' writings in 1958, working together for five years to complete three volumes of notes titled "War and Me," which then served as a basis for their research on the Vietnam War in the late 1960s.[51] They attempted to get beyond ideological viewpoints and reassess the experiences at a more basic, "instinctual" level. However, as was typical of most wartime recollections, they generally saw themselves as victims of the war, rather than as among the aggressors.[52]

Memories of wartime repression were also key to the Grass Seeds' reaction to the sudden introduction of the revised Police Duties Bill in the Diet in October of 1958. The bill sought to expand the powers of the police for search and seizure when they suspected criminal activity. Kishi's precipitous proposal suggested to many an attempt to revive the hated military police (Kenpeitai) and the so-called Thought Police (Tokkō) who violently suppressed dissent during the war years under the auspices of the 1925 Peace Preservation Law. Some of the Grass Seeds felt the bill was an urgent matter that needed to be discussed immediately, and the liaison committee gathered within the week. The Grass Seeds had also been asked by the Women's Council for the Protection of Human Rights (Jinken o Mamoru Fujin Kyōgikai) to join a coalition of groups protesting the bill. They sent a questionnaire out to all the local branches asking whether they knew of the bill; whether they approved of it or not; and if they opposed the Bill, whether the group should join with the Women's Council for the Protection of Human Rights or act independently.[53] Twenty-nine of the thirty branches said they opposed the bill, but there was no clear consensus on what to do. Eventually, the Grass Seeds both joined the coalition and submitted their own short letters of protest to the administration and the media. In addition, local branches of the Grass Seeds staged their own acts of protest.

The push toward political activism within the group reached a peak during the 1960 protests against Anpo. The Anpo issue had increasingly come into the public eye during 1959 through the united actions of the People's Council to Stop the Revised Security Treaty and through discussion in the media, even being raised in some of the popular women's magazines. *Women's Forum (Fujin kōron)*, one of the premier general interest magazines for women, began to run special features on Anpo from 1959, unlike its chief rival, *The Housewife's Friend (Shufu no tomo)*, which never covered political events. Not surprisingly, a later survey of women who had participated in the Anpo protests showed that most of them were regular readers of magazines like *Women's Forum*, while virtually none of them read *The Housewife's Friend*.[54] The Grass Seeds began to examine the issue in their own magazine from November 1959, putting out a questionnaire to the members about the controversy. The results were that most members generally opposed the treaty, but they were not necessarily opposed to the security system, and they felt that it would be difficult for Japan to maintain a position of unarmed neutrality in the cold war. This "weak" general position only sharpened the dilemma regarding the nature of the group as events progressed during 1960. Some members, mostly younger ones, wanted the group to be more activist and take a more radical stance regarding Anpo, while others wanted to retain the Grass Seeds' emphasis on discussion and research. It was difficult for women who had grown up during the war and who were raised to believe that they should not show any overt interest in politics to take an aggressively activist position.

The forcible ratification of the treaty on May 19, however, dramatically altered circumstances for the Grass Seeds, because they saw Kishi's actions as a fundamental attack on democracy. The Liaison Committee met the following day, unanimously agreeing that they should take some action as a group, and proposed drafting a letter to the prime minister and the House leader. The letter to Kishi decried the unilateral, forcible ratification and called for him to take responsibility by resigning, dissolving the Diet, and holding a general election, and by consulting the will of the people on whether or not to approve the treaty. They also sent a request to the press to reflect the opinions of the public accurately and to be vigorous in defending democracy.[55] On May 30, roughly one hundred members took part in the united action demonstration in Tokyo, delivering their letters to the Diet and various newspaper, radio, and TV offices. The group even received public exposure when a photograph of members at a rainy demonstration carried a caption about "parasol" protesters. At the same time, individual branches engaged in protest actions in their own areas, sending telegrams and petitions and participating in local demonstrations.

The bloody events of June 15 made a deep impression on the Grass Seeds, especially because it was a woman who was killed in the protests. They called another emergency meeting of the Liaison Committee and composed another letter of protest, this time condemning the police for the violence and criticizing the administration for continuing to ignore the people's anger over the forcible ratification. On June 17, they once more delivered letters to the prime minister as well as to the police and the media. They had been shocked and upset to read the Joint Declaration of the Seven Newspapers that had come out the previous day. A month later, they sent a final letter to the newspapers chiding them for reporting the events of June 15 inaccurately and raising doubts regarding how they were fulfilling their journalistic task. They called on reporters to make the utmost effort to reflect public opinion accurately.[56]

The Joint Declaration exacerbated the tensions that the group had with the press. After Anpo, the Grass Seeds' relationship with the *Asahi* and the "Hitotoki" column became attenuated, owing in part to the newspaper editors' swing to the right. The Anpo issue was also internally divisive, and those who had been less activist-oriented and more concerned with how to be better wives and mothers wanted the group to pull back from more confrontational forms of political engagement. Those members sought a return to the gossip session model of existing primarily to meet and talk (*hanashiaishugi*). They criticized the group's increasingly political orientation for making their gatherings less enjoyable, and many of them eventually dropped out of the organization.[57] Over the course of the Anpo protests, the membership had swelled to 1,500 women, but afterwards the numbers fell off to roughly a thousand.

Those who remained in the group tended to have more political concerns, although the group continued its very deliberate style of gathering information and engaging in lengthy debate in order to reach a general consensus on actions taken in the group's name. For example, the Grass Seeds created important new research groups in the early and mid-1960s that focused on peace issues (which linked to the life histories group that was collecting stories of people's wartime experiences), on protecting the postwar constitution (1964), and on problems in education (1966). The latter group was especially concerned with the lawsuit that Ienaga Saburō had brought against the Ministry of Education for censoring the contents of his history textbooks.

This research set the stage for a renewed bout of activism in the late 1960s with the protests against the Vietnam War. The Grass Seeds became involved in these at an early stage, prompted by the U.S. bombings of north Vietnam in February 1965. As Beheiren began to organize its citizens' movement in April, the Grass Seeds were sending letters to U.S. president Johnson expressing their unease at the escalation of hostilities against the Vietnamese as fellow Asians and as mothers who despaired at anyone sending their young off to war.[58] Two years later, the group set as a research theme "The Vietnam War in the Midst of Our Regions," which produced a wide range of investigations from the Chiba group that looked into connections between U.S. military operations and the construction of the new Tokyo International Airport at Sanrizuka to various Tokyo groups that researched the effects of the war at Yokosuka and Atsugi, where the United States maintained naval and air bases, and at Oji, where it had a field hospital. Still other groups investigated what Japan's Self-Defense Forces were doing in the war effort.

The level of political involvement that the Grass Seeds maintained over the years was not a function of leisure time afforded the urban middle class by an improving economy and the spread of labor-saving appliances for the household. Certainly, women in 1960 had to devote considerably more time to housework than women today; according to a survey taken that year by the *The Housewife's Friend*, housework took an average of seven hours twenty minutes a day.[59] According to a more recent survey of housewives who did not participate in the Anpo protests, roughly half of them said they were too busy to get involved, usually with housework or raising their children. However, the same survey also revealed that a much higher than average percentage of those women owned the "three sacred treasures" that could have freed up some of their time. Seventy-four percent of them had washing machines, 56 percent had refrigerators, half had electric rice cookers, and 41 percent had vacuum cleaners.[60] By contrast, only 50 percent of urban families had washing machines, 17 percent had refrigerators, 42 percent had rice cookers, and 15 percent had vacuum cleaners.[61] Material conditions therefore did not determine women's participation in political actions.

Nor did lack of awareness prevent women from participating in the Anpo protests. Virtually all of the nonparticipants in the survey were aware of the controversy, and nearly two-thirds said they were concerned about the issue.[62] Many of them felt they lived too far away in the countryside, but some also cited objections their husbands or parents made to their joining the protests, and a few felt that the demonstrations seemed too "red." By contrast, the husbands of women in the Grass Seeds were often supportive of their activities in a general way, although they did not involve themselves in the working of the group.

The example of the Grass Seeds indicates that attitudes like the desire to break free of the prewar "good wife, wise mother" ideology and political socialization through alternative communities were the key to women's participation in Anpo. Housewives who engaged in the protests generally saw a continuity between Anpo and later citizen and resident movements, unlike women students who tended to feel that the energy from the protests quickly evaporated.[63] Women students were disillusioned with their inability to revolutionize the political system and with people's apparent abandonment of politics in favor of pursuing higher incomes. Housewives, in contrast, felt that their consciousness as women, not just as Japanese citizens, had been raised over the course of the Anpo protests, and as a result they felt politically empowered by the process.[64]

Legacies

THE CONDITIONS that gave birth to the Grass Seeds began to change dramatically during the 1960s so that few women from the younger generations are members of the group today. For the next generation of women, the war and the Occupation were either distant memories or not experienced at all. They did not feel "the menace and dread of war" that those who formed the Grass Seeds spoke of. Having grown up in an era of ever-increasing economic prosperity, they found the group's premises and ways of doing things to have little relevance.

Also, with the "failure" of the united front style of mass mobilization during the 1960 Anpo protests, social movements tended to become smaller and more independent with more specific objectives and constituencies. The change was analogous to the way that general-interest journals began to lose their readership to weeklies and specialty magazines. Mass organs were seen as having broad but shallow support, while movements with a narrower focus would draw those having a deeper commitment to the cause. As a member of the Grass Seeds commented, the specialized focus of groups after Anpo facilitated very passionate, energetic activity, while broader groups seemed to have only a vague sense of direction.[65] Increasingly, new consumer, environmental, and feminist movements became the key outlets for women's political activism in the late 1960s and early 1970s. Early postwar consumer movements like the Japan Housewives Alliance with their rice ladle demonstrations seemed outdated to younger women even by the mid-1960s. As one citizen movement activist noted in 1966:

> The biggest problem for the consumers' movement is that young people are not interested in a women's federation (*fujinren*) type

of movement. The groups that are popular are sponsored by particular corporations and try to dispense some consumer information, for example, the BLC (Better Living Circle) or the BHC (Better Home Council). You could also include those like the ALC (Asahi Ladies Circle) that take the form of holding occasional expositions instead of having a membership system. . . .

If one compared the people who gather in these groups to the Shufuren type, many of them are fresh, young wives. These groups relate closely to everyday life by teaching [housewives] to be clever consumers, but unfortunately they are not organizations of consumers themselves.[66]

These so-called consumer groups were merely fashionable forms of advertising unable to survive without corporate sponsorship, whereas when consumers themselves created independent bodies, they often did so out of environmental concerns about the quality of the products they were buying. These concerns eventually led to the development of what activist-theorist Mutō Ichiyo has termed "alternative livelihood cooperatives," which sought to create organic ties with organic farmers, on the one hand, and to give consumers a direct voice in the operation of services, on the other.[67] At the same time, another type of environmental movement developed from residents' concerns about industrial pollution at production sites near where they lived.

The adaptations that groups like the Tanashi-Hōya Acorns (Donguri) made in the 1960s indicate three important aspects in the changing nature of social movements. First, local residence became more crucial as the focus of action and concern. Movements no longer strove to expand to a national level, but concentrated instead on local public spheres. Second, social movements turned more and more to environmental issues and resisted the tendency to be made cogs in the machinery of rapid economic growth. Heavy urbanization prompted the government and large corporations to locate major state projects such as massive petrochemical industrial complexes in less populated, outlying areas. The construction and operation of these projects were largely unregulated, prompting local residents to question the direction and social costs of such modernization. Third, the newsletters and magazines that these movements produced were considered to be an essential element of their evolving democratic praxis. Internally, they fostered dialogue and group participation, but they were also used for public purposes, disseminating information not carried in the mass media and reaching out to groups and individuals facing similar struggles to create loose networks of solidarity.

The Acorns were started in 1957 by housewives living in Tanashi, a suburb west of Tokyo, and although the group expanded slightly to include the neighboring city of Hōya in 1969, it never tried to widen its scope beyond the immediate area. They began to put out a handwritten, mimeographed, newsletter in 1962 named after the group, and by the time they converted to typewriters in 1965, they were printing and distributing about 2,500 copies each month.[68] The group focused on the local system of education and government rather than on the national-level bodies, so one of the key issues for them was the board of education's accountability to the community and its openness to input from related groups such as the Parent-Teacher Association, especially regarding the use of scholastic achievement tests.[69] Another major campaign they took up after Anpo called for the public disclosure of local election results. At the time, election tallies were announced publicly only for national-level representatives, so the Acorns used their newsletter as a means to mobilize support for full disclosure of the local political processes. Later they also began to attend city council meetings and to report on the proceedings in their newsletter. By insisting on citizens' right to know, they implied that politics should not be the exclusive domain of professional politicians, and they indirectly posed a challenge to male control of the political system by insisting on their participatory rights as women. They considered the role of being a watchdog over the local administration to be a key function of their group.[70]

The Acorns also thought it crucial to reform local politics

when the city government impeded solutions to environmental problems affecting their daily lives. For years, the group had called for public debate on a proposed sewage treatment plant in Tanashi, and when the local government failed to respond, Acorn members sent out their own questionnaires and conducted their own surveys. They then reported the results in their newsletter to inform local residents and to help build their movement. Their struggle was characteristic of the residence-based environmental movements that sought to prevent the introduction of polluting state projects into their areas. Whether city leaders were aligned with the Liberal Democratic Party or with the progressive parties, what mattered to the movement was their position on allowing the projects to be implemented. Practical objectives took precedence over ideological stances.

The feminist movement has been perhaps the most important channel for the second generation of postwar women's activism. Feminism began to take off from the time of the campus struggles in the late 1960s, and it started by questioning the primary identification of women with the roles of wife and mother.[71] Feminists pointed instead to other areas of identification, such as that of women as workers. This shift reflected the changing household contexts for women during the period of rapid economic growth. While the labor force participation rate for women has remained relatively constant from 1960 to the present, there has been a dramatic shift in the sectors in which women work. The numbers of women who were employed in companies rose from 5.3 million in 1955, to 7.4 million in 1960, to 9.1 in 1965, and to 11 million in 1970.[72] However, the number of women who were self-employed, working in family businesses, or engaged in agriculture steadily fell. Because young women employees in the 1950s generally left the work force permanently once they got married, in 1955, over 65 percent of women employed in the business and industrial sectors were single, while only 20.4 percent were married. By 1965, only half of women employees were single while 38.6 percent were married, and by 1975, 38 percent were single and over 51 percent were married.[73] That is, during the decade from 1955 to 1965, more and more women were reentering the labor force once their children had grown to middle or high school age, creating an M-shaped age distribution curve for women's employment that is more pronounced than that of any of the industrialized economies save Britain.[74]

Women's work became episodic, and it was regarded as supplemental to the household's income. Companies increasingly tracked women returning to the labor force into temporary or part-time work as male workers pushed the companies to provide them a family wage during the 1950s. Larger corporations therefore used women as economic buffers. They could absorb losses during recessionary periods by firing women while retaining a greater number of "permanent" male employees. However, during economic booms, they could quickly and cheaply expand their production by bringing in more part-time and temporary women workers, who did not receive any significant company benefits.[75] This strategy was clearly demonstrated during the recessionary spells in the 1970s and the subsequent recovery in the 1980s. Overall, women increasingly had to shoulder the double burden of domestic reproductive work and productive labor in the industrial sector.[76] They had to grapple with their identities as workers as well as wives and mothers, and thus movements like the Grass Seeds seemed out of date and had difficulty attracting younger women.

Given the limitations imposed by this discriminatory labor structure and the double burden that they had to bear, it was more advantageous for women to find work closer to home, which served to reinforce their concerns with the environs of their residential areas. Women, therefore, were usually more active than men in the residents' movements of the late 1960s and 1970s. By contrast, middle-class men's daily lives became more restricted by the organizations in which they worked. They generally had to commute farther to and from work, and they increasingly were expected to engage in after-hours activities with their coworkers.

They were thus for the most part physically absent from the places they lived. Hence, few men felt free enough from work-related constraints to become involved in these movements.[77] Some activists also perceive a gender separation and tension between a predominantly male labor movement with its ties to the established opposition parties and Marxist ideological language and the more women-oriented citizens' movements based on issues of daily life.[78] All of these factors contributed to the numerical dominance women had in the residents' movements to the point that gender has often been considered a defining characteristic.

Because of the prominence women have had in the residents' movements, their small-scale publications, or mini-communications (mini komi) as they came to be called in the 1970s, are also typically thought to reflect a "feminine" style of writing. Feminist activist and founding editor of the magazine Agora Saitō Chiyo characterizes the mini-communications style as one of personal narratives of self-discovery, using language that is often seen as "emotional" and close to the form of oral tales.[79] While she acknowledges that the newsletters serve as a crucial outlet for women suffering a "staggering" degree of alienation, she also criticizes mini-communications for pushing overly individualistic points of view and not being more pluralistic and dialogic. Thus, she tries to avoid "women's language" in her own self-proclaimed midi komi magazine, which she positions somewhere between the male-dominated mass media and the female-dominated mini-communications.

However, these mini-communications express the same principles that the Grass Seeds used in organizing themselves. The movements that produce these publications emphasize face-to-face contact and decentralized, horizontal forms of association. They typically insist on local autonomy and existential over ideological positioning.[80] Later consumer, feminist, and residents' movements all moved in new directions and focused on different aspects from the Grass Seeds, but they all derived from the same current, like an underground stream (fukuryūsui) that surfaces now and again at different locations, in the imagery of Grass Seeds' member Imai Yaeko.[81] The statement of purpose that the Grass Seeds continue to put on the inside cover of every issue of their magazine serves as a reminder that they began as a kind of self-cultivation program established to explore alternative forms of community. Characteristically, when contacted, they wanted to be interviewed as a group, each of them bringing her own interests and viewpoints to discuss issues collectively.

6

THE VOICELESS VOICES
AND THE DISCOURSE
ON PUBLIC CITIZENRY

NLIKE THE MOUNTAIN Range or the Grass Seeds, the
Voiceless Voices (Koe Naki Koe no Kai) formed in the
midst of the Anpo protests in direct response to the forcible ratification of the Security Treaty and Prime Minister Kishi's
disdain for those who criticized his actions. They reflected the
large numbers of people who were concerned with the government's program of retrenchment in the years leading up to the
Anpo controversy and finally felt compelled to take action. It was
these previously unmobilized protesters who accounted for the
marked increase in the size of the demonstrations. The Voiceless
Voices took this mobilization one step further by aiming their
appeals at the many bystanders who had come out to see the
marches.

The experience of the Voiceless Voices has shown that the
number of people actually marching around the Diet represented
only a portion of the sentiment against Kishi and the treaty. Bystanders formed another layer, and they were more than just
curious onlookers. They showed their support for the protest
marchers by waving to them and shouting encouragement, even

from the windows of the surrounding buildings.[1] The marchers could act as proxies for a wider body, not just for those who lined the streets of Tokyo but for those around the country who were unable to travel to the capital. Groups like the Voiceless Voices helped break down the sense of separation between political activism and everyday life. They represented a general spirit of political engagement by ordinary citizens.

The Voiceless Voices posited the notion of an engaged citizenry rather than the working class as the agent of historical change. The fact that they appealed to a different group of people from industrial workers meant that their political philosophy diverged from the classic Marxist formulation. They considered direct democratic praxis more important than ideology. Because they felt that democracy was defined by its processes rather than its institutions, groups like the Voiceless Voices also began to re-inscribe a notion of the public sphere (or multiple public spheres) that had previously been heavily identified with the state. These citizens' movements sought alternatives to the repressive hierarchies that pervaded the government, including the opposition parties, as well as society in general. Thus, they tried to create more horizontal forms of organization as an integral aspect of their democratic praxis.

One of the Voiceless Voices, Takabatake Michitoshi, referred to the way in which they formed as a process of "organizing the spontaneous."[2] What he meant by the term "spontaneous," however, was not that the members were unconscious or irrational or chaotic but rather that they generated their own group. Groups like his were not created at the behest of the Socialist or Communist parties or their affiliated labor federations, nor were they unilaterally committed to participate in the demonstrations by their leaders or central offices, as was common with labor unions and organs of the opposition parties.[3] Instead, the members of the Voiceless Voices and similar citizen groups came to the protests of their own volition as freestanding individuals and organized themselves through face-to-face contact.

A Time to Decide

DESPITE THE treaty's unpopularity, Kishi had dramatically asserted his authority over the formal representation of citizens' participatory rights and interests by forcibly ratifying it on May 19. Demonstrations took place daily around the country, and the united actions mushroomed in size, owing largely to the influx of citizens from a wide range of local circle movements, women's organizations, professional associations, artistic and cultural groups, rather than a greater mobilization of organized labor. Movements that were already active immediately issued statements denouncing Kishi's actions. The Assembly of Jurists to Stop the Treaty (Anpo Soshi Hōritsuka Kaigi) declared the ratification invalid,[4] and the Association of Japanese Literary Persons (Nihon Bungeika Kyōkai) voiced their fears that the Liberal Democratic Party's unilateral actions over the treaty would result in curtailed freedom of expression.[5] On the twentieth, the Federation of Japanese Women's Organizations (Nihon Fujin Dantai Rengōkai) also demanded that the Cabinet resign and the Diet be dissolved, and the YWCA declared that the government had to reform itself to bring about a political system that the people could trust.[6] All of the major daily newspapers, including the conservative *Nihon keizai shinbun*, condemned Kishi's unilateral actions and his use of force. The media referred to this policy as the "tyranny and violence of the majority" and complained that Kishi gave no consideration to dissenting opinions or compromise between the ruling party and the opposition.[7] It was, according to the newspapers, an "unprecedented day of shame" and an "indelible blot" on Japanese democracy.[8] The common thread to the outcries of these movements and the media was the fear of a fascist revival and the loss of postwar democratic gains.

Takeuchi Yoshimi, a prominent China scholar and translator of Lu Xun, used a different strategy to make his protest, one that had important implications for the citizens' movement in general. On May 21, Takeuchi resigned from his post at Tokyo Metropolitan University and issued a statement that said:

When I accepted my position as professor at Tokyo Metropolitan University, I took an oath as a public official to respect and uphold the constitution.

However, I believe that from May 20, we were bereft of parliamentarianism, a chief object of the constitution. Moreover, those responsible for depriving the Diet of its function as the nation's highest body were none other than the chair of the Lower House and our top public official, the prime minister. To continue my professorship at Tokyo Metropolitan University when the constitution is flouted in this way would violate not only the oath I took when I was hired but also my conscience as an educator. I have therefore resolved to resign.

I reached my decision independently, not through the intervention of anyone's wishes. No one pushed me to take such measures nor am I in any way urging others to do the same. I have the means to eke out a living through my writings, and, given that, I chose this path after careful deliberation as one possible way for me to make a protest.

I ask forgiveness for any trouble my resignation ends up causing my colleagues and students, and hope for their continued friendship in the future.[9]

May 21, 1960
Takeuchi Yoshimi

Takeuchi had settled on his course of action before he had decided on his reasons for doing so. As he listened to the radio reports on the evening of the nineteenth, he knew that he had to resign in protest, but on what grounds? Significantly, Takeuchi does not mention the treaty in his statement, nor does he refer to any ideological framework in talking about his motivations. After pondering the question all night, "the word 'constitution' suddenly sprang to mind like a bolt from the blue."[10] Takeuchi had been a member of the Research Group on Constitutional Issues (Kenpō Mondai Kenkyū Kai) from its inception, and during the late 1950s he was active in causes to protect the postwar constitution.[11] But like most he had forgotten about the oath that teachers at public universities had to take when they were employed.[12] The clause was aimed primarily at restraining bureaucrats from engaging in overt political protest, and teachers did not generally see themselves as public officials. However, by categorizing himself as such, Takeuchi established a common ground on which he could upbraid Kishi for *his* failure to uphold the constitution, implying that the prime minister ought to resign and dissolve the parliament.

Takeuchi's public protest was also motivated by personal experience. He had visited the prime minister's residence the day before as a representative of the Committee to Criticize the Security Treaty (Anpo Hihan no Kai) in order to secure Kishi's promise to respect the people's wishes expressed in the massive number of petitions submitted against the treaty. Thus, Takeuchi felt that Kishi had both broken a personal promise and violated the public trust by his actions on the nineteenth. For him, to remain silent and not protest in such a situation would be tantamount to allowing Kishi to violate his very humanity and subjectivity and destroy any possibility for independent action.[13]

Takeuchi's declaration therefore exhibited dual impulses. On the one hand, he claimed to be making a personal gesture as an individual, but, on the other hand, he used his intellectual prominence and his supposed status as a government official to give the act public significance. Although he wrote later that his statement was intended as a notice to his friends rather than a public declaration, Takeuchi sent the text to some three hundred people, and it was immediately picked up by the newspapers and announced on TV.[14] He knew that the words of a well-known intellectual would carry some weight. As an indication of the effect Takeuchi's declaration had, the *Asahi shinbun* ran a three-quarter-length body picture rather than the usual head shot along with an extended interview with Takeuchi about his resignation. In the days following the forcible ratification of the treaty, Takeuchi became even more of a public figure, speaking at a number of rallies and meetings, and writing articles for weekly and monthly magazines.

His resignation stirred up academic circles, whose visibility in the protest lent the movement greater legitimacy in the eyes of the public and inspired many students to demonstrate.[15] Takeuchi's protest agitated the Kishi administration as well, and Education Ministry officials reacted so strongly to it that they began to draft a Bill to Control the Universities.[16]

The key point that Takeuchi stressed during this period was that "the aspect of politics completely changed after the twentieth. Even given the Anpo issue, the focus now is how to defend democracy."[17] According to Takeuchi, Kishi had raised the specter of prewar fascism through his actions and polarized politics to such an extent that there could no longer be any middle ground. As the title of Takeuchi's May 23 speech stated, it was "time to decide" (*ketsudan no toki*) between democracy and dictatorship, and he exhorted his audience to rise up and form a people's front against fascism.[18]

On the evening of the twenty-fourth, Takeuchi went on to say that Kishi had already established a dictatorship by destroying the function of the Diet itself, so the only recourse open to the people (*kokumin*) was to organize a protest movement and force Kishi to resign. He asserted that the right to protest was the very foundation of democracy and that the core of the parliamentary system resided in the people's direct exercise of sovereignty, not the internal machinations in the Diet.[19] Protest, then, was the only way for the people to recover their subjectivity.

It is important to keep in mind here that Takeuchi had accused both Kishi and House Speaker Kiyose Ichirō of destroying constitutional government in his resignation statement. Both of these figures had been indicted (but not tried) as Class A war criminals during the Occupation, and the mention of Kiyose both reinforced fears of a fascist revival and suggested that the crisis of democracy was systemic. Moreover, Kishi had locked up the Diet after extending the Diet session and forcing through the treaty, so there was no longer any representative government being exercised even though the Diet was supposedly still in session. Therefore, Takeuchi felt that protest in the streets was the only recourse for political action.

Many other progressive intellectuals shared Takeuchi's sense of crisis and quickly organized themselves to register their opposition. On the twenty-fourth, some 2,500 scholars gathered at the Kanda Education Hall (Kanda Kyōiku Kaikan) in Tokyo from twenty universities and ten research groups as far away as Gunma, Aichi, and Hiroshima. Maruyama Masao, the professor of political science at Tokyo University who was instrumental in organizing the Kanda rally, delivered a speech whose title, "A Time to Choose" (Sentaku no toki), and contents echoed those of Takeuchi's speech the day before.[20] In his brief talk, Maruyama stressed that Kishi's actions on May 19 were different from his previous attempts to reinstitute prewar structures, because this time he did not even attempt to pay lip service to peace and democracy. He simply exercised raw, naked power and thus changed the nature of the dispute. This act condensed all the various struggles of the postwar period and simplified the issue to that of either accepting capricious authoritarian rule or protesting the current order and defending democracy.[21] After listening to the speeches, the participants marched on the Diet, and a group of representatives went to the prime minister's residence to demand, unsuccessfully, an interview.[22]

These scholars' elite position made them feel they had dispensation to ask for an audience with Kishi, and as educational leaders, they could exert great influence over their students. However, their calls for the public to join the protests were based on everyone having equivalent status as citizens with as much say as politicians in running the government. Ultimately, these scholars and intellectuals would have to forgo the privileges of their elite status if they wanted to retain their credibility with the students and citizens. Those professors who stood by as the police clubbed their students at demonstrations and tried to sidestep the attacks by saying they were teachers were vilified by the students afterwards. Takeuchi had made an important symbolic sacrifice in resigning his post and its privileges, but it was a sacrifice that only the elite could afford to make.

Takeuchi's resignation encapsulated a crucial shift taking place during the Anpo protests. It indicated the enormous influence that intellectuals could have with the general public through their access to the media, but it also showed the sense of elite privilege that intellectuals felt they shared with those in power. At the same time, his resignation signaled the beginning of a decline in the influence intellectuals had, in part necessitated by the turn to a citizen ideology. Takeuchi's concern with the postwar Peace Constitution and the gains that the people (*kokumin*) had made under it, his fear of fascist revivals and the comparatively weak resistance he felt that the Japanese had displayed, the ambiguity in his status as an elite "public intellectual" supposedly acting solely as a private individual, and the idea of self-sacrifice for the sake of the nation implicit in his statement of resignation all had important implications for citizens' movements.

Lending an Ear to the Voiceless Voices

WHEN KISHI sequestered himself in his prime minister's residence following the vehement reaction to the forcible ratification, he tried to arrange a meeting with the top three opposition leaders in hopes of negotiating a deal to quell the unrest. Since Kishi viewed the demonstrations as a result of Communist and Socialist manipulation, he thought that behind-the-scenes negotiations might resolve the problem. However, he failed to realize that the nature of the protests had been fundamentally altered, and the opposition parties would have found it almost impossible to disperse the demonstrators. Since Kishi was unsuccessful in reaching a settlement, he turned to chastising the press for their uniform criticism of his actions. Kishi's secretary claimed that they had received a great volume of mail supporting Kishi and the treaty, some of which had even been penned in blood.[23] When Kishi finally granted a press conference on May 28, he shifted his attack to the protesters, whom he called a violent, vocal minority. He vowed that he would never yield to their demands for his resignation or for the dissolution of the Diet in order to hold new elections. Instead, he insisted that he would only bend his ears to the "voiceless voices"—the "silent majority" he claimed supported him.

By using the term "voiceless voices," Kishi had actually appropriated a phrase that some demonstrators were already using to describe their participation in the treaty protests, and the opposition immediately sought to reclaim the term. At the next united action, the June 4 general strike, a placard appeared that identified its two bearers as Voiceless Voices and encouraged onlookers to join them in disproving Kishi's claim. By the time they had reached the end of the course, their ranks swelled with hundreds of "nameless citizens" (*mumei no shimin*). As Kobayashi Tomi described it, "There were about thirty of us by the time we had reached Hibiya Park from Toranomon, and after we had gone around the Diet to the front of the Ministry of Education, there were about three hundred of us. I was so moved by the dramatic way in which our numbers had increased."[24]

The idea for the placard arose from members of a small study circle called the Subjectivity Group (Shukan no Kai), who had come together to work through different ideas on the problem of objectivity versus subjectivity in recording people's lives. In doing so, they went to visit people in various occupations that shed light on social problems—kindergarten teachers, picture card storytellers (*kami shibai*), dressmakers, juvenile delinquents—making detailed observations and recording interviews.[25] Several of them had come from a twenty- to thirty-person Record-Taking Methods circle associated with the *Science of Thought (Shisō no kagaku)* magazine. But despite the social and behavioral science origins of the circle, the Subjectivity Group had a heavy artistic bent, including a cartoonist, a film critic, a play manager, an assistant director at Shōchiku films, and Kobayashi, who was an artist and schoolteacher and became the most steadfast member of the Voiceless Voices over the years.[26]

The intellectual leader of the Subjectivity Group was Tsurumi Shunsuke, one of the founding members of the Science of Thought group, whose goal was to produce research through empirical methods.[27] Tsurumi was a strong adherent of William James, George Mead, and other American pragmatists, and he considered the central maxim of pragmatism to be, "Thought means what can be revealed in the form of action."[28] These groups were one way of putting this philosophy into practice as places to test social theory against actual experience. Tsurumi also immersed himself in political activities in the days following the forcible ratification, taking a cue from Takeuchi and resigning from his teaching post at the Tokyo Institute of Technology on May 30 in protest. Unlike Takeuchi, he did not issue a written statement or make any disclaimer that people should not follow his example, but he did talk with reporters about his protest.[29] Because of the media crush surrounding his protest, he was late getting to his meeting with the Subjectivity Group the next day.

The circle had gathered on May 31 to conduct interviews with youths at a juvenile detention center in Hachiōji. Afterwards, the members began to discuss Tsurumi's resignation and a demonstration that one of them had attended the previous day. That member was particularly impressed by a cook who had overcome the reluctance that most onlookers felt and joined the marchers. His impression was that many of those who lined the sidewalks to watch the demonstrations were actually anxious to join in and express their opposition to the government but found it hard to do so without belonging to a formal body like a union. He felt that something should be done to encourage more onlookers to cross over into the streets.

Kobayashi herself was in an analogous position to the onlookers. She had talked with those who had gone to demonstrations and was sympathetic to the cause, but she hesitated to go herself, since she did not consider herself to be political and she had no affiliation with the groups involved in the organized opposition. However, with the forcible ratification and the daily protests around the Diet, she was anxious to do something. As she and the others in the Subjectivity Group talked on the train home from their May 31 meeting, they decided to take part in the next major demonstration and to prepare some signs to get individual bystanders to join them as they marched.[30] This was a crucial step for Kobayashi and many others in the citizens' movements, because they moved from being interested observers to active participants in politics.

As the artist of the group, Kobayashi drew up the sign saying, "Anyone can join the 'Voiceless Voices' group." The group had agreed to assemble on June 4 at the tail end of a block of artists and intellectuals behind the Committee to Criticize the Security Treaty, but only Kobayashi and Fuha Mitsuo were able to find each other that day. The location was fortuitous, however, because when Fuha later turned the sign around to the rear, bystanders rushed in to march with them. Once the barrier between people marching in the street and those standing on the sidewalk was breached, those who first joined were quick to encourage others, calling out "it's okay" and "let's walk together." As one woman told Kobayashi, "I just couldn't stay at home today, so I brought along my son who's going to a prep school to take a look around the Diet, but when I saw this nonpartisan group, I joined in. This is really great. Something would have been missing if we'd just gone home. I came down on May Day this year, too, but with those labor unions carrying red flags, it was hard to join them somehow."[31]

As this woman's comments indicate, she was not drawn to the protests by the established opposition or a belief in Marxist ideology. The ideological trappings of the union movement made her uncomfortable. Furthermore, taking part in a demonstration was thought of as requiring a certain amount of training and discipline, because it was potentially hazardous. Unionists and students had experience in closing ranks and protecting themselves from attacks by the police and violent right-wing groups. However, citizen groups generally lacked this experience and did not perform the zigzag demonstrations that the students used to cut a wider swath in the streets and fend off blows. It was also much more difficult for women to engage in the marches, because protest organizers felt that they had to be protected and stuck them toward the rear of the main body, surrounded by men. Moreover, politics was still considered a male domain, and women were generally discouraged from such public action. Still, this woman and many others who lined the streets felt that Japan had reached a critical juncture and they had to express their disapproval of the government's actions.

Kobayashi was so exhilarated by the experience that, after having a bowl of noodles, she decided to go back for a second round, gathering hundreds more with her placard. As the protesters staged a sit-in in front of the American embassy, they began to exchange names and telephone numbers so that they could meet at the next demonstration, and by the time this group had reached the end of the march, Kobayashi had collected two hundred names and one thousand yen in contributions.[32] Since they had no formal organization or office, they used the phone numbers of volunteers for making contact and developed the pattern of meeting at the next rally or demonstration. They made no attempt to create a leadership or establish membership criteria.

The Voiceless Voices also garnered a good deal of exposure in the newspapers and on television. When reporters asked Kobayashi who made up their group, she replied that anyone who had gathered and did not belong to any particular organization was a member. This comment inspired a plethora of signs at the next demonstration on June 11 announcing other Voiceless Voices groups and citizens' bodies with names like "Anyone Can Join the Voice of the Citizens' Group" or the "Citizens' Group You Can Join Even as a Solitary Individual." All of these slogans emphasized the principle of individual participation and identified this principle with the notion of the citizen as political subject.

To encourage more people to come out, the Voiceless Voices promoted voluntary participation, even on a limited, part-time basis, and stressed a willingness to act over adhering to a particular ideology. Takabatake Michitoshi and Yasuda Takeshi wrote up a flyer for the June 11 protest that summarized these principles.

ANYONE CAN JOIN THE VOICELESS VOICES!

Citizens! Let's all walk together. If only for five minutes or a hundred meters, let's walk together. We don't have any particular grand point of view nor are we loudly staking some claim. But even the "voiceless voices" can distinguish what is right and what's not, and we really want to protest to the government. So let's walk together and quietly show our opposition. Maybe you're busy with work every day and maybe you're embarrassed to take part in a demonstration, but if we give up and keep silent here and now, Japan will never get any better. We don't want to feel ashamed when our children ask some day, "What was everyone doing then?" In order to keep the deeds of May 19 from becoming an accepted fact, the Diet should be dissolved immediately and the treaty revoked. As for Prime Minister Kishi, who in his duty to America has trampled on his own people, he should resign. And until we see that happy day, the prime minister should postpone Ike's state visit to Japan, which he is using [for his own purposes]. Citizens all, be brave! Walk with us; show them how we feel.[33]

This philosophy of "just do what you can" was a key factor in attracting bystanders to join the protests. Along these lines, the group also coined the phrase "money from those who have it, power from those with strength" (*kane aru mono wa kane o, chikara aru mono wa chikara o*), a variation on the Marxist saying "from each according to his abilities, to each according to his needs."[34] Some onlookers found it difficult to become involved because they could not afford to take the five or six hours required to go through the whole demonstration. Unlike organized laborers, whose unions negotiated time off for them to attend the protests and provided them with transportation and lunch money, other protesters had to create their own time and forgo any compensation. This meant that small shop owners, housewives, and students had the most flexibility to go to the protests. For example, Mochizuki Sumiko, who joined the Voiceless Voices on June 4, was running a grocery store with her husband in Azabu, and from the middle of May she began to go watch the demonstrations at the Diet nearly every day after she finished the housework.[35] If office workers wanted to attend, they might go to the protests in the evening after finishing work. They could also be more surreptitious by going after work, although they might talk about it in whispers with others at the office the next day.[36] Full-time activism required monetary sacrifice and a major commitment of time. However, the Voiceless Voices asked people to contribute only what they felt comfortable doing without damaging their positions in the home, local community, or workplace. Ultimately, this approach had drawbacks in terms of long-term commitment and continuity, but during the demonstrations it helped create an alternative to the obligatory participation demanded by the opposition parties.[37]

The Voiceless Voices also began to create their own culture of protest. Students and workers had their own songs of struggle, and revolutionary melodies like the "Internationale" were ubiquitous at demonstrations, but other citizens found it hard to identify with these songs. Therefore, Nakada Yoshinao took the lead lines and conclusion from the flyer that Takabatake and Yasuda had written and set the words to music so the group could have their own song.[38]

The Voiceless Voices debuted their marching song on June 15, when the words "citizens all, be brave" took on special meaning. March organizers were more concerned than usual for the safety of the demonstrators because of all the women and children who had shown up for the protest, and they continually warned the marchers as they waited in Hibiya Park to be on their guard. The Voiceless Voices therefore sang their new song to allay their fears and to overcome their sense of vulnerability.[39] Those fears were soon realized when they heard about the violent attacks the Restoration Action Corps (Ishin Kōdōtai) had made on members of the New Drama (Shingeki) troupe and Christian and citizen activists. They also heard that the police stood by without intervening to stop the violence. When Kobayashi and others reached the main gate to the Diet, they saw the ambulances go by, and when they reached the official residence of the prime minister, they saw students lying by the side of the road with their heads wrapped in blood-soaked bandages. These were the Bund students who had forced open the South Gate and poured into the Diet compound only to be beaten back by the riot police. Some of the other students ran over to the main line of marchers to plead with them to join their sit-in.[40]

Japan Communist Party leaders, however, tried to stop people from going near the area. They sought to isolate the Bund students, who had once more defied party directives and forced open the gates to the compound.[41] Organizers told marchers to keep moving, but despite these obstacles some of the women rushed to the site to tend to the injured. The ideological position of the students or the party leaders did not matter to them. They were moved to act by a desire to alleviate the human suffering they saw.

People were deeply shocked to hear that Tokyo University student and Zengakuren officer Kanba Michiko was killed that evening. The Keio Hospital autopsy concluded that Kanba had been strangled to death, which implicated the riot police, who were using their billy clubs to put choke holds on those they were arresting.[42] Although the police later denied any responsibility and claimed that Kanba had been trampled to death by other students retreating from the compound, most protesters saw her as a victim of state violence. Kanba's death became a touchstone for the Voiceless Voices, and members continued to commemorate it for decades to come by bringing flowers and incense to the South Gate every June 15. They continued to reassess the significance of her death in relation to changing events such as the Vietnam War and to reflect on their basic principles. The events of June 15, like the forcible ratification of the treaty, reinforced their mistrust of authority and confirmed their fears that the government was re-imposing the violent oppression of the war years. As Hattori Akira remarked at the following year's commemoration: "I don't think you can ever trust authority no matter what form it takes, because no matter who wields it, some kind of violence accompanies it. Oh, sometimes the authorities seem to refrain from exercising their power over us, but then suddenly when we aren't looking, they run riot over us and go out of control. Since we're always so busy, we tend to neglect this and just trust them, but you'd better be careful."[43]

Hattori points to the need for citizens to take individual re-sponsibility in holding the abuses of governmental power in check. Widespread distrust of the authorities was reinforced by the shift in attitude that the media took toward the protests in the wake of Kanba's death. In the month after the forcible ratification, the tone of newspaper editorials seemed to turn away from the protesters. Then, on June 16, the *Yomiuri, Mainichi, Asahi, Nihon keizai, Sankei, Tōkyō shinbun,* and *Tokyo Times* newspapers printed an unprecedented joint editorial calling for the opposition parties to lay aside their differences with the ruling party and return to the Diet as the way to end the violence.[44] People were outraged at the suggestion that it was the protesters who were responsible for the bloodshed, and they began to picket the press club. Satō Eiichirō wrote in the Voiceless Voices' newsletter that May 19 was the death of parliamentary politics, June 15 was Kanba's death, and June 16 was the death of the public media.[45]

The change in the press coverage of the Anpo protests was due in large part to the widening split between editors and rank-and-file reporters over the issue. Disagreements with the editors had arisen months earlier over the terminology used to describe the protests, such as whether or not to use the words "vio-lent break-in" (*rannyū*) to characterize the Zengakuren students' charge into the Diet compound during the November 27, 1959, demonstration.[46] Reporters on the street tended to be more sym-pathetic to the protesters than their editors, and most rank-and-file newspaper employees belonged to the National Federation of Press Workers (Shinbun Rōren) union, which because of its affiliation with Sōhyō held a number of study sessions on the treaty. Kishi was imperious and disdainful of news reporters and did not enjoy good relations with the press. He felt that reporters ought to fulfill the role of supporting the administration rather than acting as independent watchdogs, so he was hostile to critical questions. The focus of his administration's Mass Media Counter-Measures Committee, therefore, was on wooing editors and getting them to control their reporters, change the coverage of the protests, and blacklist opposition figures. The degree to which the joint declaration was reprinted around the country and broadcast on radio and television seemed to indicate how much the administration's countermeasures had succeeded in altering the function of the media to that of manufacturing publicity for the state, in the words of Habermas.[47] For the Voiceless Voices, Kanba's death also showed that they needed to create their own vehicles of expression and channels of communication.

Kanba's sacrifice was also a motivation for the group to continue despite the imminence of the moment the treaty would take effect. On the day of the students' joint service for Kanba at Tokyo University, the Voiceless Voices gathered some two thousand people who once again exchanged names and numbers while staging a sit-in at the prime minister's residence.[48] The next day at the Sōgetsu Meeting Hall rally, the two hundred who gathered decided to start a campaign to collect money for Kanba's family. Although the Bund students were despondent when the treaty automatically took effect, the Voiceless Voices were not.[49] The group drew their biggest following on June 22, as Sōhyō led another limited general strike and 120,000 protesters rallied around the Diet.[50] Then on July 2, some two hundred Voiceless Voices joined a national rally against ratification that drew 100,000 to march through Ginza in Tokyo.[51]

On June 23, after exchanging the instruments of ratification for the treaty, Kishi announced that he would resign from office, although he did not actually step down until July 15. Despite

Kishi's resignation, the Voiceless Voices decided to stay together and further develop their political engagement. They felt it would be a waste simply to quit after continuing to draw people out to the demonstrations even after the treaty came into effect, so they started a small newsletter called *Tayori* (Correspondence) to keep in touch with each other. The first issue carried short pieces on people's impressions of the demonstrations and messages from other groups that had contacted them during the month. It also announced that the owner of a small coffee shop by the Yaesu exit of Tokyo station was letting the group use the place late on Saturday afternoons to get together for informal conversation. The issue also carried Tsurumi Shunsuke's proposal for a nonpartisan citizens' assembly to discuss the current political situation. In it, he urged a detached, scientific discussion that went beyond utilitarianism in politics, but what resonated most with the group was his call for direct democracy and political expression instead of entrusting matters to professional politicians. He also warned the Voiceless Voices against becoming an umbrella organization that subsumed other groups or creating a central home office that oversaw outlying branches.[52]

In the second issue of *Tayori*, Takabatake Michitoshi urged a residentially based movement even though local groups might find it hard to sustain themselves over the long haul because of the wide range of issues each would have to address. Still, the only way to counter the local pork-barrel politics, which enabled Diet representatives to ignore the Anpo protesters' demands without threatening their electoral base, was a residents' movement. Therefore, he urged forming a loose network of local groups and individuals demanding participatory rights rather than monetary benefits. In the same issue, Sakaguchi Masaaki wrote in to suggest that the group get together to talk about where to go from here, his hope being that they would organize themselves only "to a degree," not turn to formal agendas and structures. He also stressed that they had to listen to other voiceless voices who had not yet spoken publicly rather than try to enlighten them.[53]

Tokyo-region members did finally gather for an assembly on

September 25, but significantly they called this meeting an *ido-bata kaigi*, a village gossip session around the local well, rather than a formal meeting with set speakers giving lectures.[54] The meeting differed from Tsurumi's proposal in that they did not discuss national politics so much as reexamine their movement self-critically in order to set a general course for the future. In line with Takabatake's thinking, the attendees organized themselves according to residential area (discussants were identified in the minutes by ward), but any suggestion of a central office, even in the form of a facilitating committee (*sewanin kai*), was vigorously opposed because it would tend to encourage executive decision making. By the same token, the idea of having lectures by experts or any action intended to "enlighten" the masses was also sharply criticized. The attendees made no attempt to draw up any kind of manifesto beyond adopting the general theme of noncooperation with any war effort. That is, they consciously aimed at a formless solidarity that was nonsectarian and nonpartisan and focused on debate and political engagement.

Local autonomy was key to taking action because, as one member from Tosa Shimizu City in Kōchi Prefecture wrote, organization men in the countryside often feel unable do anything without orders from above. Associations can only truly develop when people are independent enough to decide on their own course of action and then get the central bureaucracies to acknowledge their freedom to do so.[55] Another letter called for greater inclusion of those who had not, for whatever reasons, taken part in the protests by using the newsletter as a forum for participation and for extending the group's formless solidarity to a wider group of people.[56]

Historical Memory and Organizing the Spontaneous

THE OPPOSITION to Anpo and the government exhibited by the Voiceless Voices and the citizens who flooded the streets after

May 19 was conditioned by historical memories of what had happened in World War II and the immediate postwar period. The Anpo generation comprised people who had direct experience of the war and then saw the sudden transformation of their leaders into "democrats" with the coming of the Occupation after Japan's defeat. World War II had ended only fifteen years earlier, and people were acutely sensitive to the possibility of a second descent into the "valley of darkness," especially since many of the same prewar government figures had returned to power. These very real fears of a fascist revival and the possibility of another war, this time an all-out nuclear one, made the slogan "protect peace and democracy" an effective one during Anpo.

Kobayashi Tomi made it clear that her memories of World War II were a key factor in her political participation with the Voiceless Voices.

> No matter if it's for the country or whatever, those who start wars, those so-called big shots, never become its victims. When a war starts, it's always people like us who are the victims that suffer, who are wounded or killed. Wrath burns in my heart over that, and while I believe that we must never start another war, I didn't do anything about it until 1960. Certainly, the forcible ratification of the 1960 Anpo treaty compelled even people like me to turn toward the Diet. In my case, I hate war and, feeling that way, I thought it would be really terrible if we got steamrollered into one.[57]

Maruyama Masao, one of the most influential theorists for the citizens' faction (*shimin-ha*) during Anpo,[58] linked the spirit of the protests to the desire the Japanese people had to transform the nation after their defeat in World War II. In his speech on June 12, for example, he explained that his title, "Fukusho no setsu," meant returning to the beginning or restoring the original spirit.

> Speaking concretely, returning to the beginning means going back to May 20 and not forgetting it. Remembering that day is not just

a matter of keeping in mind the events that occurred. It is also a matter of realizing the significance of that day, drawing out its meaning, and continuing to give life to it. "Remember Pearl Harbor" was the American motto during the Pacific War, and it worked the same way. The motto was used to recall what Pearl Harbor symbolized. If we go back to the significance of May 20, I think this leads us back once more to August 15. "To return to the beginning" is to go back to the moment of defeat, to go back to August 15. That was when we resolved to construct a new Japan from amidst the ruins.[59]

Maruyama sought to shift people's recollections of the war from painful memories of oppression to memories that could inspire them to overcome the past. His call for a "return to the beginning" was also a reminder that the problems of war responsibility and the lack of wartime resistance were still unresolved. Fostering a movement against the government's authoritarian actions during Anpo was a logical consequence of his efforts to create a "community of contrition" in the wake of the wartime defeat.[60]

The reforms that the Occupation implemented after the defeat had been welcome correctives to the prewar state. SCAP quickly initiated a number of major reforms. Among other things, it eliminated the Home Ministry (Naimusho) along with the Special Higher Police (Tokkō) and the Peace Preservation Law, which were used to curb dissent; it began to break up the business conglomerates (*zaibatsu*) and to encourage labor by laws that extended workers the right to unionize, engage in collective bargaining, and strike; it instituted a land reform program to reduce tenancy and rural poverty; it enfranchised women with the right to vote and abolished the Civil Code to change their legal and social status; it decentralized the educational system, abolished state-authorized textbooks, and purged curricula of ethics (*shūshin*) courses. The key symbol of these reforms was the postwar "Peace Constitution," so dubbed because of Article 9, which renounced the maintenance and use of military forces. Even though this constitution was dictated by SCAP, it had wide popular support, and SCAP used the threat of submitting the constitution to a popular referendum to get reluctant conservatives to pass the document in the Diet.

However, SCAP soon shifted its focus from purging prewar right-wing fascist influences to suppressing what it saw as Communist threats. Changes in America's global policy in 1947 led Dean Acheson and George Kennan to formulate a policy of Communist containment in Asia using a defense perimeter that Acheson likened to a "great crescent" that stretched from Japan to Southeast Asia to India.[61] Japan was to be the linchpin for the region, and Kennan urged MacArthur to "reverse course." With the 1949 Communist revolution in China and the outbreak of the Korean War, the Occupation took a hard-line cold war stance and allowed wartime leaders such as Kishi to reassume power. It also softened the dissolution of the conglomerates and reduced the reparations they were to pay, and it purged suspected Communists from organized labor and government positions.

SCAP's reverse course rekindled people's fears about the remilitarization of their country, and SCAP was, in fact, responsible for the creation of the postwar Japanese military. Despite his personal hand in putting Article 9 into the postwar constitution, General Douglas MacArthur authorized the formation of a 75,000-man National Police Reserve force in August of 1950 to fill the gap left by the departure of American troops for Korea. The ranks of this "police force" were filled with large numbers of former imperial military officers, a practice that Prime Minister Yoshida Shigeru promoted, so the officer corps of this "police force" became overwhelmingly populated with veterans. When the San Francisco Peace Treaty and original Anpo accords were signed, the allocation for troops jumped to 110,000. The appellation of "police" was gradually removed, and the Reserve transformed into the National Safety Forces (Hoantai) in 1952 and the Self-Defense Forces in 1954.[62] The Anpo treaty was one way that the United States could ensure that Japan remained militarily and economically bound to the Western bloc after the Occupation ended, and it opened up the possibility for the return of prewar militarism.

After the Occupation ended, the Japanese government continued the push to remilitarize the country. However, the existence of Japan's military forces in the postwar period posed a legal contradiction, since the mutual defense agreements and the concomitant provisions for military purchases presumed an entity that had no constitutional standing. Therefore, the Liberal Party (Jiyūtō) formed an Investigative Committee on the Constitution (Kenpō Chōsa Kai) in 1953 to explore ways to revise the constitution and legalize the military forces. Kishi was made chair of this committee, a position that carried over when the Liberal Party merged with the Democratic Party (Minshutō) in 1955, and he also headed the League for an Autonomous Constitution, which had similar aims.[63] The procedural difficulty in striking Article 9 from the constitution was that a two-thirds vote of both houses in the Diet was required before the matter could be put to a popular referendum, and the Liberal Democratic Party was never confident of achieving this number of votes even after gerrymandering the election districts during Hatoyama Ichirō's administration. Still, when Kishi took power in 1957, he followed in the footsteps of his predecessors by pushing for revision of the constitution and strengthening the now 210,000-troop Self-Defense Forces. In March of 1959, Kishi even went so far as to tell the Upper House Cabinet Committee that, "speaking in terms of legal interpretation of the constitution, there is nothing to prevent the maintaining of the minimum amount of nuclear weapons for the purposes of self-defense."[64]

Given the development of the ban-the-bomb movement in Japan in the latter half of the 1950s, Kishi's words were highly provocative. However, the Anpo treaty more often raised fears that the U.S. military might store nuclear weapons or transport them in and out of the bases. Since the treaty granted extraterritorial status to the bases and since American policy was to neither confirm nor deny the presence of nuclear weapons, these fears could not be allayed (and the United States later admitted that nuclear arms were in fact stored at and shipped through the bases on occasion).

Anti-bases movements developed in the early 1950s as incidents such as the Girard Case brought out other problems with the bases' extraterritoriality and the difficulties of prosecuting base personnel for offenses committed in the surrounding communities.[65] The Sunagawa protest against the expropriation of farmland for the purpose of extending the runway at the Tachikawa airbase near Tokyo also highlighted the problem of Japanese sovereignty in relation to the bases. Local farmers and residents tried to block the land surveys, and several protesters were arrested under the administrative agreement in July 1957 for breaking into the base. Although the Tokyo District Court acquitted the protesters on the grounds that the Security Treaty violated the constitution, the Supreme Court reversed the decision at the end of 1959.[66] In both of these cases, the Japanese government and courts were perceived as bowing to U.S. military pressure, and protesters felt that the bases and the treaty threatened Japan's sovereignty. The bases were also unpopular with communities around them, because they created social problems such as prostitution and entertainment districts and because base workers felt the treaty restricted their efforts to improve poor wages and work conditions.[67]

Ironically, while the Liberal Democratic Party pursued remilitarization in the political arena, their postwar economic plans were predicated on a demilitarized economy engaging in nonaligned overseas trade. In 1946, a group of influential economists produced a document that the government used to set its economic policy, and its basic premise was that peace, democracy, and international neutrality were the best foundations for economic growth.[68] The group later argued that the Federation of Economic Organizations (Keidanren) and American economists were incorrect in thinking that a large military would provide "spin-off" opportunities for the civilian economy. Instead, they held that the economic boost that Japan received from military procurements during the Korean War was an anomaly and would not recur, given that most of the economic expansion was created by U.S. aid.[69] They thought that turning the economy toward military production would be wasteful, draining social welfare resources and making it difficult to achieve a more equitable distribution of wealth.[70] Japan's productive capabilities had recovered to peak prewar levels only in 1955, and the hint of prosperity that Japan had achieved by the time of the treaty crisis was fragile.

In addition to movements that developed from problems directly connected with the treaty, numerous groups organized to oppose the ruling party's drive to revise the constitution. The term "constitutional revision" was understood to mean not only re-militarization but the entire range of government initiatives aimed at undoing the reforms of the early Occupation.[71] The political agenda of the Liberal Democratic Party's reverse course included attempts to weaken organized labor, strengthen centralized control over education and undercut the militant Japan Teachers Union (Nikkyōso), reinstitute ethics courses, curb the powers and autonomy of local governments, and significantly increase the search and seizure powers of the police. Kishi himself embodied this agenda because of his wartime prominence, his sudden "conversion" to democracy after the war, his return to political power, and his aggressive drive to revise the constitution as soon as he assumed the prime ministership. Thus, his use of police force to ratify the Anpo treaty was seen as the culmination of the ruling party's decade-long reactionary crusade.

The opposition to the Police Duties Bill (Keisatsukan Shokumu Shikō Hō) was particularly strong because the bill so clearly raised the specter of prewar fascism. Kishi suddenly introduced the bill in the Diet on October 8, 1958, and it was widely viewed as an attempt to revive the prewar "Thought Police," because it would greatly expand police powers with regard to interrogation, search, and arrest. Since the bill was introduced in conjunction with the opening of negotiations between Ambas-

sador Douglas MacArthur II and Foreign Minister Fujiyama Ai-
ichirō over the Security Treaty, people also suspected that Kishi
would use the police to ensure the treaty's passage or even to revise
the constitution.[72] Police had in fact been mobilized once before
to ensure the passage of a bill, appropriately enough for the 1954
Police Law, which recentralized the police under a national administration and weakened locally autonomous units. The Yoshida
government was determined to push the bill through the Upper
House and had already extended the Diet session three times in
trying to do so.[73] Finally, on June 3, Socialist Diet members tried
to block off the chambers physically to prevent the Speaker from
entering and declaring yet another extension. Yoshida mobilized
the police to the Diet to clear his path. The opposition declared the
extended session illegal and refused to recognize the June 7 approval of the bill, which was passed in their absence.[74] This was
the same session in which the Diet passed the act that turned the
Safety Agency into the Japan Defense Agency and its Safety Forces
into Self-Defense Forces, a measure required under the Mutual
Security Agreement in order to receive military aid from the United
States.[75]

Given this recent history as well as memories of the wartime
"Thought Police," opposition to the 1958 Police Duties Bill spread
rapidly. People could easily relate the issue to their daily lives, and
the mass media were nearly unanimous in criticizing the bill, so
there was little difficulty in drawing large crowds of protesters.
Sōhyō, the Japan Socialist Party, and various labor bodies formed
a People's Council against the Police Duties Bill (Keishoku Hō
Kaiaku Hantai Kokumin Kaigi) eight days after it was introduced,
and by the first united action on November 5, they were able to
mobilize six million workers in a protest strike and ten million
people in mass actions nationwide.[76] Factions within the Liberal
Democratic Party also severely criticized Kishi for his handling of
the bill and used popular opposition to the bill to erode Kishi's
power. Thus, on November 22, the administration worked out a
compromise with the Japan Socialist Party to have the bill shelved.

The success of the People's Council in blocking the Police

Duties Bill encouraged the participating bodies to form a similar coalition to try and generate a mass movement against the Security Treaty. The Japan Socialist Party immediately proposed a permanent People's Council for the Protection of Peace and Democracy for that purpose, but the process of converting one movement to another was neither simple nor direct. Although seven of the groups composing the secretariat of the People's Council against the Police Duties Bill were willing to form another coalition against Anpo, the All Japan Labor Union Congress (Zenrō) on the right wing of the Japan Socialist Party tried to prevent the Japan Communist Party from having any role in the council,[77] and the Socialist Party's central committee sought to exclude the Communist Party from the secretariat. The labor federation Sōhyō, in contrast, was willing to work with the Communist Party even though it was affiliated with the Japan Socialist Party. Furthermore, neither political party was willing to give Zengakuren full status in the council. It took nearly four months for the leadership to work out a compromise.[78] Once this compromise was reached, these groups sponsored a general call to form an official body to oppose the treaty.

The sponsors sought to build a united front–style organization that was as broadly inclusive as possible, and 134 groups encompassing a wide range of concerns responded to the call, sending 620 representatives to the founding meeting of the People's Council to Stop the Revised Security Treaty (Anpo Kaitei Soshi Kokumin Kaigi) on March 28, 1959. Some of these groups had concerns directly related to the treaty, for example, groups formed to defend the constitution, peace groups opposed to nuclear weapons, movements against the military bases, and amity associations with China and Korea. However, the council also drew groups that wanted to develop or protect their political representation and enfranchisement, such as outcast (*burakumin*) organizations, various types of women's groups, farmers' unions, child protection agencies, youth groups, and teachers' associations. The dominance of the Japan Socialist Party, Sōhyō, and the

Japan Communist Party did not prevent nonaffiliated bodies, such as Christian peace activists, human rights groups, merchants associations, and local citizens' movements, from joining. The People's Council also established regional branches to incorporate local movements that might support the cause.

Director Minaguchi Kōzō would claim that the People's Council had also inherited a legacy of organizational confusion and weak party leadership from the struggle over the Police Duties Bill. None of the parties or labor federations held hegemony over the council, according to Minaguchi, and much of their energy was expended on "internal adjustments" to deal with Zengakuren's "adventurism," the conflicts between the Japan Socialist Party and the Japan Communist Party, and the friction between labor groups and the political parties.[79]

However, the council was structured hierarchically with the established opposition parties and the labor federations wielding the greatest power. The original sponsors composed the council's thirteen-member secretariat, and the Japan Communist Party held observer status.[80] Their decisions were binding and committed all the regional affiliates to carry them out, even though the affiliates were often not involved in the process of determining what their actions should be. Later in April of 1960, a Strategy Committee comprising the Japan Socialist Party, Sōhyō, the Japan Communist Party, the National Federation of Neutral Labor Unions (Chūritsu Rōren), and the Tokyo Joint Struggle Committee was formed to take over tactical decisions, which further strengthened the authority of the parties and big labor federations. The regional affiliates were organized along a democratic centrist model, so local struggle committees were overseen by prefectural councils, which in turn sent representatives to a national council. The national representative council functioned as a liaison group to the secretariat rather than a decision-making body, and communication flowed more heavily from Tokyo down to the local level rather than the reverse.[81]

The main activity of the People's Council was organizing a

series of united actions that coordinated demonstrations in Tokyo with labor strikes and local rallies and marches in other cities across Japan. While these were organized partly to provide a channel for people to express their opposition to the treaty, they were also set up to "enlighten" the masses about the implications of the treaty relative to their situation.[82] The push to "enlighten" the masses was reinforced by the top-down organizational structure of the council and by the elitism of the opposition parties' leaders. These leaders cast themselves as the political vanguard by virtue of their advanced political consciousness, which they would then impart to the working masses to help them fulfill their role as the subjects and agents of the eventual socialist revolution. Therefore, the People's Council basically treated citizen groups as fellow travelers who ought to submit to the leadership of the established opposition.

In that sense, the People's Council was organized much like the government. They both emphasized vertical integration on a nationwide scale, and the leaders of the opposition parties shared the elitist attitudes of government bureaucrats and the Liberal Democratic Party leaders. The Voiceless Voices, however, consciously rejected the characteristics that the People's Council and the opposition parties shared with the government, which was why they reacted so strongly to any suggestion of central office or leaders, executive decision-making, ideological manifestos, or actions to "enlighten" the masses. All of these characteristics were legacies of the prewar system and anathema to them. Instead, they insisted on local autonomy, egalitarian relations, and "formless solidarity" as implicit critiques of what Tsurumi dubbed the government's "dictatorial bureaucratism" as well as the democratic centrism of the Communist and Socialist parties. The group's "spontaneous," self-generating origins implied an organic, transmutable form conditioned by environmental factors rather than rigid and mechanical rules, and their principles of voluntary, individual participation were, in effect, a critique of both the state and the People's Council.

Although some groups failed to develop a systemic critique of the political process, those like the Voiceless Voices went beyond partisan politics to assert a new basis for political subjectivity.[83] Citizen opposition to Anpo was both profoundly conservative and radically progressive because of historical memory of the war and early postwar period. It was conservative in seeking to preserve the democratic reforms of the early Occupation, symbolized by the constitution, but it was progressive in rejecting any return to wartime political or social structures, ideology, or personnel.[84] Memories of the war also caused citizens' movements such as the Voiceless Voices to look for a new model of political subjectivity. That is, they countered the government's attempts to reimpose a model of the passive, obedient (imperial) subject (*shinmin*) by putting forward a modern subjectivity—an active, politically engaged citizen (*shimin*) publicly expressing his or her political will (*ishi hyōji*). After May 19, people stated over and over again in street interviews that they came out because they simply could not remain silent any more, implying some need to atone for keeping silent during the war by protesting against current attempts to revive the wartime system.

A Rectification of Names:
The Modern Citizen and the Public

THE INDETERMINACY of the term "citizen" was an important part of the appeal of such movements. Other than being an alternative to ideological terms like "the masses" and apart from an association with urban dwellers, the word "citizen" was difficult to pin down. It did not explicitly refer to the nation, as the word *"kokumin"* did with its combination of characters. In the Japanese context, the word "citizen" (*shimin*) could be contrasted with the agrarian ideology of the prewar state, and the citizens' rallies (*shimin taikai*) during the Rice Riots of 1918 offer an intriguing analogy to the Anpo protests. Although the term *"shimin"* might imply the bourgeoisie, the urban protesters in the Rice Riots were ordinary working people concerned with shrinking real wages and their lack of political rights to change the situation. The protesters demanded rights to representation within the context of being, at the same time, imperial subjects.[85] The Anpo protests also became a site for debating and establishing the character of the citizen and his or her political participation (*seiji sanka,* or the term reflecting the influence of French existentialism, *engagement*), but this time in the context of postwar democracy and a revamped notion of the public sphere (*ōyake*).

The debates over what constituted the citizen were an extension of the early postwar debates among Japanese intellectuals regarding subjectivity (*shutaisei*), that is, the agent of the democratic revolution.[86] As Sakuta Keiichi wrote, "In the immediate post-World War II era, a single theme virtually pervaded the Japanese intellectual world: the need for complete renunciation of the 'feudal legacy.'"[87] The perceived need for a thoroughgoing transformation of society entailed theorizing which elements would be the agent of change. With the resurgence of Marxist discourse, debates in fields ranging from social science to philosophy and literature arose, especially in the general-interest magazines, regarding how Japan would modernize. Marxist ideologues argued that at the present stage of historical development a broad spectrum of forces had to emerge in a united front, but the proletariat had ontological priority as the true subject of the revolution.[88] Other writers and intellectuals chafed at the constraints the Communist Party tried to impose on them by demanding that their writing be limited to social realism and serve only to raise the workers' consciousness. They argued that as petty bourgeois elements, they had to write from their own perspective but could still play a role in the reconstruction of society.[89]

The liberal perspective of the citizen movement theorists came in part from this resistance to the orthodox Communist Party line and also in response to mass society theory, which was prevalent in the latter half of the 1950s. This response was evident in the essays of both Kuno Osamu, a member of Science of Thought who then became a mainstay in the Voiceless Voices, and Maruyama Masao. Both of these men helped develop the theoretical perspective of the citizens' movement during the Anpo protests, and both of their ideas were at the same time altered by citizens' actual experiences. The debates over mass society theory were sparked by a special issue of the magazine *Shisō* in November 1956. Matsushita Keiichi was the theory's main proponent in Japan, and for him it explained perfectly the situation of prewar Japan. In his article "The Formation of the Mass State and Its Problems" (Taishū kokka no seiritsu to sono mondaisei), he claimed that the overwhelming majority of the population were turned into proletarians, which produced an atomized society. Mass culture also formed with the development of certain social technologies, and social forms were transformed through political equality. These processes produced a society that was polarized into mass versus elite, which Matsushita identifies with monopoly capital. The state, which represented monopoly capital politically, was then able to coopt the masses through ameliorative social welfare and limited political enfranchisement.[90] Thus, while society spawned numerous mass movements, the masses in these movements were acquiescent to state power instead of becoming a revolutionary force.

If prewar Japan was already a modern mass society, having destroyed the rationalist form of nineteenth-century civil society, which in turn had broken down the aristocracy and feudal forms of community through urbanization and industrialization, then the question for the postwar era was what form society would take now that the imperial state had been dismantled. Various positions can be advocated within the theory's framework, from an elitist stance that the phenomenon of mass society would destroy critical standards and political stability to a democratic view that mass society was too prone to manipulation by elites. However, in both the aristocratic and democratic critiques, the word "masses" (*taishū*) carried the negative implication of being uncultured. As with mass society theory in the West, mass movements were seen as basically irrational and destructive. Therefore, its theorists tended to assume that the masses had to be made civilized if they were to be turned into a politically engaged public (*kōshū*), and they often displayed a strong enlightenment ethic in their writings with perhaps a Tocquevillian sense of loss over aristocratic standards. For citizen movement theorists the problem was how to make mass society democratic and to transform the alienated imperial subject into an autonomous citizen. One common approach was to call for intermediary groups that would sever the direct link between elite and mass, thus blocking or at least mitigating elite control and manipulation.

Some ambiguity existed as to whether or not mass society theory was anti-Marxist and intended as an ideological cold war weapon. Matsushita denied that the theory was an attack on Marxism, claiming it to be a more general theory that allowed for a Marxist subset.[91] He did, however, assert that the idea of the masses was too vague and had to be updated to twentieth-century realities,[92] and he criticized the Japan Communist Party for failing to realize that even the Soviet Communists had shifted to thinking of the masses as national units rather than as a single international working class.[93] Marxists like Shibata Shingo claimed that mass society theorists in essence sought to deny Marx's theory of class struggle and that they disparaged and distrusted the masses while glorifying elite culture. Shibata also claimed that mass society theorists reduced politics to an intellectual operation of making symbols that could mobilize the masses.[94] However, the Japan Communist Party was equally prone to view the masses as being in need of enlightenment to raise their class consciousness. Party theorists generally asserted that, owing to feudal anomalies still present in the Japanese situation, the masses were unprepared to fulfill their historical role as the agent of socialist revolution. Therefore, the party had to assume the role of the vanguard in place of the proletariat, asserting its authority on the basis of its advanced theoretical understanding.

Although Matsushita described how conditions such as urbanization, industrialization, and mass communications set the stage for mass society by leveling and atomizing all sectors and classes, he tended to slight the question of how these conditions actually produce a particular kind of political subject.[95] When he later discussed the "civil minimum," the minimum social conditions required for a modern democracy, he again assumed that these social forces, with some additional political training, would automatically result in active civic political participation.[96] However, a vibrant democracy does not necessarily result from attaining this "civil minimum."[97] Even though the postwar reforms of the Occupation had established a language of democracy and Japan had urbanized and industrialized to the "civil minimum," its democracy had "no heart," as Takabatake put it.[98] Thus, citizen movement thinkers focused on political values rather than material conditions in their writings and were especially concerned with overcoming half-feudal attitudes in realizing the modern citizen. Kuno Osamu presented his own formulation in his article "Creating the Political Citizen" (Seijiteki shimin no seiritsu), dated June 15, the day that Kanba Michiko was killed.[99] The article is written in the form of a dialogue, conveying a sense that Kuno and an interlocutor are arriving at a joint conclusion through their discussion. That is, Kuno engages in a stylistic experiment to reinforce his point that citizens are created through a dialectical process, not authoritarian pronouncements. The dialogue also indicates how the practical experience of protesting forced Kuno to rethink his theoretical perspective.

First, person A asks what kind of relationship exists between the idea of the masses (taishū) in mass society theory (taishū shakai ron) and that of the citizen masses (shimin taishū) being so widely discussed. B replies that the term "citizen masses" seems to be applied only to everyday life, but when he was out protesting, he felt deeply for the first time the "classical" sense of the word "masses." This observation suggests that while the notion of citizen masses tends to be divorced from politics, that is an inadequate way of understanding the term. In other words, Kuno tried to get away from the image of atomized, alienated people losing themselves in a mass movement in order to recover some sense of community. B considers the term "masses" a positive appellation, defining it as a group that is bound together by a shared mood and emotion for joint action, especially in response to the political situation. At the same time, he says, the masses do not act thoughtlessly but are conscious of their mood and direction. They are internally directed, not subject to control from the outside, but because politicians like Kishi do not understand, they take to calling the Anpo protesters an uncontrolled mob.[100]

A says that in this case the citizen must be considered as the subject and asks B for a contemporary definition of "citizen." B asserts that the contemporary citizen is someone who supports his or her life through some particular occupation (*shokugyō*).[101] However, B also insists that one's life (*seikatsu*) has to be separated from one's occupation for a citizen consciousness to emerge. Farmers find it difficult to think of themselves as citizens, because their entire lives are subsumed in the work of farming, that is, farming is not a job but a way of life. Teachers as well may find it hard to think of themselves as citizens outside of work, because they cannot separate their job from their station in life.

Kuno's emphasis on occupational groups hinges on the claim that such groups should be essentially independent from state authority. In civil society, such groups ought to be self-governing, self-regulating, independent bodies that determine their own rules and standards like guilds, but this notion, B admits, is hard for Japanese to grasp. This is not to say that citizens can only be born out of urban guilds. Self-governing bodies that exist in any area or job can give rise to one's self-awareness as a citizen.[102] Kuno stresses this idea of occupational groups apparently because he sees them as intermediary bodies that mitigate elite manipulation of mass society. He also takes quite seriously the strength of the union movement, but he wants to go beyond the social bifurcation according to class that it implies and broaden the base of antigovernment protest.

As Maruyama points out, however, occupational autonomy

and ethics tend to be replaced by a sense of belonging and loyalty to an all-embracing company or bureaucratic order, thus making sustained, widespread political activity and resistance difficult in the business sector.[103] Moreover, the dual structure of permanent versus temporary and part-time employment at such enterprises weighed heavily against occupational solidarity, tending to compartmentalize workers along status and gender lines. Kuno felt that citizen awareness in residential organizations was still weak as well, owing to, as he says elsewhere, the hierarchic order of Japanese-style community from the Meiji period on.[104] Thus, during the Anpo protests political conservatives controlled the local districts even though progressives controlled the streets. Therefore, Kuno asserts, Liberal Democratic Party politicians could ignore the outcry against Anpo, because they controlled the flow of funds at the local level, and until it becomes integrated with local residential groups, the citizens' movement as a whole is bound to fail.[105]

The most important wrinkle that Kuno presents here, however, lies with the idea of the public (*ōyake*), especially the notion of responsibility accompanying the public's rights. Unlike Matsushita's notion of political participation (*seiji sanka*), which consists primarily of electoral behavior, Kuno suggests a deeper involvement. He says that local citizens not only have the right to elect representatives, they ought to summon them, register grievances, and remove them from office if they violate the citizens' trust. That is, political engagement means citizen responsibility for what occurs in the public sphere.[106] Thus, Kuno insists on the active creation of the public sphere by citizens, rather than a more passive notion like Matsushita's civil minimum.

Kuno continued to develop this theme and expanded his notion of the public in a speech given October 2, 1962, titled "What Is Active Democracy?" (Kōdō suru minshushugi to wa nani ka).[107] Since democracy, he said, is a method of solving public problems, the first task is to define the public. He does this first by opposing it to the private (*watakushi*) and drawing a qualitative distinction between the two spheres. The difference between public and private is not a quantitative one of majority versus minority or individual, as mass society theory was inclined to posit.[108] Rather, he says, the private sphere is the source of autonomy, creativity, and identity, and, reiterating Maruyama Masao's famous essay on the psychology of ultranationalism, he insists that the public sphere must not transgress the boundaries of the private as the state did during World War II through groups such as wartime aid societies and neighborhood associations.[109]

Kuno distinguishes private from public by claiming that private interests are limited in scope, while the public sphere deals with effects beyond the immediate parties concerned. He explains this distinction by recourse to Western etymologies, saying that the Latin word for state (*kokka*), "*respublica*," means property held in common (*kyōyū zaisan*) and that the word in English is "commonwealth."[110] People engage in the public sphere by virtue of sharing in the "common wealth," and in his Rousseauian formulation, elected officials are public servants who are entrusted with the care of those common interests. In China and Japan, however, the idea of the public was identified traditionally with the imperium, which laid claim to all lands and peoples. No private domain existed, or to look at it the other way around, the public was wholly contiguous with a single private sphere, that of the emperor.[111] Therefore, elected officials feel little obligation to those who elect them and do not act as public servants (*kōboku*, another term not intuitively obvious to Kuno's listeners), tending instead to represent or act on behalf of the interests of their political superiors or wealthy enterprises. But no matter how large the company or how many people it employs, its interests are private and limited, Kuno claims, and so representatives who choose company interests over those of the "common wealth" should be forced from office.[112]

This logic foreshadows that of the environmentalist residents' movements of the 1970s, although at a more pragmatic level the distinction between the different spheres of interests is not clear-cut, especially at a place in which, for example, a polluting company employs most of the town's people and provides their livelihoods while threatening their general health. But Kuno was concerned with fostering a sense of public responsibility and sustaining political engagement among citizens who could only devote part of their time to such activities. Most citizens leave matters up to the professional politicians after they cast their ballots in an election, a practice Kuno disparages as democracy that asks for favors (onegai).[113] Not being revolutionary, they have to be pushed nearly to the breaking point before they take to the streets, and then they are quick to cool down.[114] Thus, by the October 1960 issue of Science of Thought (Shisō no kagaku), he focuses on nonelectoral forms of political engagement in an article originally titled "Methodological Self-Criticisms Regarding Political Participation" (Seijiteki sanka e no hōhōteki hansei).[115]

While Kuno considered one's occupation to be the proper foundation for citizen consciousness and placed a stronger emphasis on experience over theory, he largely recapitulated themes that Maruyama Masao developed. While Maruyama was often associated with mass society theorists, Matsushita Keiichi excluded him from their ranks on the basis of his Lecture Faction (Kōza-ha) style "two-stage" analysis regarding the transition from feudal to modern society. That is, Maruyama felt that Japan still had not become a fully modern society and that a feudal layer within it continued to exert significant influence.[116] Thus, on the eve of the Anpo protests he expressed two related concerns: one was that the nonmodern elements of Japanese political thought inhibited the realization of the autonomous citizen, and the other involved developing Japanese democracy.[117]

Maruyama participated throughout the 1950s in a number of groups with political concerns. He was a member of the Roundtable Conference on the Peace Issue (Heiwa Mondai Kondan Kai) throughout its existence, and he joined several other groups, such as the Science of Thought group (Shisō no Kagaku) and the Committee to Investigate Constitutional Issues (Kenpō Mondai Chōsa

Kai). All of these groups were oriented toward academic study more than activism, and he carefully avoided any involvement with political parties. He also resisted taking sides in the cold war, so those who knew Maruyama well considered it highly unusual for him to become involved in the Anpo movement.[118] However, the citizens' movement during Anpo allowed Maruyama a way to avoid being forced into one or the other cold war camp and to consider an independent path for Japan.

Maruyama's presence lent credibility to the treaty opposition, but he preferred to work unobtrusively and did not make his first public appearance until May 3, 1960, at a meeting sponsored by the Research Group on Constitutional Issues (Kenpō Mondai Kenkyū Kai). Even then, he only came to the forefront after the May 19 forcible ratification. He was a key organizer of the May 24 meeting at the Kanda Education Hall, and he subsequently spoke at numerous teachers' meetings and student rallies. Still, his activism did not really extend to demonstrating in the streets, only to observing and discussing with others what had occurred on the marches.[119] While Maruyama may have considered the Anpo protesters to be "an engaged public . . . embodying the ideals of democratic subjectivity he had sought to translate to the Japanese body politic,"[120] he did not see much chance of stopping Anpo and was pessimistic from the start about being able to sustain such a movement.[121] Afterwards, he went back to a quiet, academic life—at least until the Tokyo University campus revolt of 1969 forced him into the limelight again.

From the early postwar years, Maruyama had grappled with the idea of the public and its political consequences. In prewar Japan, all aspects of life were politicized in the sense of being subject to state regulation, but the initiative for political decision making was severely restricted to those at the top of the state bureaucracy and a few economic and social elite.[122] Consequently, Maruyama maintained, the Japanese had failed to develop a private, internal sphere of values that could resist the prewar state ideology. Without any formal, legal demarcation between public and private domains, morality became identified with state power.[123] The public realm belonged to one's superiors (*okami*) and ultimately to the emperor rather than the common people (*tami* or *min*). Ordinary people partook of the public sphere only insofar as they were *subjected* to and received benevolence from the emperor. As Maruyama noted in the article "August 15 and May 19: The Historical Significance of Japanese Democracy," the term *"shinmin"* (subject) derived from the combination of a character standing for the emperor's retainers (*hyakuryō yūshi*) and one for the people (*tamigusa*), and so the prewar system emphasized almost exclusively self-sacrifice and devotion to the (imperial) "public" (*messhi hōkō*) and "the support of a hundred million" (*ichioku yokusan*).[124]

The postwar period, however, began with an enormous backlash against such ideology as subjects (*shinmin*) turned back into common people (*tami*) again. This backlash, he claimed, split into two main currents—one that turned the notion of *messhi hōkō* inside out by valorizing self-interests above all else and another that retained a trace of sacrifice for the sake of society through an active reform movement of the people. Even though he argued that prewar fascism succeeded because it allowed no private autonomous space within Japanese life, Maruyama clearly favored the latter current over the former. He was concerned that postwar rulers would support the former current using people's apathy toward politics to deprive them of the right to determine the public realm. Thus, Maruyama advocated a citizen ethos that insists on both the autonomy of the private sphere and service to the general public, primarily in terms of vigilantly watching the authorities and opposing any undemocratic acts they might commit.[125]

Democracy, he claimed, had to be exercised constantly. As he made clear in his lecture " 'Being' and 'Doing' " *("De aru" koto to "suru" koto)* around the time of the Police Duties Bill controversy, Maruyama considered democracy to be an activity, not simply a structural condition.[126] Articles 12 and 97 of the constitution, he said, can be read as admonitions that the people will lose their sovereignty if they do not exercise their democratic rights and freedoms.[127] That is, it is not enough to turn over the handling of political decisions to others, meaning politicians, even though "such things as freedom or rights in modern society could be considered extremely burdensome."[128] Maruyama also used this same argument to dispute the government's claim to being democratic, which it made simply on the basis of declaring itself to be so. During Anpo, the government claimed to operate by the rule of law but surreptitiously replaced the principle of using legal debate and consultation to settle matters with the omnipotence of positive law. It declared itself democratic but violated the exercise of those processes.[129]

Maruyama also drew out concretely what the exercise of democracy means in a speech at Tokyo University on May 31 titled "Political Issues in the Present Situation" (Kono jitai no seijiteki mondaiten).[130] The strong emphasis he placed on education was only partially due to the audience he was addressing. He harked back to Nakae Chōmin in describing the actual functions of the parliamentary system as, first, integrating interests and coordinating differences of opinion and, second, educating the people through the deliberative process of Diet sessions. The kind of democratic education Maruyama had in mind, however, was not one in which the audience passively received pronouncements, nor did it consist of abstract academic studies. Education here meant that people had to engage in and experience the political process if they were to learn anything.[131] One reason Maruyama had such a high regard for the act of petitioning the government for grievances was that he saw it as both active and educational. However, he did not confine himself solely to this technique; he promoted multifaceted political engagement, urging people to send letters and telegrams to Kishi and Diet members and to explore all legal forms of protest. Maruyama also saw the exercise of democracy as a deliberative process. As he considered democracy to be a method of conflict resolution, not simply majority rule, he viewed the ratification of Anpo as highly undemocratic because the Kishi administration abandoned the process of discussion to resolve the conflict.[132]

Unlike Matsushita, he did not believe that social conditions determined modernity or that a "civil minimum" would necessarily result in democracy. "For Maruyama, modernity denoted a mode of thought, a leitmotif, a set of presuppositions about consciousness marked by a powerful sense of the irreducible difference between what is and what ought to be."[133] He was much more concerned with "interiority" (the Hegelian term, *naimensei*) and the generation of subjectivity (*shutaisei*) than with promoting certain classes or communities, and he "nowhere specified how social groups are to function in a Japanese democracy."[134]

Maruyama also saw modernity as an incomplete project and was concerned with the feudal remnants still embedded in the social structure and psychology of the Japanese, such as subservience and acquiescence to authority.[135] He did not believe, however, that these "nonmodern" modes of thought could easily be dislodged, as his lecture " 'Being' and 'Doing' " indicates. "Being" (*"de aru" koto*) in the title signifies a mode of thought that organizes society in terms of ascriptive attribute and social status. Social relations are determined most heavily by the knowledge of who another person is, that is, his or her social station in relation to one's own.[136] Kuno's mention of farmers and teachers being unable to consider themselves apart from their work as citizens is an illustration of this point. "Being" societies are static with fixed relationships and by implication are hierarchic and premodern. By contrast, "doing" (*"suru" koto*) stands for modes of social organization based on accomplishment or merit. This mode, Maruyama claims, becomes more dominant as division of labor among social functions makes a person's roles too numerous and complex for societies organized by ascriptive status to prescribe how one should act.[137] Therefore, the society develops horizontal relations based on functional efficacy, which he identifies as modern. "The organization of functional groups—companies, political parties, educational groups and so on—which sociologists see as a distinctive feature of modern societies, is essentially based on the principle of achievement (*suru koto*)."[138] But Maruyama says several times that *de aru* thinking is stubbornly persistent even in the "progressive" camp. It permeates every nook and cranny of society, inundating people so they are not conscious of it. In a modern society with strong *de aru* modes of thought, function tends to be turned into attribute so that politics, for example, is seen as something only professional politicians should do.

> When that tendency becomes very pronounced, political activities become the special possession of politicians and groups in political circles, which seals up politics inside the Diet. Thus, political activities that are performed outside in general society by people other than politicians are regarded as overstepping one's basic role or as "violence." Of course, democracy originally developed as a movement to liberate politics from the monopoly of those with special status and broaden it to the citizens. In addition, the great majority of citizens shouldering democracy pursue occupations outside of politics during their everyday lives. Thus, it would not be too much to say that democracy, rather paradoxically, is first of all supported by *political* concerns of *non*-political citizens and political expressions and acts coming from *outside* of political circles.[139]

Given these stubbornly persistent nonmodern features of Japanese society, Maruyama acknowledged that its modernization could produce a variety of cultural and political forms. The process would not necessarily lead to cultural convergence with the West, nor would it perforce result in democracy.[140] This indeterminacy is what made the constant engagement of citizens in politics so crucial for Maruyama. He saw democracy as an active process rather than an institutional condition. It was an ideal that could never be fully realized, even in the West. For Maruyama, "ultimately democracy inhabits all institutions only provisionally; it is a vital 'fiction.' The question of democracy is not how to fix it within institutions, but how to expand the scope of participation in the making and inevitable remaking."[141]

A major stumbling block for the progressive camp in the postwar period was having to defend a constitution that was dictated by the United States while at the same time opposing political domination by the West. For Maruyama, the key to resolving this dilemma was for the Japanese to make the constitution their own through exercising its provisions. Similarly, it was necessary for the Japanese to lay claim to their own tradition of protest against undemocratic governments if they were to activate any sense of politics as a field in which individual citizens bore responsibility.

Maruyama's thought had profound implications for the Voiceless Voices, who embodied his notion that democracy is maintained by the political activities of "amateurs," that is, people without the vested interests or social status of government officials. Furthermore, Maruyama implies that the key function of these citizen amateurs is anti-authoritarian, that is, to hold the grasp of the state in check.[142] This opposition has to be internally generated to be effective, something that the Voiceless Voices and other citizen groups emphasized when they described their movements as spontaneous and insisted on the need to express their (political) will publicly.

One consequence of Maruyama's line of reasoning, however, is that the citizen can only be conceived of in relation to the state. For him, citizens were defined by their engagement in the public sphere, which he saw as the contested space where the state and private spheres intersect. He saw democracy in terms of direct individual engagement with the government rather than as mediated through class or the mass organs of the state or political parties. Certainly the Voiceless Voices viewed democracy in terms of activity rather than institutional structures, as their participation in demonstrations and public debates show. However, because citizen participation is by nature part-time, Maruyama felt that it necessitated sacrifice on the part of the individual for the sake of the nation's welfare. This type of altruism had its limits. During the treaty crisis, the direct threat posed to everyday life by the Kishi administration's remilitarization of society seemed clear, and so the appeal to citizens, defined by their participatory rights in the nation, was broadly effective. However, the level of daily involvement in public affairs was difficult to maintain after the treaty crisis had passed.

After the Flood

THE NATURE of the Voiceless Voices' activities shifted with the end of the Anpo demonstrations toward debates on rethinking the nature of political movements, and their newsletter *Tayori* became a key vehicle for these debates. Issue 5 reported on their September 1960 *idobata kaigi,* and issue 12 (July 20, 1961) featured a series of reflections by different members on creating a new image for movements with regard to the mass media, the Japan Socialist Party, the antiwar movement, and the newly proposed Law to Prevent Political Acts of Violence (Seijiteki Bōryoku Bōshi Hō) in June 1961, which the Liberal Democratic Party drew up to stave off any repetition of Anpo-like demonstrations.

The newsletter supported the kind of flow of information that the mass media were unable to provide, and in keeping with the free exchange of information, the front cover of every issue carried an unusual "disclaimer" that said the contents could be freely copied and quoted as long as the person or group sent a copy of the piece in which the material appeared. As the title *Tayori* suggests, the main idea of the newsletter was to facilitate correspondence from individuals, whether they identified themselves with the Voiceless Voices or not, and from other grassroots organizations announcing their activities or engaging in dialogue. This purpose distinguished *Tayori* from typical movement organs like the Japan Communist Party's *Akahata.* The type of pieces that appeared in *Tayori* varied widely from theoretical essays by scholars like Maruyama or Kuno to personal reflections by ordinary people on current events such as the coal miners' strike in Miike or the assassination of Japan Socialist Party chair Asanuma Inejirō in October of 1960. *Tayori* also published poetry, photography, and artwork from its members and reviewed counter-culture films and plays, foreshadowing the trend to make culture a more significant field of political resistance and the development of alternative lifestyle movements in the 1970s and 1980s.

The Voiceless Voices also used their newsletter to report the responses that the four major political parties at the time had made to a series of questions posed in conjunction with the fall elections of 1960. This report was a follow-up to their fifth issue of *Tayori*, which carried a list of all the representatives of the Lower House and their positions on Anpo. Interestingly, the group tailored their queries to each party's particular policies or situations rather than asking them all the same four questions. For example, they asked the Liberal Democratic Party what it would do with members who did not cut their ties with right-wing ultranationalists as the party had promised, whereas they asked the Democratic Socialist Party if it would punish those party members who violated the Election Law.[143] In other words, they tried to present information their members could use in deciding how to cast their ballots, and they repeated a similar survey two years later together with nine other citizens' groups in preparation for the scheduled Upper House elections.[144]

One of the most important aspects of the Voiceless Voices' movement was their attempt to break down the boundary between politics and everyday life, but like Maruyama they focused primarily on direct engagement with the national government rather than the local, as their questionnaires to the parties show. Despite their principle of local autonomy, the notion of citizenry that they employed assumed the nation as the primary field of political engagement. Their actions were taken first and foremost for the sake of the nation rather than for their own specific locale, and they had more difficulty theorizing the public good or public welfare solely at the community level. In the absence of major national conflicts, some of the group's enthusiasm and numbers waned, but with the Vietnam War and the growth of the antiwar movement, the political activities of the Voiceless Voices hit another peak.

The legacy of citizens' movements such as the Voiceless Voices may appear to be the supplanting of mass collective action, as defined by the Old Left, with absolute individualism. However, the Voiceless Voices placed the autonomy of the individual citizen within a context of collective action. They aimed at modifying the terms of collective action to replace the visions of ideological and organizational homogeneity that both the state and the Old Left were promoting with forms that allowed for a diverse, flexible political response.[145] Kuno, for example, had hoped that by making occupational groups the primary organs for political action, people would engage politics in their daily lives, but residentially based groups proved to be more viable, given the citizen movement's emphasis on shared living experiences and the rejection of ideologically based movements. The most crucial consequence of the Voiceless Voices' experiments with political action and organizational forms was that they raised the value of heterogeneity in communities as a creative force.

7

EPILOGUE

THE PROLIFERATION OF specialized social movements in the late 1960s and the weakening of mass organizations have led commentators to speak of the 1960s as a decade in which progressive forces fragmented into myriads of pieces. The student movement is said to have splintered into so many factions that one needs an organizational flow chart showing the genealogy of each group and pictures of the various colors and helmet designs to distinguish the factions at demonstrations. It would be a mistake, however, to describe the Anpo protests as the Big Bang from which thousands of separate worlds were generated. The protesters had never been a unified body despite government and media characterizations of them as a mindless mob or the dupes of international communism, and despite the Japan Communist Party's attempt to impose ideological and organizational conformity on the participants.

Many of the streams that the 1960 Anpo movement comprised, moreover, continued their activities on a smaller scale or at a local level once the anti-Anpo actions had finished. With the exception of the Poets of Ōi, the movements discussed in this book have continued to operate down to the present, at times taking part in larger, more visible protests, but mostly continuing to do what they had done before Anpo. In the imagery of the Grass Seeds' Imai Yaeko, the movements flowed like underground streams, welling up to the surface on occasion and merging with other streams for a time before branching off and slipping from sight again below the earth.

The groups have survived because of their flexible organization and their emphasis on dialogue rather than dogma. They see themselves as a community of friends and seek to maintain the bonds they have formed over the years even with former members who have dropped out of the group. Those who left a particular movement did not necessarily give up their social activism. Often when former participants moved to a new city or region, they involved themselves in local issues and movements, sometimes becoming key figures. However, the comparatively small scale of these movements has frequently rendered them invisible to scholarly analysis.

An event-oriented approach to analyzing the 1960 Anpo struggle—one that focuses on political leaders and party rivalries or diplomatic negotiations between the United States and Japanese governments—diverts attention from the mass that lies below the tip of the iceberg.[1] Such approaches "make analytically invisible a crucial network of relationships that underlie collective action before, during and after the events."[2] Limiting the scope of analysis to the vortex that briefly engulfed the Diet and then rapidly subsided after the treaty went into effect obscures the submerged reality of the social movements that produced the vortex. It also obscures the connections that the Anpo era movements had to the new waves of circles and social movements that followed.

Robin LeBlanc makes a similar point by comparing her "bicycle" methodology to research by "taxi."[3] In examining the political activities and networking of Japanese housewives, LeBlanc's research mirrored her subjects' use of bicycles to get from one task to another in their daily lives. Their networks operate primarily within local neighborhoods and are predicated on face-to-face contact. They tend to form or join groups that characteristically strive to be egalitarian and autonomous, and therefore these women are leery of the hierarchies of politics and business.

Taxis, in contrast, are used by politicians to hop quickly from one area to the next and to escort them to the seats of power. These passengers travel on large thoroughfares and elevated highways and avoid the narrow winding side streets. LeBlanc thus characterizes "taxi research" as taking a big suitcase of data as quickly as possible to a major rail station, making assumptions about the proper categories (major arteries) to follow, and "flattening out" crucial differences in the way that the objects of study perceive themselves and their situations.[4] In the process, a researcher might speed past particular neighborhoods and "make analytically invisible" the networks of relations that are crucial in determining how nonelites such as housewives act politically.

The "invisible" citizens' networks of the Anpo era, however, informed and shaped later "cycles of protest" and provided them with "master frames," in the words of David Snow and Robert Bedford.[5] Snow and Bedford use this language of "master frames" (collective action frames by which grievances and injustices are understood) to suggest the importance of ideational factors over material conditions in generating social movements and demarcating their parameters. They also suggest some reasons for the persistence or disappearance of protest movements, claiming, on the one hand, that later movements are indebted to progenitors that create innovative "master frames," but also saying, on the other hand, that in order to sustain themselves later movements must be imaginative in extending and reshaping those frames, even while being constrained by them, and in making tactical innovations.

Movements in the decades following the 1960 Security Treaty protests indeed often trace their genealogies back to the groups that emerged in the Anpo era, because they see legacies and continuities in the participants, the constituent groups and identities, the forms of organization, and an evolving notion of the citizen ethos. They also have adapted their forms, ideas, and tactics according to the changing historical conditions in which they found themselves.

Continuities in Participants

MANY WHO took part in the protests surrounding Anpo later became active in the anti–Vietnam War effort, local environmentalist movements, alternative lifestyle groups, and consumer movements. Their experiences with direct democracy and the processes of political socialization during the Anpo era led them to become involved in other causes and to draw connections between the different movements. Studies by Ellis Krauss of student activists after the 1960 Anpo protests and by Margaret McKean of citizen movement activists in the 1970s attest to the importance of prior experience and the process of political socialization for those who continued to engage in social and political activism.[6]

In the case of the Voiceless Voices, many members became heavily involved in Beheiren, short for Betonamu ni Heiwa o! Shimin Rengō (Citizens' Federation for Peace in Vietnam), one of the key anti–Vietnam War groups in Japan. Hundreds of them showed up at Beheiren's first rally in 1965 at Shimizudani Park in Tokyo, which was used frequently for demonstrations during the 1960 Anpo struggle. The choice of this site of historical memory symbolized the continuity between the new cycle of protests and the previous one. The Voiceless Voices came to the rally because they felt that once again Japan was undergoing a national crisis related to the Security Treaty. The Vietnam War was the sort of situation they had feared would result from Japan's military obligations under the treaty; that is, Japan was being dragged into a war not of its own making. Leading figures such as Tsurumi, Kuno, Takabatake, and even Maruyama soon immersed themselves in the antiwar effort, and the June 10, 1965, issue of *Tayori* presented the new movement's goals and methods along with a report on the Shimizudani demonstration.[7] This issue foreshadowed the major focus of the group's energies over the next decade.

In the early 1970s, members of the Voiceless Voices also became involved with the Sanrizuka farmers who were resisting the construction of the new Tokyo international airport (Narita) on their land in Chiba.[8] A special issue of *Tayori* and subsequent articles showed the logic of involvement that motivated these members.[9] The pieces they wrote were more than reportage; they also articulated the basis for identification with other movements. Perhaps the biggest motivation for their participation in the Sanrizuka struggle was that the government had unilaterally imposed its plans for the airport without consulting the farmers or obtaining their consent. When the government was unable to get the farmers to give up their lands voluntarily, it began forcibly expropriating their property in 1971 under the rubric of national interests. The farmers' experience deeply resonated with those of the citizens who had protested the way that the Security Treaty had been imposed.

It was also widely rumored that the construction of the airport was related to heightened U.S. military activity due to the Vietnam War, since under the Security Treaty, the U.S. military had priority over much of the airspace around Tokyo.[10] People's experience in Beheiren made them more concerned about the possibility that the new airport would be used for military purposes. The airport also raised ecological concerns, because it destroyed productive farmland for the sake of international trade and industry and because it created significant noise and air pollution. These problems made the forcible expropriations seem even more outrageous. So although most participants from the Voiceless Voices were not farmers and did not live in the immediate vicinity of the airport, they still felt an affinity toward the Sanrizuka protesters based on parallels to their own experiences during the Anpo protests and clear connections to the Security Treaty.

Members of the Grass Seeds also joined in the anti–Vietnam

War effort through Beheiren. Their participation was a logical extension of their continuing involvement in antiwar and disarmament movements, ties that they have maintained down to the present. In the 1970s, they, like the Voiceless Voices, also joined groups with more specific concerns when the issues raised by such movements had larger national implications. They actively supported the lawsuit brought by the historian Ienaga Saburō against the Ministry of Education for censoring the contents of his textbook, especially those parts related to Japan's conduct during World War II. The suit struck a chord with them because of their long-standing involvement with the Parent-Teacher Association and their concern for their children's democratic education, which they felt was being threatened by the Ministry of Education's censorship of history textbooks. The Grass Seeds also carried out ongoing research about Okinawa because of the issue of reversion to Japan in the early 1970s and the presence of massive U.S. military facilities there. They and the Voiceless Voices saw themselves as generalist organizations, and they related the most strongly to national-level issues. However, the Grass Seeds originally formed to deal with concerns of everyday life, and the logic of their involvement with other movements depended to a large degree on connections they could draw to problems in their own daily lives.

Members of the Mountain Range also see their movement as arising from their experiences of everyday life, and they think of their group as an alternative lifestyle not restricted by the social and political hierarchies of contemporary society. Therefore, many of the members simultaneously explore other movements with a similar penchant. One of the reasons that the group rotates the site of its biannual gatherings is to give its members a chance to get acquainted with other movements in an area where local members have connections.

Students were also active in these and other Anpo era citizens' movements, and the "Anpo generation" had a major impact on the student movements of the late 1960s. Many student activists in the independent joint struggle councils (Zengaku Kyōtō Kaigi, or Zenkyōtō for short) at the end of the decade were graduate students who had participated in the 1960 Anpo protests.[11] Others from the "Anpo generation" helped train the Zenkyōtō generation when they became teachers and served as an active support group for the students in the campus revolts. Afterwards, students from both generations were crucial elements in the Sanrizuka struggle, environmentalist movements from Minamata to the opposition to nuclear power, the feminist movement, cooperatives and consumer groups, and communities pursuing alternative lifestyles and cultural forms. The common perception is that more of the Zenkyōtō generation joined these alternative social movements, but according to Ellis Krauss' research, student activists in the 1960 Anpo generation often chose occupations like teaching and publishing that allowed them more flexibility to continue their political involvement.[12] This was the case for some members of the Tokyo branch of the Mountain Range who had been students at the time of the Anpo protests. They went into publishing in part to continue their activities with the group, and they later drew some of their colleagues from work into the Mountain Range. Robin LeBlanc notes that founders of the Seikatsu Club Cooperative had participated in the Anpo protests as youths and came away from the experience with the conviction that movements had to relate to daily life.[13]

People could be active in more than one movement at once, because citizens' movements did not generally conceive of membership in their group as exclusive. Being a member of the Voiceless Voices, for example, did not preclude deep levels of commitment to Beheiren, because neither group demanded that it take precedence over the other. They saw their activities as complementary and equally important. The degree of involvement depended on an individual's own volition, not on one's ascriptive status or directives from a central authority.

Many of the later residents' movements comprised heterogeneous elements across a range of constituencies. Individuals could choose particular roles in the movement to fit varying levels of commitment and still be considered essential to the movement as a whole. Such flexible notions of membership facilitated fluid movement of people from one group to another, and with the shift away from the pre-Anpo paradigm of class-based movements, people began to conceive of their subjectivity in terms of multiple identities rather than a singular, unitary attribute.[14]

Constituent Groups and Identities

THE NEW constituencies and actors that appeared in citizens' movements of the Anpo era continued to be the most vital elements in subsequent social movements. The most conspicuous of these were youth and women, whose recent political enfranchisement motivated them to defend their entitlement as citizens when it was threatened by the state. Their sensitivity to discrimination and exclusion gave new social movements potential bonds of affinity and solidarity with other groups that previously had been marginalized or ostracized, such as the disabled, atomic bomb victims, victims of industrial poisoning, and minority groups like the *burakumin*, Ainu, Okinawans, and Korean residents in Japan.

During the 1960s and 1970s, the labor movement began to lose its dynamism compared to the students, feminists, local residents fighting pollution, and groups exploring alternative lifestyles. Labor's decline was attributable to the increasing prosperity of the economy, the weakening of the unions as they were absorbed into corporatist structures, and the changing nature of industrial work and workplace culture. From the early 1960s, the number of workplace culture circles fell precipitously, and in order to survive, the National Congress of Culture had to acknowledge the dissatisfaction that workers' circles felt with being subordinated to centralized organizations and ideological dictates. Thus, it turned to being more of an information center than an organ by which Sōhyō could mobilize the working masses.

The different perspectives that Nakamura and Inaba from the Poets of Ōi had about organized labor suggested larger trends among workers in the 1970s and 1980s. Although acutely aware of its limitations, Nakamura maintained a strong relationship with the union throughout his career, at one point even traveling around the country as a reporter for the union organ. Inaba, however, decided early on that the union leadership had become accommodationist and useless. He was more impressed with the student protests against the war in Vietnam, the educational system, and the 1970 renewal of the Anpo treaty. These actions stimulated him to produce more volumes of poetry about the world outside of work, and in the 1970s, Inaba experimented with new channels of expression. He started his own magazine called *Tom and Jerry*, after the cartoon characters, and then began another magazine called *Point-to-Point Communiqué (Ten-ten tsūshin)* that combined essays with poetry.

In contrast to labor, women have played an increasingly important role in new social movements since Anpo. Older groups like the Grass Seeds have continued their activities based on their identity as housewives. The Grass Seeds maintain their research-action groups on the elderly, peace issues, education, and recording life histories, but the constitution is their touchstone, because it granted women the rights to political participation and free expression that were extended to the household with the revision of the Civil Code. The group's formation lay at the juncture between political enfranchisement and concerns of everyday life, and was reaffirmed in their struggle against government attempts to do away with the constitutional reforms. Because the constitution is so fundamental to them, the Grass Seeds continue to distribute free copies of it, especially to young people who they worry are not being taught about its provisions.

The rise of "Women's Lib" in the 1970s brought new emphases and concerns to the fore. Although the formative experiences women had in the student movement in the late 1960s gave impetus to the "Women's Lib" movement, feminism was not simply an extension of Zenkyōtō philosophy but also partly a response to its inadequacies. The marginalization that women had suffered in the 1960 Anpo student movement informed the new direction of Zenkyōtō in the late 1960s, but women still encountered discrimination in progressive student circles at male-dominated universities a decade later. As a result, the Women's Lib movement developed as a critique of patriarchy both in society at large and at the university.

The feminist movement had a significant impact on public awareness regarding problems with the gendered structure of Japan's economy such as discriminatory hiring and career-tracking practices, unequal pay and benefits, and sexual harassment. It also brought attention to the severe underrepresentation of women in public office and other problems with Japan's closed political system.[15] The women's movement has also highlighted the problems of domestic labor, reproductive rights, and sexploitation. However, feminists worry that in response to this attention, the patriarchic economic and political structures in Japan will simply recast themselves in a slightly altered form. The problematic nature of the Equal Employment Opportunities Act of 1985 was highly symbolic in this regard. The law was enacted ostensibly to prevent discriminatory hiring practices and workplace inequalities, but in fact it provided no punishment for offenders and was used by companies to remove restrictions that prevented even further exploitation of women's labor, such as limits on compulsory overtime, holiday work, and graveyard shifts. Thus, ironically, many feminist and progressive groups opposed the law while corporations and the state promoted it for both image and profit. Not surprisingly, the wage gap between men and women remains nearly unchanged, as do hiring practices and the gender stratification of the work force.[16]

A common line of analysis in feminism is that discrimination against women in Japan is based on a system that confines women's role nearly exclusively to that of housewife. While the identification of women solely with the domestic sphere has been problematic in terms of changing the economic system of labor, it also has certain advantages for women involved in local citizens' movements. Housewives became the major component of residents' movements because of their larger stake in the local community compared to their husbands, who usually worked outside of their place of residence and were thus typically marginal to it. LeBlanc also shows that the image of housewives as political amateurs and outsiders can give them greater credibility in terms of being seen as uncorrupted by the system.

The housewives' campaign in Zushi City against the expansion of U.S. military housing into the Ikego Forest is a good example of LeBlanc's point about the image of women qua housewives in citizens' movements.[17] When the Japanese government announced the housing project, local residents, primarily housewives, led a long campaign to stop the plan and to reconfigure local politics in the process. The housewife image was useful in confirming their standing as local residents with a major stake in the ecology of the area, for its associations of environmental protection with women as nurturing mothers (one of the groups dubbed itself the "Citizens' Association for the Protection of Nature and Children in Opposition to the U.S. Military Family Housing Construction Plan"), and for the connotations of being political amateurs without the taint of corrupt politicians or business leaders receiving the benefits of the construction project. The Grass Seeds supported the Zushi housewives' movement in part because the national government claimed it was obligated to supply the housing under the terms of the Security Treaty, and therefore local residents had no say in the matter. Here again, local people were marginalized and denied rights to consultation and self-determination.

Similarly, the identification of women with the role of housewife, and therefore consumer, has facilitated their dominance in organic food cooperatives and alternative lifestyle movements. Although housewives' role as producers continues to be glossed over and ignored, women are able to exercise some political power as consumers.

The women's movement exemplifies both the problems and

the possibilities inherent in identity politics. Once the unitary identity of the worker as the primary agent of historical change began to decline, other constituents and identities became more important as the basis for social movements. Marginalization and exclusion, for example, could provide a common basis for solidarity or "equivalences," which facilitate commitment to groups beyond one's local area or social status.

Organizational Legacies

ORGANIZATIONAL CHARACTERISTICS adopted and adapted from the Anpo era movements by later social movements comprised another key legacy. Yoshimoto Takaaki astutely called the 1960 Anpo struggle "an end to fictions," at least in terms of the Japan Communist Party's style of organization. Although the party seemed unaware of it, the huge throngs of people who came out to protest the treaty's forcible ratification were not there because of its hierarchic control of a mass and class-based united front. Numerous student and citizens' groups chafed at this style of organizing, which stifled their energy, vitality, and creativity. It was the pattern of smaller, egalitarian, autonomous groups with flexible memberships and diverse ideologies that became dominant as the power of the opposition parties steadily declined in the decades that followed.

The Anpo era movements had organized themselves in these ways to promote certain values, so their form expressed their political philosophy. The groups examined here were affirming the values implied in the Peace Constitution—free expression and full and equal participation in decisions affecting their own lives. Social movements that developed after Anpo did more than just follow this new paradigm when they organized themselves; they made a conscious decision to use similar organizational forms, because they shared the same values and philosophies as the Anpo era movements. They sought to enact direct democracy in their groups, so they organized themselves as rhizomes, organic networks of horizontally spreading roots, rather than as vertical pyramids.[18]

Beheiren, for example, took a freely associative, decentralized form similar to the Voiceless Voices, the Grass Seeds, and the Mountain Range. Participation was voluntary and individual. Individuals or groups could join Beheiren and use the name if they accepted the aims of peace and self-determination for Vietnam and an end to Japanese complicity in the war.[19] As with the Voiceless Voices, anyone could participate freely in Beheiren's loose network of some four hundred affiliated groups, and each affiliate was considered autonomous.[20] Affiliates set their own agendas and activities and were free to determine their own programs and contributions to the antiwar effort. Groups that chose not to participate in activities undertaken by other affiliates could do so without fear of censure or ostracism from the network. Actions were not directed by an executive committee, and Beheiren did not establish a central headquarters, although they did maintain an office in Tokyo for the purpose of facilitating communication between the groups. Beheiren and other movements took the form of a loosely connected horizontal network, in part to give their organizations a broader base of appeal and to protect local, small group autonomy.[21]

Citizens' movements also adopted the model of decentralized, antihierarchic networks as a way of ensuring free expression and open debate. They promoted these values by producing their own newsletters and magazines as alternative forums that addressed the limitations of the mass media. The idea of mini-communications spread rapidly in the 1970s following the Mountain Range example in which each local body was encouraged to produce its own publications. The form of mini-communications again reflected the principles inherent in citizens' movements—autonomy and autopoesis, anti-authoritarianism, and individualism and independence.[22] Implicit in the notion of the citizens' movement and *mini komi* was that the movements had arisen out of the concerns of daily life and that they were self-generating and self-motivating, not established or directed by another group. The idea of networking gave rise to the Residents' Movements Library that was established in 1976 to house the various mini-communications that circles and citizen movements were circulating. It ultimately led to the formation of a citizens' movement network in 1989, composed of locally autonomous groups who assemble once a year to get acquainted, compare experiences, and carry on face-to-face dialogue. This type of gathering has become especially important because recent movements are much more localized and specialized, running a greater risk of becoming isolated.

A corollary to these organizational principles was the perceived need to avoid subordination to political parties. Like the Voiceless Voices, Beheiren refused any partisan affiliation. Its form of organization reflected the members' disillusionment with the Old Left's dogmatism and hierarchic elitism,[23] and they rejected any uniform adherence to a particular ideological stance beyond that of seeking an end to the war. Beheiren conceived of itself as a citizens' movement rather than a proletarian movement claiming ontological priority in the struggle. Thus, the Japan Communist Party and Japan Socialist Party sharply criticized the group for being an unenlightened bourgeois movement and seemed to consider it a worse threat than the Liberal Democratic Party.[24] Zenkyōtō, however, chose to work together with Beheiren, partly because of its own rejection of Japan Communist Party control and the party's stifling of what it deemed "heterodoxy."

The student movement, in fact, shared several organizational traits with Beheiren and other citizens' movements. The key principle that distinguished Zenkyōtō from the student movement at the time of the Anpo protests was that of local autonomy for participating groups. Student organizations were free to abstain from certain actions while still taking part in later decisions and actions.[25] This loose form was in part a reaction to the Japan Communist Party's attempt to quash internal dissent in the Anpo struggle, and early Zenkyōtō theorists stressed the need for an egalitarian structure that allowed members to maintain positions of difference.[26] Zenkyōtō never claimed to speak for the entire student movement and did not consider itself an umbrella organization that directed all the campus movements. "Zenkyōtō seemed to make debate the entire point of the movement. Thus, instead of closing off debate for the purposes of action, Zenkyōtō organizations often postponed action until participants decided that they had enough debate."[27] The students considered this *performance* of direct democracy to be essential to any movement devoted to the transformation of society. "Zenkyōtō was a form or a method, rather than an organization with a membership list."[28]

The environmentalist movements of local residents against polluting industries and disruptive state projects in the 1970s also typically adopted a nonpartisan stance, although their reasons were somewhat different. These movements arose in response to the contradictions of Japan's postwar "economic miracle," especially the problem of pollution resulting from unregulated industrialization. Much of this industrialization, and therefore the worst cases of pollution, occurred outside of major metropolitan areas, so the movements insisted on local autonomy and leadership. The residents' movements found that in order to gain broad community support for their issue, they had to deal with and include a wide range of participatory bodies. They often worked together with sympathetic elements in the local government at the same time that they garnered support from autonomous community organs, each of them playing different roles within the movement. Moreover, in some cases the movements were opposed by conservative Liberal Democratic Party politicians representing the interests of business, and in other cases they were opposed by progressive party politicians who chose the economic growth that projects like industrial parks would bring over the social costs that pollution and community disruption created. The residents' movements, thus, took a nonpartisan (or multipartisan) stance in order to draw support from as many sectors as possible.

Movements that developed after the Anpo era exhibited still

other crucial organizational differences from the earlier groups. Beheiren differed from the Voiceless Voices, for example, in defining itself as an ad hoc organization that would only continue until it accomplished its specific, concrete, limited objective. It promised to disband once peace in Vietnam had been achieved, and when the Paris Peace Accords were signed and the United States had committed to withdrawing from Vietnam, Beheiren gradually shut down, finally dissolving in January 1974.

Beheiren's self-definition as an ad hoc body, in turn, influenced the Voiceless Voices. By the mid-1970s, key members such as Takabatake Michitoshi decided that it was time for the Voiceless Voices to take a different path. Those members felt that the group ran the risk of becoming irrelevant as a political action group if its energies were devoted to organizational continuity rather than concrete objectives. Consequently, many of them moved on to other groups while those who remained in the Voiceless Voices turned to more research-oriented activities in the 1980s. The group still holds monthly meetings and continues to publish a newsletter, but they also involve themselves with other citizens' movements, make visits to their local communities to learn more about them, engage in dialogue, and lend support to their actions.

Beheiren's pattern of setting concrete, limited objectives signaled a trend that was also repeated in the environmental struggles of local residents against state projects. The movements set limited, concrete goals for themselves and made a commitment to accomplishing those goals the main precondition for inclusion rather than partisan affiliation or ideological viewpoint. They also resolved to disband once the goals were achieved rather than create permanent organizations with unending ideological commitments. The limited objectives made it easier to see progress toward their goals and to sustain greater community enthusiasm and energetic participation in the struggle. Since the immediate goals of residents' movements were confined to the community, these organizations focused on problems with local administration, not reforming national politics. This localism created the danger of becoming isolated and quietly overpowered by the state and large corporations. In some cases, it also led to a self-interested not-in-my-backyard attitude in which movement participants were satisfied if the polluting industry was simply moved to another location. Therefore, residents' movements had the opposite problem from the Voiceless Voices, who felt that they needed to be more firmly rooted at the local level. The residents' movements, conversely, needed to have their vision constantly broadened so they could connect with similar groups around the country and see the systemic nature of their particular problem.

Philosophic Legacies

THE ANPO era legacy most frequently pointed to in later movements is philosophical, that is, the idea of the citizen as the key social actor operating in public spheres. During Anpo, the notion of the citizen actor was somewhat ambiguous compared to the old paradigm of the proletariat as the agent or subject of historical change, and although the new paradigm seemed to appeal most to the urban middle class, it encompassed a much broader range of people. Social movements after Anpo retained the same pragmatic concern to employ a more encompassing, less ideological term to appeal for support. Beheiren specifically called itself a citizens' federation, not a workers union or a student group, to address the problem of Japan's complicity in the Vietnam War, and residents' movements later consciously invoked the citizen ideal promoted by the Voiceless Voices and Beheiren of "pursuing the common good and public welfare by the enlightened civic action of concerned citizens."[29]

But while residents' movements down to the present have continued to invoke this ideal, they have also adapted its formulation to their own situations by shifting its referential field of action to the local community.[30] In order to apply the "citizen ideal" of individuals becoming politically engaged for the sake of the nation's public welfare to a local community's struggle against large state industrial projects, residents' movements had to reformulate the notion of public interests and challenge the state's exclusive claims to speak for them.

The government justified the environmental impact of projects like massive petrochemical plants, the Bullet Train, Narita International Airport, and nuclear power plants by asserting that the projects' "public benefits" outweighed any sacrifices local communities might have to make. The government logic was a postwar variation of the prewar ideology of "suppressing private interest to support the nation" (*messhi hōkō*). When residents' movements tried to block such ventures, they were accused of "local egoism" and placing their own selfish interests above those of the nation. That is, state bureaucrats asserted that they rather than ordinary citizens should be the ones to determine what was best for society.

In response, activists in the 1970s argued that state projects did not actually serve the public welfare when the state acted unilaterally without the consent of local grassroots communities. The situation recapitulated the problem of Kishi's forcible ratification of the Anpo treaty at the community level. The state argued that opening large industrial complexes would have a major impact on local and national economies by employing hundreds or thousands of people at the plants and subsidiary industries. Residents' movements, however, argued that planning projects without consulting the communities where they would be located, forcibly implementing them over residents' objections, or displacing residents and endangering the health and well-being of the entire community could not claim to benefit the "public welfare." Furthermore, they argued, the main purpose of the projects was to generate private wealth for the corporations involved, and any resulting benefit to the public was an *accidental* attribute. Therefore, local protest movements in fact better served the public interest, because their concerns reflected those of other communities and were aimed at the common good.[31]

In the course of their struggles against polluting industries,

residents' movements began to develop a critique of modernization that earlier citizens' movements generally lacked. Thinkers
such as Maruyama and Kuno and most Anpo era citizens' movements were insufficiently critical of the direction of Japan's modernization and the costs it imposed. Given the recent memories of
economic hardship in the early postwar period, it took time for
citizens' movements to develop a critique of the Ikeda administration's income-doubling plan and its promotion of industrial
modernization. However, by the end of the 1960s it was clear that
unregulated industrial development and economic growth were
also destroying the capacity to enjoy that increased income. The
residents' movements, therefore, still used the language of citizens
acting on behalf of the public welfare, but they also revised Maruyama's notion of the public sphere.

Many of the new social movements also implicitly critiqued
Japan's course of development by choosing to disengage themselves to varying degrees from existing social and political hierarchies. In the 1970s, communes sprang up around the country as
people explored alternative lifestyles and relations of production.
These groups provided alternate visions of social networks outside of the "managed" or "controlled society" model that the government promoted in the 1980s. The critique of Japan's economic
development also led to a greater consumer focus. Polluting state
projects were often located away from urban centers in more
rural farming and fishing areas, so local communities had direct
concerns with how pollution affected locally produced food. In
Minamata, the Chisso Corporation dumped mercury into the
bay as a waste product from the manufacture of fertilizers and
plastics. The mercury poisoned the local waters and the fish caught
there, which in turn poisoned the people of Minamata, especially fishermen's families. This outcome prompted some of the
local farmers to turn toward producing organic foods, such as
the oranges that the region is known for. At Sanrizuka, the struggle against the airport forced the farmers to rethink the way that
they produced food, and they began experiments in collectivized

organic farming such as the One-Pack vegetable movement. These organic foods initiatives provided movement participants with a connection to the larger society and raised awareness of pollution problems. They also forced people to rethink the economic arrangements between producers and consumers, and spurred a tremendous growth in consumer cooperatives. The co-ops sought to increase the percentage of profit going to the actual producer, reduce the cost to the consumer, and ensure the quality of the produce.[32]

Kurihara Akira has noted, however, a fundamental difference in the philosophical stances of later movements, such as those at Minamata and Sanrizuka, and the earlier citizens' movements. The citizen mentality was based on a legalistic or political notion of inclusion within the field of the nation, while groups that have suffered radical marginalization and exclusion seek what he terms "heterotopia" rather than inclusion.[33] The goal of these people's movements is not to secure reincorporation into the same system that has victimized and marginalized them. Instead, they seek to invert their hellish situation by affirming symbiosis with, rather than control over, nature. The government has dealt with the Minamata victims by providing limited monetary compensation but sees their suffering as an unavoidable consequence of economic growth. The victims, however, are not placated by mere compensation and seek instead to end their suffering and that of any future victims. In the case of Sanrizuka, the farmers' slogan has not been "give us more compensation," but rather "turn the airport back into green fields again." Thus, these movements constitute a radical critique of technological progress and the economic development on which it is based.

A Question of Historicities

PERHAPS THE key legacy of the Anpo era movements is their approach to historical memory. While it may be tempting to view these groups as precursors to or progenitors of new social movements by virtue of their position at the cusp of "advanced capitalism,"[34] movement participants had a very different notion of historical analysis. What mattered to them was not the theoretical scheme that was applied to an analysis of the past so much as how they grappled with their dissatisfactions with the past in order to rectify the present situation. The groups discussed here viewed history in personal terms and thought that personal responsibility had to be attached to the past if they were to turn memories into prophesy, as Shiratori put it. In their minds, the most important legacy they gave to the new social movements was a tradition of resisting authority and reclaiming the past. They were unwilling to let the reactionary state or vanguard party intellectuals or the mass media be the "custodians of the past." To do so would rob them of their subjectivity and their ability to transform themselves by detaching the past from the present. For them, the postwar reconstruction was not premised on getting over the past and laying to rest the hungry ghosts of history through benign neglect or blissful amnesia. The legacy of these groups is one of critical engagement based on shared experience, and ultimately this legacy speaks to the historian's responsibility as well.

NOTES

CHAPTER ONE

1. See Carol Gluck, "The Past in the Present," in *Postwar Japan as History*, ed. Andrew Gordon (Berkeley: University of California Press, 1993), 64; Carol Gluck, "The Idea of Showa," in *Showa: The Japan of Hirohito*, ed. Carol Gluck and Stephen R. Graubard (New York: W. W. Norton and Company, 1992), 4–5.

2. Haruko Taya Cook and Theodore Cook, *Japan at War: An Oral History* (New York: The New Press, 1992), 16–17.

3. Fernando Calderón, Alejandro Piscitelli, José Luis Reyna, "Social Movements: Actors, Theories, Expectations," in *The Making of Social Movements in Latin America*, ed. Arturo Escobar and Sonia Alvarez (Boulder, Colo.: Westview Press, 1992), 27.

4. The only major work in English on the protests is George Packard's *Protest in Tokyo: The Security Treaty Crisis of 1960* (Princeton, N.J.: Princeton University Press, 1966), written a few years after the events, and Packard is unable to refrain from the cold war rhetoric. He sees the People's Council to Block the Revised Security Treaty as an arm of the Japan Communist Party (118–199), and he ascribes the media's criticism of the government to socialist and communist unionists (282–284). He likewise accuses progressive and radical intellectuals of organizing and controlling citizen demonstrations (344–346, 348). Despite presenting an impressive amount of detailed information, Packard's analysis of the protests frequently lapses into the simplistic claim that Anpo was the result of an international communist conspiracy.

Packard was apparently concerned that this cold war rhetoric, to say nothing of his job at the U.S. Embassy, might be construed as coloring his account's objectivity. Thus, in his preface, he touts the usefulness of quickly publishing an account of the protests by asserting that later interpretations would obscure what was "objectively evident" at the time of their occurrence. He quotes General Sir Ian Hamilton, who said, "On the actual day of battle naked truths may be picked up for the asking: by the following morning they have already begun to get into their uniforms" (v). However, his account shows that "naked truths" go into battle with their uniforms already on. The battle could hardly have taken place without the combatants first donning those uniforms.

5. Kishigami Daisuke, "Ishi hyōji," in *Haraguchi Junzō—Hatachi no echuudo, Kishigami Daisaku—Ishi hyōji, Ōtake Ayumu—Shi to hangyaku to shi, Nihon kyōyō zenshu* 16 (Tokyo: Kadokawa, 1974), 93.

6. For a description of what are considered typical characteristics and themes of new social movements, see Alan Scott's *Ideology and the New Social Movements* (London: Unwin Hyman, 1990), 18–20, 30.

7. In Latin America, for example, a mosaic of forms develops in the 1980s under a severe economic debt crisis and repressive politics, conditions not necessarily conducive to popular mobilization. "From squatters to ecologists, from popular kitchens in poor urban neighborhoods to Socialist feminist groups, from human rights and defense of life mobilizations to gay and lesbian coalitions, the spectrum of Latin American collective action covers a broad range. It includes, as well, the movements of black and indigenous peoples; new modalities of workers' cooperatives and peasant struggles; middle- and lower-middle-class civic movements; the defense of the rain forest; and even cultural manifestations embodied, for instance, in Afro-Caribbean musical forms (such as salsa and reggae) and incipient antinuclear protest in some countries." Arturo Escobar and Sonia E. Alvarez, "Introduction: Theory and Protest in Latin America Today," in Escobar and Alvarez, *The Making of Social Movements in Latin America*, 2.

8. Scott, *Ideology and the New Social Movements*, 34.

9. Ibid., 6. As Takabatake Michitoshi has pointed out, the Anpo protesters sought both to resist Kishi's exercise of political authority and at the same time to defend the principles of the Peace Constitution.

10. Stuart Hall, *The Hard Road to Renewal* (London: Verso, 1988), 169.

11. Kurihara Akira, "New Social Movements in Present-Day Japan," *Journal of Pacific Asia* 5 (1999): 10.

12. Carol McClurg Mueller, "Building Social Movement Theory," in *Frontiers in Social Movement Theory*, ed. Aldon Morris and Carol McClurg Mueller (New Haven, Conn.: Yale University Press, 1992), 3–25.

13. Ibid., 3. Mueller points to a number of major scholarly journals, for example, and notes that during the 1970s over half of the articles on social movements and collective action took the resource mobilization approach but that this figure jumped to three-quarters in the early 1980s. The subtext to the proliferation of resource mobilization is also its popularity as an alternative to Marxist-oriented thought both in terms of its materialist orientation and emphasis on the objective conditions of exploitation and with respect to its ideological focus on class as the key concept.

14. Ellis Krauss and Bradford Simcock, "Citizens' Movements: The Growth and Impact of Environmental Protest in Japan," in *Political Opposition and Local Politics in Japan*, ed. Kurt Steiner, Ellis Krauss, and Scott C. Flanagan (Princeton, N.J.: Princeton University Press, 1980), 204–215. While Krauss and Simcock say that two essays in the same volume by Margaret McKean and Jack Lewis show the utility of resource mobilization theory in analyzing the environmental protest movement, neither article explicitly makes such a claim. Nor does McKean's book *Environmental Protest and Citizen Politics in Japan*, published a year later (Berkeley: University of California Press, 1981), align itself expressly with a particular theoretical perspective.

15. Samuel Popkin, *The Rational Peasant* (Berkeley: University of California Press, 1979), 17–31, 243–267.

16. James Scott, *The Moral Economy of the Peasant* (New Haven, Conn.: Yale University Press, 1976), 13–55.

17. Mueller, "Building Social Movement Theory," 7.

18. Ibid., 13.

19. Escobar and Alvarez, "Introduction: Theory and Protest in Latin America Today," 5.

20. Alan Scott holds that resource mobilization theory fails to address the question of *why* social movements develop, whereas identity-oriented approaches tend to slight the question of *how* they come about. *Ideology and the New Social Movements*, 8. The analysis here argues that exploring the question of "why" actually informs the ques-

tion of "how" and considers the philosophies as well as the social and political contexts within which the Anpo period movements developed.

21. Robin LeBlanc, *Bicycle Citizens: The Political World of the Japanese Housewife* (Berkeley: University of California Press, 1999), 131.

22. Ibid. LeBlanc discusses the application of new social movement theory because some of the leaders of the Seikatsu Club co-op themselves refer to the group as a new social movement. Note the difference in the theoretical works LeBlanc refers to and those cited by Nancy Abelmann, also mentioned in this section. LeBlanc cites Mario Diani, "The Concept of Social Movement," *Sociological Review* 40, 1 (1992): 1–25, and Russell J. Dalton, "The Challenge of New Movements," in *Challenging the Political Order: New Social and Political Movements in Western Democracies*, ed. Russell J. Dalton and Manfred Kuechler (New York: Oxford University Press, 1990), 3–20, for her description of new social movement characteristics. Abelmann looks instead to Melucci, Touraine, Escobar, and a few postmodernist authors.

23. Jeffrey Broadbent, *Environmental Politics in Japan: Networks of Power and Protest* (Cambridge: Cambridge University Press, 1998), 181, 359.

24. Ibid., 182.

25. Ibid., 360.

26. Nancy Abelmann, *Echoes of the Past, Epics of Dissent: A South Korean Social Movement* (Berkeley: University of California Press, 1996), 5.

27. Ibid., 6.

28. Gluck, "The Past in the Present," 70–79.

29. Mueller, "Building Social Movement Theory," 6. For further elaboration of these points, see also ibid., 10–11.

CHAPTER TWO

1. Article 9 of the Japanese Constitution reads, "Aspiring sincerely to an international peace based on justice and order, the Japanese people forever renounce war as a sovereign right of the nation and the threat or use of force as a means of settling international disputes. In order to accomplish the aim of the preceding paragraph, land, sea, and air forces, as well as other war potential, will never be maintained and the right of

belligerency of the state will not be recognized." Therefore, Japan's military forces were dubbed "Self-Defense Forces," which, the government claimed, were not restricted under this article.

2. The figure of sixteen million is taken from police records and includes various forms of protests including petition drives, rallies and meetings, demonstrations, and strikes. Ōtoshi Shigeyuki cites a figure of ten million signatories to petitions against Anpo in *Anpo sedai sennin no saigetsu: Kokkai totsunyū no hi kara* (Tokyo: Kōdansha, 1980), 284–285. However, Robert Scalapino and Masumi Junnosuke claim that thirteen million people signed petitions. *Parties and Politics in Contemporary Japan* (Berkeley: University of California Press, 1962), 1.

3. The People's Council to Stop the Revised Security Treaty (Anpo Kaitei Soshi Kokumin Kaigi), the quasi-official opposition, was a coalition of 134 groups such as those listed. The council's thirteen-member secretariat, however, was dominated by the Japan Socialist Party and three major labor federations with the Japan Communist Party holding observer status.

4. Miyazaki Katsuji, "Time to Reevaluate the Security Treaty," *Japan Quarterly* 37, 4 (October–December 1990): 417–418.

5. Ishida Takeshi and Ellis Krauss, "Democracy in Japan: Issues and Questions," in *Democracy in Japan*, ed. Ishida and Krauss (Pittsburgh: University of Pittsburgh Press, 1989), 16.

6. Noted by Ienaga Saburō during his testimony in the suit he brought against the Ministry of Education for censoring his history textbook. Ōe Shinobu, "Anpo hantai tōsō o dō hyōka suru ka" (How Does One Evaluate the Anpo Opposition Struggle?), section 3, part 3 in *Kyōkasho saiban: Nihonshi no sōten*, vol. 2, ed. Tōyama Shigeki (Tokyo: Ayumi Shuppan, 1983), 225.

7. Scalapino and Masumi, *Parties and Politics in Contemporary Japan*, 150.

8. The Japanese government's 1956 Economic White Paper made the famous declaration *"mohaya sengo de wa nai,"* that it was no longer the postwar.

9. See, for example, Matsushita Keiichi, "Citizen Participation in Historical Perspective," in J. Victor Koschmann, ed., *Authority and the Individual in Japan: Citizen Protest in Historical Perspective* (Tokyo: University of Tokyo Press, 1978), 177–182.

10. Masumi and Scalapino, *Parties and Politics in Contemporary Japan*, 150.

11. Kōsai Yutaka, *Era of High-Speed Growth: Notes on the Postwar Japanese Economy*, trans. Jacqueline Kaminski (Tokyo: University of Tokyo Press), 129.

12. For example, Chief Cabinet Secretary Shiina Etsusaburō called the June 15 demonstration "a planned action dictated by international communism to destroy democracy by violent revolution." Robert Trumbull, "Tokyo Mob Storms Parliament; 870 Police and Rioters Injured; Eisenhower's Party Concerned," *New York Times*, June 16, 1960, 12. Reprinted in *Japan*, Great Contemporary Issues series, advisory ed. Edwin Reischauer (New York: Arno Press, 1974), 272–273. See also Ide Busaburō, ed., *Anpo tōsō: "Sengo shi" o tsukuru daitōsō no kiroku* (Tokyo: San'ichi Shobō, 1960), 188.

13. "Japan: Democracy or Anarchy?" *New York Times*, June 13, 1960, 26.

14. These photos can be found in *Asahi shinbun*, May 30, 1960, morning edition, 12 (housewives); Mainichi Shinbunsha, ed., *Kōdo seichō: Shōwa 31–38 nen*, vol. 15 of *Shōwa shi* (Tokyo: Mainichi Shinbunsha, 1984), 33 (noodle-shop owners); Asahi Shinbunsha, ed., *Shōwa 35-nen, Asahi Gurafu ni miru: Shōwa no sesō*, vol. 13 (Tokyo: Asahi Shinbunsha, 1976), 102 (artists and actors); Sunday Mainichi, Economist, Mainichi Graph, eds., *"Anpo" ni yureta Nihon no kiroku: 1960-nen 5–6 gatsu*, (special issue, September 10, 1960), 26 (farmers); and ibid., 2–3 (union workers).

15. I am using the term "equivalences" in the sense that Ernesto LaClau and Chantal Mouffe employ in *Hegemony and Socialist Strategy: Towards a Radical Democratic Politics* (New York: Verso, 1985), 183–184. For them, "equivalence is always hegemonic insofar as it does not simply establish an 'alliance' between given interests, but modifies the very identity of the forces engaging in that alliance. For the defence of the interests of the workers not to be made at the expense of the rights of women, immigrants or consumers, it is necessary to establish an equivalence between these different struggles. It is only on this condition that struggles against power become truly democratic, and that the demanding of rights is not carried out on the basis of an individualistic problematic, but in the context of respect for the rights to equality of other subordinated groups."

16. Filipino activists often used the image of the caribou (water buffalo) to symbolize the masses and spoke of how the caribou patiently suffers blows and heavy burdens until one day it reaches some particular threshold and rises up to throw off its cruel taskmaster. However, this image makes protest movements appear to be a subconscious reaction rather than conscious organized activity and once again portrays the opposition as unitary in nature.

17. LaClau and Mouffe, *Hegemony and Socialist Strategy*, 181.

18. These reading circles were known as *wadatsumi* groups, a name that derived from the title of the 1949 book *Kike wadatsumi no koe: Nihon senbotsu gakusei no shuki* (Listen to the Voices of Wadatsumi: Writings of Japanese Students Killed in the War), which compiled letters that kamikaze pilots and other suicide squads left for their families and loved ones just before being dispatched on their missions.

19. Mutō Ichiyo and Inoue Reiko, "Beyond the New Left: Part 1, In Search of a Radical Base in Japan," *AMPO: Japan-Asia Quarterly Review* 17, 2 (1985): 26; Masumi and Scalapino, *Parties and Politics in Contemporary Japan*, 135.

20. Packard, *Protest in Tokyo*, 238–242. Scalapino and Masumi, *Parties and Politics in Contemporary Japan*, 135–136.

21. Takeuchi Yoshimi, *Fufukujū no isan* (Tokyo: Chikuma Shobō, 1961), 118. The title of Takeuchi's May 24, 1960 speech, "Minshu ka dokusai ka?" literally asks "Democracy or Dictatorship?"

22. Ōsawa Shinichirō, "Shūdan no sengo shisōshi: Ko," in Osawa, *Kohō no shisō: Arui wa chōsei e no shuppatsu* (Tokyo: Shakai Hyōronsha, 1971), 8–44; and "Saakuru no sengoshi," in *Kyōdō kenkyū: Shūdan* (listed hereafter as *Shūdan*), ed. Shisō no Kagaku Kenkyūkai (Tokyo: Heibonsha, 1976), 68–92.

23. Ota Takashi pointed to "village gathering spots" as predecessors to circles, while Tazawa Gisuke looked to youth groups. In the countryside, youth groups continued to be active even after the war, and many of the young repatriated soldiers who joined these groups on their return later went on to become (for the most part, Liberal Democratic Party) politicians. Kyushu activists in a group called Circle Village saw their own origins in mutual aid societies and pilgrimage groups. "Sōkan sengen: Sara ni fukaku shūdan no imi o," *Saakuru Mura* 1 (September 1958): 6.

24. Ibid. The statement was written primarily by Tanigawa Gan together with Morisaki Kazue and Ueno Eishin.

25. Tsurumi Kazuko also looks at writing circles as a forum for women to debate their changing roles in the postwar period. See chapters 6, 7, and 8 of *Social Change and the Individual: Japan before and after Defeat in World War II* (Princeton: Princeton University Press, 1970), 213–303.

26. The accounts were a method of constructing a "countermemory" to what had been hidden or excluded from existing prewar and wartime histories. For a discussion of countermemory, see George Lipsitz, *Time Passage: Collective Memory and American Popular Culture* (Minneapolis: University of Minnesota Press, 1990), 213.

27. J. Victor Koschmann, *Revolution and Subjectivity in Postwar Japan* (Chicago: University of Chicago Press, 1996), 43–47, 51–54.

28. As the only woman on SCAP's constitutional drafting committee and the only person with experience living in Japan, Beatte Sirotta Gordon was singularly influential in the changes put into the constitution related to women. She sought to include the kind of provisions she found in other constitutions around the world, but the men on the committee were often reluctant to go along with her suggestions, and she had to be persistent to get as much as she could included. *Reinventing Japan* (video), a coproduction of PBI/Jigsaw Productions in association with NHK-Japan, KCTS/Seattle, and Teleac/Holland (Pacific Century 5) (S. Burlington, Vt.: Annenberg/CPB Project, 1992).

29. Tsurumi, *Social Change and the Individual*, 259.

30. Sometimes Dr. Yasui Kaoru, one of the early leaders of the council, is also credited with developing the movement, but he was brought to the position later on in order to take charge and lend further legitimacy to the effort.

31. Foreign Minister Okazaki Katsuo made this statement March 25, 1954, in a question and answer session in the Diet. He said that because of Anpo, Japan would try to cooperate with the United States in protecting secrecy about the tests. Shibagaki Kazuo, *Kōwa kara kōdo seichō e: Kokusai shakai e no fukkatsu to anpo tōsō*, vol. 9 of *Shōwa no rekishi* (Tokyo: Shogakkan, 1989), 170.

32. See Koschmann, *Revolution and Subjectivity in Postwar Japan*, 231–232.

33. Ibid., 237.

34. Tsurumi, *Social Change and the Individual*, 309–310, 369, 371.

35. The analysis that Matsuzawa Hiroaki applies to the Japan Communist Party during the repression of the war years is also relevant to its postwar structure. See " 'Theory' and 'Organization' in the Japan Communist Party," in Koschmann, *Authority and the Individual in Japan*, 112–113, 121–122.

36. Anpo Jōyaku Kaitei Soshi Kokumin Kaigi Chōsa Iinkai et al., *Rekishi e no shōgen: 6.15 no dokyumento* (Tokyo: Nihon Hyōronsha, 1960), 120–125.

37. For a complete list of names and injuries, see ibid., 147–152. Sixteen were hospitalized for more than five days, thirteen others for more than a week, twelve for over ten days, nine for more than two weeks, four for over three weeks, and six for more than a month.

38. Hidaka Rokurō, *1960-nen, 5-gatsu, 19-nichi* (Tokyo: Iwanami Shinsho, 1960), 230.

39. Ōe Shinobu and Fujii Shōichi, eds., *Sengo Nihon no rekishi 2* (Tokyo: Aoki Shoten, 1971), 116.

40. Oda took his trip from 1958 to 1960, arriving back in Japan in April just before the height of the demonstrations. He wrote his book that summer in Tokyo in the midst of the protests, and according to the commentator Ide Magoroku, this atmosphere permeates the book. "Kaisetsu" (Commentary), in *Nan demo mite yarō* (Tokyo: Kōdansha Bunko, 1979), 454.

41. Anpo Jōyaku Kaitei Soshi Kokumin Kaigi et al., *Rekishi e no shōgen*, 55.

42. Interview with Kanba Toshio, " 'Anpo tōsō' waga musume kokkai minami mon ni shisu," in *Sengo sanjū-nen* (*Shōwa shi tanbō 6*), ed. Mikuni Ichirō (Tokyo: Kadokawa Bunko, 1986), 241.

43. Margery Wolf points outs the crucial social functions that these informal gatherings perform in her book *Women and the Family in Rural Taiwan* (Stanford: Stanford University Press, 1972), 38–41.

44. Their statement against the Police Duties Bill says, "Several [recent] antidemocratic laws have been destroying the peace. . . . We housewives greatly fear such moves that indicate a revival of war." Kusa no Mi Kai, ed., *Jū-nen no kiroku: Daijūkai sōkai o kinen shite* (Tokyo: Kusa no Mi Kai), 85. Discussion of the group's actions during this time come from Amano Masako, "Kusa no Mi Kai," in *Shūdan*, 272.

45. Ibid.

46. From an interview with Grass Seeds members, November 2, 1996.

47. See the *Asahi shinbun*, May 28, 1960, Tokyo evening edition, 1, for a report on the press conference. Administration officials claimed that they received more mail supporting the treaty than opposing it, and they censured the press for criticizing Kishi and claiming to represent "public opinion"—which in Kishi's mind ought to be identified with the state.

48. One hundred eighty-two students were formally arrested that night, and many more were detained. Hosaka Masayasu, *Rokujū-nen Anpo tōsō* (Tokyo: Kōdansha Gendai Shinsho, 1986), 191.

49. The report from the autopsy conducted at Keio Hospital on June 16 concluded that Kanba had clearly died from strangulation. Two days after that report was published, the police issued their own statement denying that strangulation was the cause of death and disavowing any responsibility in the matter. For the full texts, see Anpo Joyaku Kaitei Soshi Kokumin Kaigi et al., *Rekishi e no shōgen*, 299–308. George Packard does his best to exonerate the police, saying that their violent reaction was only natural given the level of abuse they had stoically endured over the course of the demonstrations. *Protest in Tokyo*, 298–299.

50. Tsurumi Shunsuke, "Ikutsu mono taiko no aida ni motto migoto na chōwa o" (For a More Splendid Harmony among Several Drums), in Tsurumi, *Jiron, essei*, vol. 5 of *Tsurumi Shunsuke chōsakushū* (Tokyo: Chikuma Shobō, 1976), 60.

51. Yoshimoto Takaaki, "Gisei no shūen," in *Minshushugi no shinwa* (Tokyo: Gendai Shichōsha, 1966), 44–45. Yoshimoto saw the scene at Shinagawa station during the June 4 general strike as another instance in which the logistics recapitulated ideological position. At Japan National Railways' Shinagawa station, student protesters continued their sit-in on the train platform past the allotted early morning hours of the general strike and tried to convince the workers to carry their protest further. Japan Socialist Party and Japan Communist Party leaders stood outside the ticket wickets angrily demanding that the students obey their orders to end the sit-in. Members of various citizens' movements stood between the two groups trying to mediate a settlement. Ibid., 66.

52. Shima Shigeo, then chief secretary of Bund, said that storming the gates "was the most dramatic means of symbolizing the reclamation of the Diet, which had been beyond the reach of the people, on behalf of the people whose representative it should have been" (quoted in Tsurumi, *Social Change and Individual*, 333). The interview with Shima took place in July of 1962. Certainly the students' intent was not to vandalize the Diet, which would have been easy to accomplish, and it was symbolically significant that they went in through the front gate rather than climbing over the low fence surrounding the compound.

53. As Tanigawa Gan wrote shortly after the protests, Japan Socialist Party and Japan Communist Party leaders realized that the limited amount of political authority they held depended on formally representing an opposition viewpoint without ever seriously challenging Liberal Democratic Party rule itself. Their function was to bolster the Liberal Democratic Party's democratic credentials as the loyal opposition. Tanigawa Gan, "Teikei no chōkoku," in *Minshushugi no shinwa*, 17.

54. The text of the broadcast is given in Usui Yoshimi, ed., *Anpo 1960: Nihon seiji no shōten* (Tokyo: Chikuma Shobō, 1969), 190. The report was made at about 1:30 in the morning on June 16.

55. Shiba Aiko, "Kangofu—sono hi no watashi," *Yamanami 25* (Anpo Struggle special issue) (October 1961): 4.

56. Shiratori Kunio, *Mumei no Nihonjin: "Yamanami no kai" no kiroku* (Tokyo: Miraisha, 1961), 189.

57. "Joshi gakusei no Anpo tōsō," in Onnatachi no Genzai o Tō kai, ed., *Onnatachi no 60-nen Anpo*, vol. 5 of *Sengoshi nōto sengo hen* (1959.1–1960.12) (Tokyo: Inpakuto Shuppansha, 1990), 104.

58. Kanba Toshio, " 'Anpo tōsō' waga musume kokkai minami mon ni shisu," 232.

59. "Text of Statement and Replies by Premier Kishi," *New York Times*, June 17, 1960, 8. Robert Trumbull reported that the visit was cancelled because Eisenhower's safety could not be fully guaranteed, which was what Ogura Ken, chief of the Tokyo police, told the Cabinet in an emergency meeting.

60. Ibid.

61. "U.S. Treaty Is Ratified By Japan While 300,000 Parade in Protest," *New York Times*, June 19, 1960, 1.

62. Ibid.

63. Packard, *Protest in Tokyo*, 380. Packard reprints the *Asahi Evening News* translation of the text, which appeared June 17, 1960.

64. Owada Jirō and Ōsawa Shinichirō, *Sōkatsu Anpo hōdō: Sengo shi no nagare no naka de* (Tokyo: Gendai Jaanarizumu Shuppan Kai, 1970), 270.

65. Maruyama Masao, "Fukusho no setsu," *Misuzu* 17 (August 1960): 26–32.

66. The terminology belongs to Jürgen Habermas. In *The Structural Transformation of the Public Sphere*, Habermas repeatedly complains that the rise of modern mass media has wiped out the kind of critical discourse generated by the bourgeois public sphere in previous centuries. That is, public discussion deteriorated into public opinion, which in turn devolved into mere publicity. See, for example, pp. 185–195, 211, 216–222, 232.

67. Owada and Ōsawa, *Sōkatsu Anpo hōdō*, 270.

68. Ibid., 31–32, 37.

69. From an interview with Grass Seeds members, November 2, 1996. For an overview of their early years, see Amano Masako, "Kusa no Mi no jūroku-nen: Aru shufu saakuru egaita kiseki," *Shisō no kagaku* 115 (special issue, 1971): 30–42; see also Kusa no Mi Kai, ed., *Kusa no Mi: Sanjū-nen no kiroku* (Tokyo: Kusa no Mi Kai, 1984).

70. Tōkyō Daigaku Shokuin Kumiai, ed., *6.15 zengo: Ichō namiki kara kokkai e* (Tokyo: Tokyo Daigaku Shokuin Kumiai, 1960), 103.

71. Hosaka, *Rokujū-nen Anpo tōsō*, 212–214; Mutō and Inoue, "Beyond the New Left: Part I," 27.

CHAPTER THREE

1. The translation comes from F. C. Jones, *Japan's New Order in East Asia, 1937–1945* (Oxford: Oxford University Press, 1954), 474–475, cited in David Lu, *Japan: A Documentary History* (Armonk, N.Y.: M. E. Sharpe, 1997), 458.

2. This is arguably the more commonly heard translation of the phrase.

3. The emperor had stated this unequivocally during the final cabinet meeting before the announcement. "I am reminded of the anguish the Emperor Meiji felt at the time of the Triple Intervention. Like him, I

must bear the unbearable now and hope for the rehabilitation of the country in the future." The Pacific War Research Society, *Japan's Longest Day* (Tokyo: Kodansha International, Ltd., 1968), 82.

4. Translation cited in Lu, *Japan: A Documentary History*, 458.

5. Norma Field's discussion of *gyokusai* is particularly eloquent. *In the Realm of a Dying Emperor* (New York: Pantheon, 1991), 58. Tsurumi Shunsuke renders the term as "glorious self-destruction," noting that although the term is often translated as "honorable death," the word for honor is nowhere in the Japanese. *An Intellectual History of Wartime Japan, 1931–1945* (London: Kegan Paul International, 1986), 75.

6. This notion had disastrous effects in the battle for Okinawa, during which many Okinawans committed or were forced to commit collective suicide (*shūdan jiketsu*). Being told that surrender was not an option, the Okinawans endured fierce pressure to kill themselves, and in some cases they were killed by the Japanese military to make sure that this *gyokusai* was carried out. Field, *In the Realm of a Dying Emperor*, 61.

7. Higashikuni's press interview in the *Asahi shinbun*, August 30, 1945. He repeated the call in the Diet on September 5. Cited in Masao Miyoshi, *Off Center: Power and Culture Relations between Japan and the United States* (Cambridge: Harvard University Press, 1991), 104. See also the reference in the context of the victim mentality in Oda Makoto, "The Ethics of Peace," in Koschmann, *Authority and the Individual in Japan*, 157.

8. Miyoshi, *Off Center*, 109. Maruyama discusses this in his essay "Kindai Nihon no chishikijin" (Modern Japanese Intellectuals), in Maruyama, *Koei no ichi kara* (Tokyo: Miraisha, 1982), 114–115.

9. Koschmann, *Revolution and Subjectivity in Postwar Japan*, 65–67.

10. Maruyama Masao, "The Ideology and Dynamics of Japanese Fascism," in Maruyama, *Thought and Behavior in Modern Japanese Politics* (expanded edition), ed. Ivan Morris (London: Oxford University Press, 1969), 30–32.

11. Maruyama Masao, "The Theory and Psychology of Ultra-Nationalism," in Maruyama, *Thought and Behavior in Modern Japanese Politics*, 6. The article originally appeared in the magazine *Sekai* (The World), May 1946.

12. Maruyama, "The Ideology and Dynamics of Japanese Fascism," 58.

13. Tsurumi Shunsuke, *A Cultural History of Postwar Japan, 1945–1980* (London: Kegan Paul International, 1987), 14.

14. Thomas R. H. Havens, *Valley of Darkness: The Japanese People and World War Two* (New York: W. W. Norton and Company, 1978), 118–132, 161–182.

15. Mark Gayn describes just how limited the purges were in his *Japan Diary* (Rutland, Vt.: Charles E. Tuttle Co., 1981), 180–192.

16. Richard Minear, *Victor's Justice: The Tokyo War Crimes Trial* (Princeton: Princeton University Press, 1971) , 24.

17. Maruyama Masao, "The Theory and Psychology of Ultra-Nationalism" (pp. 1–24), "The Ideology and Dynamics of Japanese Fascism" (pp. 25–83), and "Thought and Behavior Patterns of Japan's Wartime Leaders" (pp. 84–134), all in *Thought and Behavior in Modern Japanese Politics*. The first essay was originally published in *Sekai* (May 1946), the second was adapted from a lecture at Tokyo University in 1947, and the third appeared in *Chōryō* in May 1949, after the Tokyo trials and the 1948 Christmas amnesty of Kishi and others.

18. Tsurumi, *A Cultural History of Postwar Japan*, 15.

19. Oda, "The Ethics of Peace," 158.

20. Hara Kazuo, dir., *Yuki yukite shingun* (Tokyo: Shisso Productions, 1987).

21. For an overview of the controversy, see *Textbook Nationalism, Citizenship, and War: Comparative Perspectives*, a special issue of the *Bulletin of Concerned Asian Scholars* 30, 2 (April–June 1998). See also Yayama Tarō, "The Newspapers Conduct a Mad Rhapsody over the Textbook Issue," *Journal of Japanese Studies* 9, 2 (Summer 1983): 301–316; Arif Dirlik, "Past Experience, If Not Forgotten, Is a Guide to the Future, or, What Is in a Text? The Politics of History in Chinese-Japanese Relations," *boundary 2* 18, 3 (Fall 1991): 29–58.

22. A group called the Japanese Society for History Textbook Reform has recently published a pamphlet in English called "The Restoration of a National History" to garner support and donations from abroad. One of the group's vice presidents is Fujioka Nobukatsu, a professor of education at Tokyo University, who also heads an association for what he terms a "liberalist view of history." His contribution to the

pamphlet is a tract calling for the excision of any reference to "military comfort women," because the present references are "inaccurate" and "fabricated" and cause Japanese schoolchildren to have a negative image of Japan and themselves. Another high-profile member of this society is cartoonist Kobayashi Yoshinori, who has penned a comic that asserts that the Japanese military was in fact protecting the comfort women from the violence of the Chinese. See Christophe Sabouret, "Moves to Redraw the Past Alarm Historians" and Michaël Prazan and Tristan Mendès France, "Cartoonist Who Challenges Japan's Status Quo," *Guardian Weekly*, February 15, 1998, 16.

23. As Tanaka Yuki notes, however, when Murama Tomiichi tried to issue his apology as the head of state at the fiftieth anniversary of the defeat, conservative Liberal Democratic Party members forced him "to apologize as an individual rather than in his official capacity of prime minister." *Hidden Horrors: Japanese War Crimes in World War II* (Boulder, Colo.: Westview Press, 1996), 8.

24. Translation in Lu, *Japan: A Documentary History*, 458.

25. For a fuller discussion of the issue, see, for example, *The Comfort Women: Colonialism, War, and Sex,* a special issue of *positions: east asia cultures critique* 5, 1 (Spring 1997); the documentary film *Sensō Daughters,* produced and directed by Sekiguchi Noriko (New York : First Run Icarus Films, 1989); and George Hicks, *The Comfort Women: Japan's Brutal Regime of Enforced Prostitution in the Second World War* (New York: W. W. Norton and Company, 1994).

26. The impetus for this reexamination resembles Tanaka Yuki's discussion of why he chose to write about Japanese war crimes. Tanaka starts with the questions "Why open Pandora's box?" "What do you hope to achieve by revealing the painful and horrifying events of the past?" to which he replies, "To master the past." For him, "this does not mean simply to comprehend events of the past intellectually but also to exercise *moral imagination.* Moral imagination requires us to take responsibility for past wrongdoings and at the same time stimulates us to project our thoughts toward the future through the creative examination of the past." As he points out, "those who fought in the Asia-Pacific War were in reality mostly ordinary Japanese men. They were our fathers and grandfathers. We need to face up to the fact that we could easily become this 'other' ourselves in changed circumstances." In comprehending that possibility, "we can gain a sense of how they [war crimes] remain our problem to this day" *Hidden Horrors*, 1, 6.

27. The second edition was published by the Tōkyō Daigaku Shuppan Kai in 1952.

28. Shiratori Kunio, "Gendai no shisō jōkyō to saakuru undō," *Yamanami no kai* 45 (August 1975): 31.

29. Ibid.

30. Ōtake Tsutomu, "Yamanami no kai: Sake no nomikata to saakuru no hōhō," *Shisō no kagaku* 115 (special issue, 1971): 44.

31. *Yamanami* 11 (July 1950), cited in Shiratori, *Mumei no Nihonjin*, 187.

32. Shiratori in fact thought he had accepted employment at a girls' school only to find out that it had become coed in the postwar period.

33. Shiratori, "Gendai no shisō jōkyō to saakuru undō," 38.

34. Tsugaru (Aomori), Odate, Ohata, Fujisato-Futatsui, Noshiro, Aizu, Tsukuba, Tokyo, Nagano, Nagoya, Tango, and Shikoku.

35. Shiratori, *Nihon dokusho shinbun* (Japan Readers' Newspaper), August 17, 1959, cited in Ōtake, "Yamanami no kai," 45.

36. Shiratori, "Gendai no shisō jōkyō to saakuru undō," 35.

37. Kuno Osamu, Tsurumi Shunsuke in *Nihon gendai no shisō* (Contemporary Japanese Thought), cited in Gerald Figal, "How to *jibunshi*: Making and Marketing Self-Histories of Shōwa among the Masses in Postwar Japan," *Journal of Asian Studies* 55, 4 (November 1996): 907.

38. Figal, "How to *jibunshi*," 907. Figal writes: "Concern for such writing education coalesced, leading to a large meeting of approximately 1,300 teachers of the National Association for Writing Education in August 1952. The first fruits of this new 'Seikatsu kiroku undō' (Recording of Everyday Life Movement) were several publications of writings from the mid-1950s by common people."

39. Tsurumi Kazuko contrasts the Mountain Range with a circle of female textile workers who also wrote their own histories of their lives and war experiences. *Social Change and the Individual*, 246, note 56.

40. Shiratori, *Mumei no Nihonjin*, 106.

41. Ibid., 44–46.

42. Ibid., 44.

43. Interview with Araya Makoto, Kimura Seiya, and Shigenaga Hiromichi, November 13, 1996. One of the reasons that Tsurumi Shun-

suke never attended any of the meetings even though he thought very highly of the group and promoted it heavily was because he did not drink.

44. Ōtake Tsutomu, "Yamanami no kai," in *Shūdan*, 119.

45. Shiratori, *Mumei no Nihonjin*, 11–12.

46. Interview with Araya, Kimura, Shigenaga, November 13, 1996.

47. Ōtake, "Yamanami no kai," in *Shūdan*, 120.

48. Ibid., 123.

49. Ibid., 128.

50. Shiratori wrote this in reply to a woman who was interested in joining the group and had come to one of its gatherings. She was, however, perplexed by the proceedings and disappointed in the encounter and wrote a letter to voice her concerns. Shiratori thanked her for being so honest and said it was difficult even for him to say exactly who or what they were. Ōtake, "Yamanami no kai," in *Shūdan*, 127.

51. Tsurumi Shunsuke explained the idea of *sankai hōshiki* as deriving from the *tenarai zōshi* (copy book), a kind of practice broadsheet on which one could write whatever one wanted, as many times as one wanted without any deadlines. Ibid., 127.

52. "Yamanami no kai no hōkoku: Kokumin bunka kaigi no yobikake ni kotaete" (Report on the Mountain Range: Answering the Call from the National Congress of Culture), *Yamanami* 25 (October 1961): 19.

53. Ibid.

54. Interview with Araya, Kimura, Shigenaga, November 13, 1996.

55. Ōtake, "Yamanami no kai," in *Shūdan*, 129.

56. Interview with Araya, Kimura, Shigenaga, November 13, 1996.

57. Tsurumi, *Social Change and the Individual*, 246.

58. Carol Gluck, "The Past in the Present," 64–66.

CHAPTER FOUR

1. Andrew Gordon, "Contests for the Workplace," in Gordon, ed., *Postwar Japan as History*, 378; also *The Wages of Affluence: Labor and Management in Postwar Japan* (Cambridge: Harvard University Press,

1998), 6. Similar figures are cited in Peter Duus, ed., *The Twentieth Century*, Cambridge History of Japan 6 (Cambridge: Cambridge University Press, 1988), 498, 647–648.

2. In Japanese, these would be the "three K's" rather than the "three D's," that is, *kitanai, kiken, kitsui* (or *kurushii*). The phrase is used to describe the kind of jobs that Japanese youth are unwilling to do nowadays, and so Asian immigrant labor is brought in to fill such jobs.

3. Interview with Nakamura Kiyoshi and Inaba Yoshikazu, November 16, 1996.

4. Paul H. Noguchi, *Delayed Departures, Overdue Arrivals: Industrial Familialism and the Japanese National Railways* (Honolulu: University of Hawai'i Press, 1990), 28.

5. Gordon, "Contests for the Workplace," 380.

6. See "General Strike of 1947," in volume 3 of the *Kōdansha Encyclopedia* (Tokyo: Kōdansha, 1983), 18.

7. Lonny Carlile, "Sōhyō versus Dōmei: Competing Labour Movement Strategies in the Era of High Growth in Japan," *Japan Forum* 6, 2 (1994): 147. See also "Sōhyō," in volume 7 of the *Kōdansha Encyclopedia*, 223–224.

8. *Inside Japan, Inc.* (video), a coproduction of PBI/Jigsaw Productions in association with NHK-Japan, KCTS/Seattle, and Teleac/Holland (Pacific Century 6) (S. Burlington, Vt.: Annenberg/CPB Project, 1992).

9. Carlile, "Sōhyō versus Dōmei," 147.

10. Ibid., 150.

11. Gordon, "Contests for the Workplace," 388.

12. Noguchi, *Delayed Departures, Overdue Arrivals*, 27, 28.

13. Gordon, "Contests for the Workplace," 376.

14. For an in-depth analysis of quality control circles, see Kumazawa Makoto, *Portraits of the Japanese Workplace: Labor Movements, Workers, and Managers*, trans. Andrew Gordon and Mikiso Hane (Boulder, Colo.: Westview Press, 1996), chapter 5, especially 114–117.

15. Interview with Nakamura and Inaba, November 16, 1996.

16. *Keihin no niji* (Keihin Rainbow) (Tokyo: Rironsha, 1952), cited in Nakamura Kiyoshi, " 'Ōi Shijin' no katsudō," in *Shūdan*, 193.

17. Interview with Nakamura and Inaba, November 16, 1996.

18. Cited in Inaba Yoshikazu, "Burūsu nanka utau mono ka," in *Kokutetsu ni ikite kita* (special issue of *Takarajima* 58 [November 25]) (Tokyo: JICC Shuppan Kyoku, 1986), 60.

19. Interview with Nakamura and Inaba, November 16, 1996.

20. Tanigawa Gan, "Hōkoku fū no fuman: Kyūshū no jōsei o megutte" (Reporterly Dissatisfaction: Regarding the Situation in Kyushu), *Kokumin bunka* (People's Culture), 3 (February 15, 1959): 13.

21. Ōsawa, "Shūdan no sengo shisōshi," 40–41.

22. Nakamura, " 'Oi Shijin' no katsudō," 195.

23. Interview with Nakamura and Inaba, November 16, 1996.

24. Nakamura, " 'Oi Shijin' no katsudō," 194.

25. Interview with Nakamura and Inaba, November 16, 1996.

26. Hamaguchi Kunio, "Kasha oshi" (Pushing a Freight Car), cited in Inaba, "Burūsu nanka utau mono ka," 61.

27. Inaba, "Burūsu nanka utau mono ka," 61.

28. *Tennō shishu* (Emperor Poem Anthology) (Tokyo: Origin Shuppan Center, 1989), 57–58. Nijū bashi is the bridge that leads to the Imperial Palace in Tokyo. The Ise Shrine is located on the Ise peninsula near Kyoto and is associated with major imperial ceremonies such as the Great Thanksgiving Ritual.

29. Interview with Nakamura and Inaba, November 16, 1996.

30. Ibid.

31. Ibid.

32. Asanuma Toshinao, Inaba Yoshikazu, Katsumata Jirō, Nakamura Kiyoshi, "Rōdō kumiai to rōdōsha no jihassei," *Shisō* 460 (October 1962): 80.

33. Nakamura, " 'Oi Shijin' no katsudō," 194.

34. Inaba Yoshikazu, "The Record," *Ōi Shijin* 25 (July 31, 1961): 26–30.

35. Interview with Nakamura and Inaba, November 16, 1996.

36. Gordon, "Contests for the Workplace," 385.

37. Kumazawa, *Portraits of the Japanese Workplace*, 131–132.

38. Noguchi, *Delayed Departures, Overdue Arrivals*, 32.

39. Ibid., 27.

40. See his diary in the May 1970 issue of the magazine π. Cited in Nakamura, "'Oi Shijin' no katsudō," 196.

41. Inaba Yoshikazu, "Rōdō o yamu" (Possessed by Work), in *Densha to rōdō* (Tokyo: Doyō Bijutsusha, 1983), 133–136.

42. Inaba Yoshikazu, "Rōdō to hyōgen," in *Shi no kakumei o meza-shite: Kokutetsu shijin ronsō shi*, ed. Kokutetsu Shijin Renmei (Tokyo: Iizuka Shoten, 1984), 165.

43. Inaba, "Burūsu nanka utau mono ka," 59–60.

44. Ibid., 61.

45. The term is Andrew Gordon's and is taken from "Contests for the Workplace," 383.

46. Hyōdō Tsutomu, "Shokuba no rōshi kankei to rōdō kumiai," in Shimizu, *Sengo rōdō*, 260, cited in Gordon, "Contests for the Work-place," 390.

47. As is typical of many workers, both of them continued working at other, less strenuous jobs once they "retired." Nakamura works for a corporation that manages buildings, while Inaba is a building caretaker. Inaba says that his work at the Japan National Railways gave him the variety of skills he needs to fix the various systems in his building, but no one bothers to ask how he got them.

CHAPTER FIVE

1. Kaji Chizuko, "Minpō kaisei" (Revision of the Civil Code), in Asahi Journal, ed., *Onna no sengo shi I: Shōwa nijū nendai* (Tokyo: Asahi Shinbunsha, 1984), 170. Unfortunately, the proposed legislation was never passed. In 1939, another bill was drafted, but with the advent of World War II, it was ignored.

2. *Fujin kōron* (Women's Forum), June 1954. Cited in Asahi Journal, ed., *Onna no sengo shi, I*, 171.

3. Kaji, "Minpō kaisei," in Asahi Journal, ed., *Onna no sengo shi, I*, 171.

4. Tsurumi, *Social Change and the Individual*, 270.

5. Ibid., 257–259, 263–265.

6. Ibid., 259–263.

7. The recent trend of writing self-histories (*jibunshi*) shares certain characteristics with the life histories movement (*seikatsu kiroku*) in producing nonprofessional pieces that are written in part for the purpose of self-discovery. They do not aspire to be literary autobiographies or memoirs, although recently "how-to" guidebooks for *jibunshi* have appeared, indicating a commercialization that was not present in the early postwar period. See Figal, "How to *jibunshi*."

8. Makise Kikue, *Hikisakarete: Haha no sensō taiken* (Torn Apart: Mothers' Wartime Experiences), ed. Makise Kikue and Tsurumi Kazuko (Tokyo: Chikuma Shobō, 1959). Cited in Tsurumi, *Social Change and the Individual*, 272–274.

9. Suda Harue in *Hikisakarete*, 58–59, cited in Tsurumi, *Social Change and the Individual*, 272.

10. Makise Kikue in *Hikisakarete*, cited in Tsurumi, *Social Change and the Individual*, 273.

11. Kathleen Uno, "The Death of 'Good Wife, Wise Mother'?" in Gordon, *Postwar Japan as History*, 307.

12. Havens, *Valley of Darkness*, 135.

13. Havens says that in 1944 the female share of the work force was only 3 percent higher than in 1940 and 7 percent higher than in 1930. These figures compare with a 50 percent jump in the United States, a 38 percent jump in the Soviet Union from 1940 to 1942, and a rise in Germany from 37.4 to 52.5 percent of the civilian labor force from 1939 to 1944. Women, however, often worked in shops and in agriculture, where their labor participation was not counted. *Valley of Darkness*, 107–113.

14. Uno, "The Death of 'Good Wife, Wise Mother'?" 308.

15. Fujioka Wake, *Women's Movements in Postwar Japan* (selected articles from Tsuji Seimei, ed., *Shiryō: Sengo nijū-nen shi* [Tokyo: Nippon Hyōronsha, 1966]) (Honolulu: East-West Center, 1968), 80–81.

16. Maruki Toshi and Maruki Iri began working on their renowned Hiroshima murals in 1948 in part because they were afraid that no direct visual accounts would remain for posterity. John Dower, "The Bombed: Hiroshimas and Nagasakis in Japanese Memory," in *Hiroshima in History and Memory*, ed. Michael J. Hogan (Cambridge: Cambridge University Press, 1996), 129.

17. Ibid., 128.

18. The most renowned piece of atomic bomb literature, Ibuse Masuji's 1966 novel *Black Rain*, revolves around the social discrimination that *hibakusha* faced, using actual journals and historical documents to tell the story of a man who tries to find a husband for his niece, who had been working in Hiroshima the day of the bombing. See also Inoue Mitsuharu's 1960 short story "House of Hands," which deals with the same subject (in *The Crazy Iris and Other Stories of the Atomic Aftermath*, ed. Ōe Kenzaburō [New York: Grove Press, Inc., 1985], 145–168).

19. For an account of indigenous movements of the Hiroshima and Nagasaki victims themselves, see Imahori Seiji, "Gensuibaku kinshi undō no hōka," in *Gyakuryū to teikō*, ed. Matsuura Sōzō, vol. 3 of *Shōwa no sengo shi* (Tokyo: Yūbunsha, 1976), 8–39.

20. Cited in Shibagaki, *Kōwa kara kōdo seichō e*, 170.

21. See Shibagaki, *Kōwa kara kōdo seichō e*, 165–177; and Tsurumi, *An Intellectual History of Wartime Japan, 1931–1945*, 98–101.

22. As is well documented in Ōe Kenzaburō's *Hiroshima Notes*, trans. Yonezawa Toshi (Tokyo: YMCA Press, 1981), severe conflict between the Japan Socialist Party and the Japan Communist Party threatened to destroy Gensuikyō by 1963. The Liberal Democratic Party joined the 1955 commemoration but had already cut its ties and contributions by 1958 after Gensuikyō denounced the Security Treaty. Thomas R. H. Havens, *Fire across the Sea: The Vietnam War and Japan, 1965–1975* (Princeton, Princeton University Press, 1987), 9–10. Despite the acrimony between the parties, "the people at the local level are ready to carry on the peace movement without any help from the JCP, the JSP, and Sōhyō. The local people are the ones who will promote the movement without losing hope, even if the Japan Council Against A- and H-Bombs should split" (Ōe, *Hiroshima Notes*, 30).

23. Komatsu Tsuneo, "Hibaku taiken," in Asahi Journal, ed., *Onna no sengo shi*, 52; Nagaoka Hiroyoshi, "Sugi no ko kai," in *Shūdan*, 210.

24. All the figures in the paragraph were culled from Shibagaki, *Kōwa kara kōdo seichō e*, 172–173. Tsurumi Shunsuke cites a figure of 280,000 signatures out of a population of 390,000 in Suginami Ward, *An Intellectual History of Wartime Japan, 1931–1945*, 100. Only Tokyo and Miyazaki, Kagoshima, and Fukui prefectures did not pass resolutions against atomic weapons. Thus, part of the vigor with which Tokyo groups pursued the petition drive may have derived from the city council's failure to pass one.

25. Nakane Chie's classic analysis of a vertical society is apt here. She says that because vertical ties are stronger than horizontal ones in bureaucratic organizations like big businesses, academia, and the government, those organizations tend to fissure along vertical lines, especially when a leader resigns or is removed. *Japanese Society* (Berkeley: University of California Press, 1970), 40–63.

26. Tsurumi, *An Intellectual History of Wartime Japan, 1931–1945*, 99.

27. Thomas O. Wilkinson, *The Urbanization of Japanese Labor, 1868–1955* (Amherst, Mass.: University of Massachusetts Press, 1965), 178–179.

28. Ezra Vogel, *Japan's New Middle Class*, 2d ed. (Berkeley and Los Angeles: University of California Press, 1963), 256–257; and *Gijutsu kakushin no tenkai: Shōwa 31-nen–34-nen* (The Development of the Technological Revolution: 1956–1959), vol. 11 of *Shōwa: Niman nichi no zenkiroku* (Shōwa: A Complete Record of Twenty Thousand Days) (Tokyo: Kōdansha, 1990), 216.

29. Hosaka claims that *danchi* residents were perceived as having a "high degree of awareness," that is, they tended toward the opposition parties. He discusses the Higashi Fujimi Danchi Anpo Hantai no Kai in *Rokujū-nen Anpo tōsō*, 138. This *danchi* group and another in Tamadaira took part in the Voiceless Voices' September 25 *idobata kaigi*. See *Tayori* (Correspondence), 5 (October 10, 1960): 14–15. The suburban families that Vogel interviewed were bitter about Kishi's tactics and about American pressure to accept the treaty, even though many felt Japan would have to approve it in some form. Vogel stresses that this feeling did not translate into anti-American sentiment, however. Vogel, *Japan's New Middle Class*, 94.

30. Vogel, *Japan's New Middle Class*, 72. See also Shibagaki, *Kōwa kara kōdo seichō e*, 249. Sepp Linhart lists the sacred treasures as the washing machine, the refrigerator, and the vacuum cleaner. As is still the case, none of these items came with rental apartments or purchased houses, so once bought, the items were taken along if one moved. "From Industrial to Postindustrial Society: Changes in Japanese Leisure-Related Values and Behavior," *Journal of Japanese Studies* 14, 2 (Summer 1988): 286.

31. Later still the three C's would become the three V's of the late sixties: *visite, villa, voyage*. The change in letters not only represented

greater opulence (also marked by the shift from English to French), it was also a switch from goods to activities. *Visite* implied domestic travel and *villa* connoted a *bessō*, a resort home, to go to in the summer. *Voyage* meant foreign travel. All of these activities imply a particular ideal of the bourgeois lifestyle. Interview with Kurihara Akira, October 9 and 16, 1990.

32. Laura Hein, "Growth Versus Success: Japan's Economic Policy in Historical Perspective," in Gordon, *Postwar Japan as History*, 112–115.

33. Vogel, *Japan's New Middle Class*, 71–85.

34. Shibagaki, *Kōwa kara kōdo seichō e*, 249.

35. Kageyama Saburō, "Nihon no bunka fūdo ni okeru fujin jaanarizumu no rekishiteki yakuwari to tenbō," in *Fujin jaanarizumu kenkyū* (Tokyo: Toyota Zaikoku Josei Kenkyū, 1977), 152.

36. Kageyama quoting Shinobu Seisaburō from a special fifth-year commemoration of Nagoya Asahi's revival (February 1, 1955). Kageyama Saburō, *Shinbun tōsho ron: Minshu genron no hyaku-nen* (Tokyo: Gendai Jaanarizumu Kai, 1968), 229–230.

37. Figures for the preceding paragraph are listed in Kageyama, *Shinbun tōsho ron*, 223–224.

38. Ibid., 223.

39. This particular individual was writing in response to a feature in *Shūkan Asahi* (Weekly Asahi) about *"tōsho fujin."* She described how she had to write her letters late at night in the kitchen after everyone had gone to sleep. Since writing was not socially acceptable for women in her area of rural Shizuoka, she would go to the next village early in the morning to find a postbox and mail the letter. However, since people gossip about any woman who writes letters, she resolved not to do it again. Kageyama, *Shinbun tōsho ron*, 232–233.

40. This continues to be the case today, and woman activist Saitō Chiyo has described the male domination of the mass media in virtually absolute terms. Sandra Buckley, *Broken Silence: Voices of Japanese Feminism* (Berkeley: University of California Press, 1997), 252–254. Despite recent gains women have made in terms of media presence (often as mere window dressing), they are still systematically excluded from the mass media's decision-making structures. For example, Andrew Painter notes that in TV very few women are allowed to become directors or

network executives, although women announcers are common. One TV station president told him that equality under the law is not realistic because, "of course, men's ability is higher. . . . Compared to men, women are less intelligent, they have less physical strength, even their bodily structures are different . . . but in order to show that the company president is *not* a male chauvinist, we are also hiring women. They are people too, after all. While they may have certain limitations, there must also be 'territories' where they can make use of their abilities, too. . . . So it's not exactly discrimination against women." Painter found that the few women who were able to succeed at the station were generally marginalized or ignored altogether by men like the president. "The Telerepresentation of Gender in Japan," in *Reimaging Japanese Women*, ed. Anne Imamura (Berkeley: University of California Press, 1996), 46–50.

41. Kageyama, "Nihon no bunka fūdo ni okeru fujin jaanarizumu no rekishiteki yakuwari to tenbō," 152–153.

42. Kageyama, *Shinbun tōsho ron*, 225.

43. Amano Masako, "Kusa no mi no jūroku-nen: Aru shufu saakuru egaita kiseki," *Shisō no kagaku* 115 (special issue, 1971): 33.

44. Ibid., 37. See also Amano Masako, "Kusa no Mi Kai," in *Shūdan*, 274.

45. Amano, "Kusa no Mi Kai," in *Shūdan*, 270.

46. Ariyoshi Sawako gives a powerful literary treatment of the question of elderly care in her 1972 novel *The Twilight Years*, and much of what she describes is still applicable. Only 10 percent of the elderly live alone and only 1.5 percent live in nursing homes, which means that the great majority of wives still end up taking care of their in-laws. One aspect that Ariyoshi does not mention, however, is the role that hospitals can play in elderly care. Hospitals can act as temporary nursing homes for the elderly or conversely as a rest spot for overworked wives. The national health system enables people to stay in a hospital for only a few dollars a day, and doctors encourage long-term care because their repayment from the government is based on the number of patient-days they can show. Thus, when any kind of physical ailment occurs, families find it convenient and cheap to house an elderly person in the hospital for as long as six months or more. Overworked housewives, however, are under great pressure to come home from the hospital as soon as possible, because generally their husbands are unable to do anything for themselves. Despite this pressure, wives are often able to get at least a few extra days

of rest from their routine in the hospital, and a hospital stay is considerably cheaper than going on vacation to a resort.

47. The bill was presented in the Diet by then minister of education Kiyose Ichirō, who had achieved notoriety in the prewar period as defense counsel for various ultranationalists and who defended Tōjō during the International Military Tribunal. During the Anpo struggle he was Speaker of the House. The position of minister of education passed to Nadao Hirokichi, a former Home Ministry official, in 1957. See Kurt Steiner, *Local Government in Japan* (Stanford: Stanford University Press, 1965), 250–255, regarding the recentralization of education, and Benjamin C. Duke, *Japan's Militant Teachers: A History of the Left-Wing Teachers' Movement* (Honolulu: University Press of Hawai'i, 1973), 136–163, on the 1956 Education Law and the Kishi administration's push from February 1957 on to institute the "teacher efficiency" rating system aimed at breaking down Nikkyōsō's union strength.

48. See, for example, Kiyose's views on education in Steiner, *Local Government in Japan*, 252; Duke's comments in *Japan's Militant Teachers*, 144; and his description on page 156 of Education Minister Araki Masuo during the Ikeda administration.

49. Duke, *Japan's Militant Teachers*, 154, table 8. However, according to the director of the People's Council to Stop the Anpo Treaty, the legacy of the teachers' strikes lay in demonstrating how to engage in widespread opposition together with autonomous bodies at the local level. Minaguchi Kōzō, *Anpo tōsō shi: Hitotsu no undō ronteki sōkatsu* (Tokyo: Shinpō Shinsho, 1969), 21.

50. Amano, "Kusa no mi kai," in *Shūdan*, 270.

51. Amano, "Kusa no mi no jūroku-nen," 40; Kusa no Mi Kai, *Jū-nen no kiroku*, 109–110.

52. Amano, "Kusa no mi no jūroku-nen," 37.

53. Kusa no Mi Kai, *Jū-nen no kiroku*, 83–84.

54. Onnatachi no Ima o Tō Kai, ed., *Onnatachi no 60-nen Anpo* (Tokyo: Inpakuto Shuppan Kai, 1990), 28.

55. See Kusa no Mi Kai, *Jū-nen no kiroku*, 90 and 85, respectively, for the texts of these letters. See the article "Parasoru sashite demo— Kusa no Mi Kai seifu e kogibun" (A Parasol-Wielding Demonstration— the Grass Seeds' Letter of Protest to the Government) on page 12 of the May 30, 1960, edition of the *Asahi shinbun* for a brief description of the action the group took that day.

56. Kusa no Mi Kai, *Jū-nen no kiroku*, 87, 90.

57. Amano, "Kusa no mi no jūroku-nen," 40.

58. For the text of the letters, see *Kusa no mi: Sanjū-nen kirokushu,* special issue of *Kusa no Mi*, 30, 5 (May 1984): 46–47.

59. Yamabe Emiko, "Shufutachi no Anpo: Sanka shinakatta shufu hyakunin no koe kara," in *Onnatachi no 60-nen Anpo*, 40.

60. The survey was conducted by the Group Inquiring about Women Today in the 1980s. See *Onnatachi no 60-nen Anpo*, 41.

61. The figures for diffusion rates of appliances for urban households come from the Economic Planning Agency's White Paper on People's Lives, cited in Shibagaki, *Kōwa kara kōdo seichō e*, 249. The statistics show a major disparity between urban and rural areas with regard to these consumer products. In February of 1961, only 14.5 percent of rural households had washing machines, 2.5 percent had refrigerators, 14.2 percent had rice cookers, and 28.5 percent had TVs. By this same time, over 60 percent of urban households had TV sets.

62. Yamabe, "Shufutachi no Anpo," 41.

63. Satō Maya, "Anpo tōsō ni sanka shita onnatachi," in *Onnatachi no 60-nen Anpo*, 27.

64. Ibid., 28–29.

65. The Committee to Promote Separate Names for Married Couples, for example, by its very name indicates its highly specialized focus.

66. Seiki Kazuko, "Shōhisha undō ni jihassei o," *Tayori* 38 (June 15, 1966): 22–23.

67. Mutō Ichiyo, "The Alternative Livelihood Movement, *AMPO: Japan-Asia Quarterly Review*, 24, 2 (1993): 4–11. Mutō emphasizes the intersection of student activists from the New Left period with women consumers who desired to make alternative communities of their own in explaining the spectacular growth of these movements in the early 1980s. Given this legacy, the two major examples he cites, the Green Co-op in Kyushu and the Seikatsu Club based mainly in Tokyo, consciously aim at the politicization of everyday life by challenging the existing order and creating alternative lifestyles.

68. Maruyama Hisashi, *Mini komi sengo shi: Jaanarizumu no genten o motomete* (Tokyo: San'ichi Shobō, 1985), 70.

69. See the first two issues of *Donguri* (September 15 and October 22, 1962).

70. Maruyama, *Mini komi sengo shi*, 71.

71. Uno, "The Death of 'Good Wife, Wise Mother'?" 307.

72. Kumazawa Makoto, *Portraits of the Japanese Workplace: Labor Movements, Workers, and Managers,* trans. Andrew Gordon and Mikiso Hane (Boulder, Colo.: Westview Press, 1996), 160. Chapter 7 of Kumazawa's book presents a useful structural analysis of the changes that occurred in women's labor in the postwar period.

73. Kumazawa, *Portraits of the Japanese Workplace,* 160. Mary Brinton gives an even lower figure of 8.8 percent of married women in the labor force in 1960. *Women and the Economic Miracle: Gender and Work in Postwar Japan* (Berkeley: University of California Press, 1993), 135

74. Brinton, *Women and the Economic Miracle,* 29. A number of factors are involved in the reentry of women into the labor force. First, falling fertility rates meant that women were ending their child-bearing years in their early to mid-thirties, and it would be possible to work once their children reached a certain age. In addition, as Japan became more affluent, household expenses also began to climb, so it became more of an economic necessity for women to go back to work, especially since their children's educational and wedding expenses peak roughly at the time when their husbands would reach the retirement age of fifty-five.

75. Ibid., 137–139.

76. Women are willing to accept temporary or part-time work, because they are still expected to take care of household affairs and their children's education. They need to find employment that allows more flexibility in their hours even if it means sacrificing wages, job security, and company benefits. Many women are also careful not to earn too much income and push the household into a higher tax bracket.

77. Movement activists have frequently made this observation. For example, see "Dialogue" between C. Douglas Lummis and Nakajima Satomi in *Japanese Women: New Feminist Perspectives on the Past, Present, and Future,* ed. Kumiko Fujimura-Fanselow and Atsuko Kameda (New York: The Feminist Press, 1995), 236.

78. Nakajima Makoto, for example, made this point in an interview, October 28, 1996.

79. Sandra Buckley, "Saitō Chiyo: Interview," in *Broken Silence,* 255–256.

80. Journalist and archivist Maruyama Hisashi asserts that mini-communications are defined by autonomy and independence, an anti-authoritarian, antiestablishment stance, and a personal, individualist disposition. That is, he identifies them as expressions of citizens' movements that display these principles, noting that small size is not necessarily a determining factor in defining mini-communications. See *'Mini komi' no dōjidai shi* (Tokyo: Heibonsha, 1985), 12–13.

81. Interview with members of the Grass Seeds, November 2, 1996.

CHAPTER SIX

1. See, for example, the May 22, 1960, installment of the "Tensei jingo" (Vox Populi, Vox Dei) column of the *Asahi shinbun*. Aragaki Hideo, *Tensei jingo 4: 1958.7–1963.4* (Tokyo: Asahi Shibunsha, 1971), 129.

2. Takabatake Michitoshi, "Citizen's Movements: Organizing the Spontaneous," in Koschmann, *Authority and the Individual in Japan*, 195.

3. Takabatake and others refer to such groups as *"gurumi soshiki."*

4. Hosaka, *Rokujū-nen Anpo tōsō*, 129.

5. Hidaka, *1960-nen, 5-gatsu, 19-nichi*, 77.

6. Hosaka, *Rokujū-nen Anpo tōsō*, 129.

7. Cited in George Packard, *Protest in Tokyo*, 244. Packard complains that the Asahi editorials were biased in favor of the opposition and should have discussed prior Japan Socialist Party "violence" and taken into account the overwhelming majority the Liberal Democratic Party had in the Diet. Implicit in Packard's complaint is a sense that numerical advantage in the Diet outweighs questions of due process and the protection of minority rights. The newspapers were sensitive to the fact that Kishi had engaged in the same kind of behavior as the wartime state that claimed legal justification (such as the Peace Preservation Law) for state violence against political dissent. The phrase "violence of the majority" also suggests that the electoral majority of the Liberal Democratic Party was not achieved by entirely democratic means. The numerical advantage that the Liberal Democratic Party enjoyed in the House was due in part to political arrangements that persisted from the prewar system, to apportionment that heavily favored areas of Liberal Democratic Party strength rather than the cities, to multiple-seat districts that favored parties with the money to flood the slate with their own candi-

dates, and so on. These means were used to ensure that the Liberal Democratic Party continued to be the sole ruling party for over four decades while claiming that Japan had the formal institutions of democracy.

8. *Tōkyō shinbun* and *Mainichi shinbun,* respectively. Ibid., 244–245.

9. *Asahi shinbun,* May 22, 1960, Tokyo evening edition, 7. Also reproduced with an introduction in Takeuchi Yoshimi, *Fufukujū no isan,* 106–107.

10. Takeuchi, "Watashitachi no kenpō kankaku" (Our Sense of the Constitution), in Takeuchi, *Fufukujū no isan,* 141–142; "Dai jiken to sho jiken" (Major Incidents and Minor Incidents), in ibid., 157.

11. Takabatake Michitoshi, "Takeuchi Yoshimi to Anpo tōsō" (Takeuchi Yoshimi and the Anpo Struggle), *Shisō no kagaku* 91 (special issue, May 1978): 54. See also Lawrence Olson, *Ambivalent Moderns: Portraits of Japanese Cultural Identity* (Savage, Md.: Rowman and Littlefield, 1992), 67.

12. Takeuchi, "Watashitachi no kenpō kankaku," in Takeuchi, *Fufukujū no isan,* 141.

13. Takabatake, "Takeuchi Yoshimi to Anpo tōsō," 55.

14. Takeuchi, "Fufukujū undō no isanka no tame ni" (For the Sake of Bequeathing a Disobedience Movement), in Takeuchi, *Fufukujū no isan,* 283.

15. Packard, *Protest in Tokyo,* 275 and 278 respectively.

16. Takabatake, "Takeuchi Yoshimi to Anpo tōsō," 53.

17. *Asahi shinbun,* May 22, 1960, Tokyo evening edition, 7.

18. Ibid., 110.

19. Takeuchi Yoshimi, "Minshushugi no saiken no tame ni" (For the Recovery of Democracy), in Takeuchi, *Fufukujū no isan,* 113–114.

20. Maruyama Masao, "Sentaku no toki," *Misuzu* 17 (August 1960): 2–5.

21. Ibid., 3.

22. Hidaka, *1960-nen, 5-gatsu, 19-nichi,* 90.

23. Packard, *Protest in Tokyo,* 245, note 61.

24. Kobayashi Tomi as quoted by Ōtoshi Shigeyuki in *Anpo sedai sennin no saigetsu,* 137.

25. Kobayashi Tomi, *Kaigara no machi: Koe naki hitobito no deai* (Tokyo: Shisō no Kagakusha, 1980), 223. Interview, October 1997.

26. Koe Naki Koe no Kai, ed., *Mata demo de aou: Koe Naki Koe no ni-nen kan* (Tōkyō: Tokyo Shoten, 1962), 13.

27. Packard makes the tendentious assertion that progressive intellectuals "liked to think of themselves masters of *ninjutsu* (occult art), working invisibly to improve the lot of the oppressed classes" (*Protest in Tokyo*, 275) and that the primary *ninja* was Tsurumi Shunsuke. That is, he implies that Tsurumi and other intellectuals were manipulating the masses and fomenting social unrest in the same way as the Communist Party. Because the basic framework for his analysis is that the Anpo protests were the work of an international communist conspiracy, Packard does not differentiate between the principles and processes of the citizens' movements and the Communist Party. He denies that the Voiceless Voices originated spontaneously at all, claiming that "behind the spontaneity, however, was the guiding hand of the Institute of Science of Thought [Shisō no Kagaku]" (ibid., 274.). He also discounts the Voiceless Voices "for its failure to attract sizable numbers of *shimin* to its cause" (ibid., 275) even though sheer numbers were never a priority for the group. Instead, the Voiceless Voices emphasized personal contact, especially face-to-face discussion, and had banded together specifically as an alternative to elite-led mass organizations. Tsurumi and other intellectuals in the groups, in fact, often felt that they had to revise their social theory as a result of the debates that took place within the group in order to fit the actions that the group took. That is, the "followers" often led the leaders. The Voiceless Voices were also independent of Shisō no Kagaku both organizationally and in terms of membership.

28. Tsurumi Shunsuke, *Hokubei taiken saikō* (Reconsidering [My] North American Experience) (Tokyo: Iwanami Shinsho, 1971), 167. Cited in Olson, *Ambivalent Moderns*, 122. Olson discusses Tsurumi's involvement in Shisō no Kagaku on pages 130–131.

29. Although Tsurumi did not issue a statement, the Science of Thought group issued one the day of his resignation. The *Asahi* paraphrased it as follows. "The administration has had no second thoughts about ignoring our right to debate and petition the government or about unjustly ratifying the treaty by force. Nor has it taken responsibility for the disorder it caused in various places. We demand that the present Diet be dissolved, the ratification be nullified, and a government be created that finally takes responsibility for its own actions. We will make efforts

to achieve this." See "Protest against the Forcible Ratification of Anpo," *Asahi shinbun*, May 31, 1960, 11.

30. Interview, October 1997. Kobayashi had occasion to talk with Tsurumi at length because she lived one stop away from him on the same train line.

31. Kobayashi Tomi, " 'Koe Naki Koe' no kōshin," *Shisō no kagaku* 19 (July 1960): 108. Reprinted in Yamada Munemitsu, ed., *Anpo to kōdo seichō*, vol. 7 of *Dokyumento Shōwa shi* (Tokyo: Heibonsha, 1975), 127.

32. Kobayashi, *Kaigara no machi*, 220.

33. Koe Naki Koe no Kai, *Mata demo de aou*, 30–31.

34. The phrase comes from Marx's *Critique of the Gotha Program* (1875), but it is in quotes in the text, indicating that he may be quoting Louis Blanc's *Organisation du travail* (1840), in which he says, "Let each produce according to his aptitudes and his force; let each consume according to his need."

35. Ōtoshi, *Anpo sedai sennin no saigetsu*, 139. She said that her eyes were opened by the Sunagawa struggle, which clarified the relationship between capitalism and war and peace. After her husband passed away in 1961, she rented out the grocery store and moved to Nerima Ward to start up a kindergarten, an antipollution group, and a housewives' movement called Yama no Kami. In 1970, she moved again to Chiba City and became involved in the Sanrizuka farmers' Opposition League, which was fighting the construction of the New Tokyo International Airport.

36. See the joint report by the Jimu no Naka no Shisō Kai, "Biru no uchigawa kara," *Shisō no kagaku* 19 (July 1960): 66–67. Office personnel such as secretaries had greater latitude to join the protests through their unions.

37. Takabatake points out that many people later dropped out of the movement when the stakes got too high, so the size and composition of citizen groups with such a philosophy shifted constantly. See "Citizen's Movements: Organizing the Spontaneous," 192.

38. See Koe Naki Koe no Kai, *Mata demo de aou*, 33, for the music. See also Kitajima Kiko, "Koe Naki Koe no kōshin uta," *Tayori* 2 (August 1, 1960): 12–13, for a brief description of singing the song at various demonstrations.

39. Ibid., 32. See also Tsurumi Shunsuke, "Ikutsu mono taiko no aida ni motto migoto na chōwa o," in Tsurumi, *Jiron, essei*, 59.

40. Kobayashi, *Kaigara no machi*, 235.

41. See, for example, the account of the conversation between Japan Socialist Party and Japan Communist Party Upper House representatives taking place at the offices of the People's Council (Kokumin Kaigi) at the time of the action. The Japan Communist Party united front director, Takahara Kuniichi, claimed that the representatives did not have to rush off to the Diet to protect the students because the students' actions had endangered the entire struggle. Hosaka, *Rokujū-nen Anpo tōsō*, 196–197.

42. The government autopsy lists the cause of death as suffocation but also indicates a strong possibility of strangulation. See Packard, *Protest in Tokyo*, 296, note 109. Doctors Sakamoto Akira and Nakada Yūya claimed strangulation as the cause of death in their June 21 medical report. See Anpo Jōyaku Kaitei Soshi Kokumin Kaigi Chōsa Iinkai, *Rekishi e no shōgen*, 305–308; also see the comments of Kanba Toshio, Michiko's father, in *Sengo sanjū-nen*, 234–235.

43. Kobayashi, *Kaigara no machi*, 236.

44. See Chapter 2 for the full text of the declaration.

45. Satō Eiichirō, "Masu komi e no 'Koe Naki Koe,'" *Tayori* 3 (August 21, 1960): 5.

46. Owada and Ōsawa, *Sōkatsu Anpo hōdō*, 88–89.

47. In *The Structural Transformation of the Public Sphere* (Cambridge, Mass.: MIT Press, 1989, 1995), Jürgen Habermas views the degeneration of critical public discourse into publicity for the state as the result of the historical transformation of the bourgeois public sphere in the eighteenth and nineteenth centuries into today's modern mass media. See pages 185–195, 211, 216–222, 232. The Anpo protesters, in contrast, felt that the media's turn was attributable to state coercion rather than historical processes.

48. Takanashi Saburō gives this estimate in his letter to *Tayori*. Koe Naki Koe no Kai, ed., *Mata demo de aou*, 16.

49. Maruyama Masao walked around the Diet as the students held vigil on June 19, but unlike the students, he says that he had no sense of experiencing a historic moment and no particular feeling welled up inside him. He claims that the massive demonstration during the day

was much more significant. "8.15 to 5.19: Nihon minshushugi no reki-shiteki imi," *Chūō kōron* 75, 8 (August 1960): 44–46.

50. Ide writes that 5.4 million workers participated in the general strike. *Anpo tōsō*, 248–249. Hidaka gives a higher figure of 6.2 million in his chronology, although he agrees on the figure for the demonstration around the Diet. *1960-nen, 5-gatsu, 19-nichi*, 276–277.

51. See *Tayori* 1 (July 15, 1960): 3, for actions the Voiceless Voices had taken part in since their formation.

52. Tsurumi Shunsuke, "Shimin shūkai no teian" (Proposal for a Citizens' Assembly), *Tayori* 1 (July 15, 1960): 5–6.

53. Takabatake Michitoshi, "Ijūchi soshiki no teian" (Proposal for a Settlers Organization), and Sakaguchi Masaaki, "'Koe Naki Koe no Kai' no kongo ni tsuite" (Regarding the Future of the Voiceless Voices), *Tayori* 2 (August 1, 1960): 3–5 and 6–8 respectively. In Sakaguchi's words, "An elite consciousness is taboo" (p. 7).

54. This meeting, reported on in *Tayori* 5 (October 20, 1960): 14–17, was held at the Musashi Commerce and Industry Meeting Hall and attended by about 150 people. The date of the *idobata kaigi* is given as June 25, but the text indicates that it actually took place in September.

55. Asano Tadashi, "Inaka hito no hiai" (The Sorrow of a Country Person), *Tayori* 11 (June 20, 1961), 15, reprinted in Koe Naki Koe no Kai, *Mata demo de aou*, 61–62.

56. Asai Tamie, *Tayori* 3 (August 21, 1960): 14, reprinted in Koe Naki Koe no Kai, *Mata demo de aou*, 56–57.

57. Kobayashi, *Kaigara no machi*, 224.

58. Andrew Barshay considers Maruyama perhaps second only to Shimizu Ikutarō as the "intellectual godfather of the anti–Security Treaty movement." "Imagining Democracy in Postwar Japan: Reflections on Maruyama Masao and Modernism," *Journal of Japanese Studies* 18, 2 (Summer 1992): 393. Maruyama, however, had a bigger following of students than Shimizu, who taught at the extremely patrician, highly conservative Gakushuin University, and Maruyama was as well published as Shimizu in both the general-interest monthlies and the weeklies.

59. Maruyama Masao, "Fukusho no setsu," *Misuzu* 17 (August 1960): 31.

60. Strictly speaking, the historical memory of August 15 as the moment the Japanese people resolved to overturn their fascist past and

remake the country was a necessary fiction to give meaning to the Anpo crisis. Maruyama cites newspaper editorials written within months of the defeat that express such sentiments, but the newspapers also had to conform to SCAP's press restrictions about criticizing the Occupation. SCAP issued a ten-item Press Code on September 19, 1945, which forbade "false or destructive criticism of the Allied Powers" as well as any wartime propaganda line supporting militarism and ultranationalism. Jay Rubin, "From Wholeness to Decadence: The Censorship of Literature under the Allied Occupation," *Journal of Japanese Studies* 11, 1 (Winter 1985): 85. But Maruyama used the fictitious memory of the Japanese people's resolve at the moment of surrender in order to create an *indigenous* tradition of protest.

61. Bruce Cumings, "Japan's Position in the World System," in Gordon, *Postwar Japan as History*, 37–41.

62. Although opposition parties were alarmed at the rate of increase for troop allocations, which jumped from 152,000 in 1954 to 231,000 by 1960, the United States originally demanded that Yoshida set the figure at a whopping 350,000, something he considered completely impractical. John Dower, *Empire and Aftermath: Yoshida Shigeru and the Japanese Experience, 1878–1954* (Cambridge: Council on East Asian Studies, Harvard University, 1988), 386. See Martin E. Weinstein, *Japan's Postwar Defense Policy, 1947–1968* (New York: Columbia University Press, 1971), 111, table 1, for a list of allocations and actual strength for the years 1954–1967.

63. Togawa Isamu, *Kishi Nobusuke to hoshu antō,* vol. 5 of *Shōwa no saishō* (Tokyo: Kōdansha, 1982), 119–120.

64. Cited in James Auer, *The Postwar Rearmament of Japanese Maritime Forces, 1945–71* (New York: Praeger Publishers, 1973), 123.

65. On January 30, 1957, while guarding the Somagahara rifle range, William Girard shot and killed Nakai Saka, who was scavenging there for empty shell casings. The U.S. military was going to surrender Girard to Japanese authorities, having decided that the shooting did not occur in the line of duty, but Girard appealed his case all the way to the U.S. Supreme Court, which eventually decided against him. Girard was tried under the Japanese Criminal Code, found guilty, and sentenced to three years' imprisonment, but his sentence was suspended. The recent trials of three marines in Okinawa who were arrested for the rape of a twelve-year-old girl show that disputes continue to occur owing to the Anpo treaty regarding legal jurisdiction over base personnel.

66. In May 1955, Japanese authorities announced their intent to expropriate farmland adjoining the base for the runway extension. The mayor and city council of Sunagawa and the affected farmers immediately formed an opposition committee, and they and their supporters blocked several attempts to survey the area from July to November of 1955, despite increasingly larger police mobilizations. On July 8, 1957, some of the protesters broke through the fence surrounding the base and ran onto the runway. Seven protest leaders were arrested for violating the administrative agreement, which was more severe than civil law, and the arrests were challenged in court. On March 30, 1959, Judge Date Akio of the Tokyo District Court ruled that the Security Treaty, the bases, and the stationing of U.S. troops violated Article 9 of the Japanese Constitution and acquitted the protesters. State prosecutors immediately appealed the decision, which was overturned on December 16, 1959. See Donald Shoop, "Sunagawa Incident" (Ph.D. dissertation, University of Denver, 1985), for a detailed account of the lengthy dispute.

67. According to Douglas H. Mendel, Jr., the majority of Japanese people had never supported the bases. See *The Japanese People and Foreign Policy* (Berkeley and Los Angeles: University of California Press, 1961), chapter 4, cited in Packard, *Protest in Tokyo*, pp. 39–40.

68. Laura Hein, *Fueling Growth: The Energy Revolution and Economic Policy in Postwar Japan* (Cambridge: Council on East Asian Studies, Harvard University, 1990), 107–116. The group included Okita Saburō, Nakayama Ichirō, Arisawa Hiromi, and Tsuru Shigeto. Nakayama formulated the original wage-doubling scheme that served as a basis for Ikeda's income-doubling plan, and Okita and Arisawa were also involved in the debates regarding the way the plan would be implemented. Arisawa and Tsuru became members of the Heiwa Mondai Kondan Kai (Symposium on Peace Problems), which formed in 1949 and continued through the 1950s. They were also cosigners of the group's final statement, which appeared in the February 1960 issue of *Sekai*.

69. The United States allocated $960 million for this from 1951 to 1957, an amount roughly 12 to 13 percent of Japan's national budget at the time. These economists considered Japanese industries undercapitalized and believed that if the money for retooling had to come from Japanese sources, the country would suffer the same capital shortfalls it had experienced during World War II. Ibid., 64–65.

70. "Anpo kaitei mondai ni tsuite no seimei," *Sekai* 176 (February 1960): 12–17. Nakayama Ichirō disagreed with Arisawa Hiromi and

Tsuru Shigeto about Anpo, but he as well thought that Japan should stay away from weapons production. He also made public statements during the 1950s reaffirming his support of the Occupation reforms of *zaibatsu* dissolution and strengthening the rights and position of labor unions.

71. "Plans to revise the Constitution in general are often characterized as a manifestation of the 'reverse course' in post-Occupation Japan. The revisionist proposals regarding local government discussed above are clearly part of this trend. They do not strike out in any new direction, and the net effect of their realization would be a return to the past." Kurt Steiner, *Local Government in Japan*, 136.

72. "The government also admitted unofficially that the bill sought to control labor unrest and violence, including zigzag parades and demonstrations in and around public buildings." "It soon became apparent, however, that the government's sudden move had touched off wider fears than had been supposed." Lawrence Olson, *Dimensions of Japan* (New York: American Universities Field Staff, Inc., 1963), 189 and 192 respectively. Kishi even tried to call out the Self-Defense Forces on June 18, 1960, to quell the Anpo protests, asking Defense Agency director-general Akagi Munemori to dispatch ground troops to protect the Diet and disperse the demonstrators. While he did place the Kantō Division of the Ground Forces on alert, Akagi turned down Kishi's request to mobilize the troops. Weinstein, *Japan's Postwar Defense Policy*, 120–121; Shibagaki, *Kōwa kara kōdo seichō e*, 339.

73. During the extended sessions in May, the administration had also succeeded in passing a bill that prohibited teachers from "political activities" and from using educational materials from the union. See Dower, *Empire and Aftermath*, 356, and Mikiso Hane, *Modern Japan: A Historical Survey* (Boulder, Colo.: Westview Press, 1986), 357.

74. See Steiner, *Local Government in Japan*, 256–258.

75. The Mutual Security Agreement was concluded on March 8, 1954, and passed the Diet on April 18. The two defense laws that reorganized Japanese military structures in concordance with the agreement passed the Lower House on May 7 and the Upper House on June 2. See Dower, *Empire and Aftermath*, 466–470, 579, note 121.

76. Shibagaki, *Kōwa kara kōdo seichō e*, 184.

77. Zenrō (Zen Nihon Rōdō Kumiai Kaigi or Japan Trade Union Congress) merged with Sōdōmei to become Zen Nihon Rōdō Sōdōmei, or Dōmei, in 1964. Shinsanbetsu (National Federation of Industrial Organizations) also dropped out of the People's Council Against Anpo.

78. Minaguchi describes the long process of proposal and counter-proposal required to make the transition from one people's council to the other in *Anpo tōsō shi*, 22–24.

79. Minaguchi, *Anpo tōsō shi*, 39. On the local level, prefectural branches of the council even argued about whether to call themselves the Council to *Abolish* the Security Treaty, which the Japan Communist Party favored, or the Council to *Stop* the Treaty, which the Japan Socialist Party considered broader and less inflammatory. The other major organizational dispute concerned whether groups should become permanent units of the united front or should come together only for ad hoc, single issue campaigns. Packard claims that since power was diffused among the major groups and since the director, although good at facilitating and arbitrating arguments, provided weak leadership, the Japan Communist Party was able to steadily "infiltrate" and "unduly influence" the People's Council (*Protest in Tokyo*, 117–120).

80. The thirteen bodies were the Japan Socialist Party, Sōhyō, Chūritsu Rōren (National Federation of Neutral Labor Unions), Zen Ninō (All Japan Farmers Union), Goken Rengō (Federation to Defend the Constitution), Zenkoku Gunji Kichi Renraku Kyōgikai (National Liaison Council against the Military Bases), Heiwa Iinkai (Japan Peace Committee), Gensuikyō (Council against the Atomic and Hydrogen Bombs), Nitchū Kokkō Kaifuku Kokumin Kaigi (People's Council for the Restoration of Diplomatic Relations between Japan and China), Nitchū Yūkō Kyōkai (Japan-China Friendship Association), Jinken o Mamoru Fujin Kaigi (Women's Committee to Protect Human Rights), Seigaku Kyōtō (Joint Struggle Committee of Youth and Students), and Heiwa to Minshushugi o Mamoru Tōkyō Kyōtō Kaigi (Tokyo Joint Struggle Committee for Peace and Democracy). Ibid., 24. For a list of 110 of the 134 groups composing the People's Council, see Tsuji Kiyoaki, ed., *Seiji*, vol. 1 of *Shiryō: Sengo nijū-nen shi* (Tokyo: Nihon Hyōronsha, 1967), 145.

81. Sōhyō played a large role in setting up the forty-six Prefectural Joint Struggle Councils (Kenmin Kyōtō Kaigi). Thirty-one of the prefectural councils were set up at Sōhyō offices, and eight were in Japan Socialist Party offices. These prefectural councils oversaw 1,686 Local Joint Struggle Councils (Chihō Kyōtō Kaigi). For a chart of the relationships between the various bodies within the People's Council, see Packard, *Protest in Tokyo*, 112.

82. Director Minaguchi saw the united actions that the council organized as having this twofold function. Packard, *Protest in Tokyo*, 116.

83. Takabatake, "Citizen's Movements: Organizing the Spontaneous," 195.

84. Takabatake Michitoshi, "'Rokujū-nen Anpo' no seishin shi," in *Sengo Nihon no seishin shi: Sono saikentō*, ed. Kamishima Jirō, Maeda Ai, Tetsuo Najita (Tokyo: Iwanami Shoten, 1988), 74–75. According to Takabatake, this preservationist impulse allowed the movement to expand its mass base very rapidly but also meant that the base quickly receded after the Liberal Democratic Party conceded to the status quo and stopped its high-profile campaign to revise the constitution.

85. Michael Lewis, *Rioters and Citizens: Mass Protest in Imperial Japan* (Berkeley: University of California Press, 1990), 82–134, especially 85, 97, 116, 122.

86. For an in-depth study of these complex debates, see J. Victor Koschmann, *Revolution and Subjectivity in Postwar Japan*.

87. Sakuta Keiichi, "The Controversy over Community and Autonomy," in Koschmann, *Authority and the Individual in Japan*, 220.

88. Koschmann, *Revolution and Subjectivity in Postwar Japan*, 33–37. The strategy was dictated in part by the situation of the Occupation and the legal status that the opposition parties enjoyed at that time.

89. Ibid., 45–54.

90. Matsushita Keiichi, "Taishū kokka no seiritsu to sono mondaisei," *Shisō* 389 (November 1956): 32, also quoted in "'Taishū shakai' ronsō" (Mass Society Debate), in *Shōkai: Gendai ronsō jiten*, ed. Matsushita Kenichi (Tokyo: Ryūdō Shuppan, 1980), 218. See Matsushita Keiichi's "Shiteki yuibutsuron to taishū shakai" for a concise recap of what he considers the provenance and main points of mass society theory. *Shisō* 395 (May 1957): 43–44.

91. See "'Taishū shakai' ronsō," in Matsushita, *Gendai ronsō jiten*, 220. This seems to be Matsushita's attitude in "Shiteki yuibutsuron to taishū shakai" as well.

92. See "'Taishū shakai' ronsō," in Matsushita, *Gendai ronsō jiten*, 217. Western writers such as William Kornhauser make it clear that mass society is not to be confused with the working-class masses or identified with modernity or industrialization in order to distinguish it from Marxist analysis. *The Politics of Mass Society* (Glencoe, Ill.: Free Press, 1959), 14, 16. Matsushita transliterates the term *"taishū"* as "the masses" when discussing mass society (*taishū shakai*) and differentiates

it from Marxist usage by translating it as "the people," as in the "people's front" (*taishū rōsen*), when employing Marxist terminology. See, for example, "Shiteki yuibutsuron to taishū shakai," 44, note 2. However, he is still given to using Marxian terms and categories while ignoring their specific connotations.

93. Matsushita Keiichi, "Marukusushugi riron no nijūseikiteki tenkan—taishū nashonarizumu to seiji no ronri," *Chūō kōron* 72, 3 (March 1957), cited in "'Taishū shakai' ronsō," in Matsushita, *Gendai ronsō jiten*, p. 219.

94. Shibata Shingo, "'Taishū shakai' riron e no gimon" (Doubts Regarding "Mass Society" Theory), *Chūō kōron* 72, 8 (June 1957), cited in "'Taishū shakai' ronsō," in Matsushita, *Gendai ronsō jiten*, p. 219. This critique would also apply to Talcott Parsons' statement that "power, considered in this special sense as a symbolic medium, involves a division of labor and a consequent need for integrative exchanges. . . . The public gives up the right to exercise direct physical force on their own behalf in return for a (symbolic) promise that organized collective power will be exercised for the common good. When civil power does not or cannot deliver on these promises, the symbolic medium breaks down and the public withdraws allegiance, taking direct power back into their own hands. Talcott Parsons, *On Social Institutions and Social Evolution: Selected Writings,* edited with an introduction by Leon H. Mayhew (Chicago: University of Chicago Press, 1982), 35–36.

95. This analysis was presented by Igarashi Yoshikuni in a paper titled "The Politics of Transgression: The Mass Social Situation in Postwar Japan," presented at the Association for Asian Studies Annual Meeting in Los Angeles, March 25, 1993.

96. See Matsushita Keiichi, "Citizen Participation in Historical Perspective," in Koschmann, *Authority and the Individual in Japan,* 177–182.

97. As Robert Bellah wrote: "Exposure to urban life, modern industry, and advanced education does not in itself create universalistic and individualistic values. 'Mass society' theorists have shown how these advanced conditions can lead to the creation of pseudo-Gemeinschaft and 'other-direction.' In Japan where Gemeinschaft, pseudo-Gemeinschaft and other-direction have always been strong, much in modern society strengthens rather than undermines them." "Continuity and Change in Japanese Society," in *Stability and Social Change,* ed. Bernard Barber (Boston: Alex Inkeles, Little, Brown and Co., 1971), 401–402.

98. Takabatake, "Citizen's Movements: Organizing the Spontaneous," p. 192.

99. Kuno Osamu, "Seijiteki shimin no seiritsu," *Shisō no kagaku* 19 (July 1960): 9–17, reprinted in Kuno, *Seijiteki shimin no fukken* (Tokyo: Ushio Sensho, 1973), 7–22.

100. Kuno, "Seijiteki shimin no seiritsu," 7–9.

101. Ibid., 10.

102. Ibid., 12.

103. Maruyama Masao, "8.15 to 5.19," 53. This was also attested to by the spread of terms such as "company men" (*mōretsu shain*) and "enterprise consciousness" (*kigyō ishiki*).

104. Kuno Osamu, "Mittsu no yakuwari," *Tayori* 5 (October 20, 1960): 11.

105. Kuno, "Seijiteki shimin no seiritsu," 19.

106. Ibid.

107. Kuno Osamu, "Kōdō suru minshushugi to wa nani ka" (October 2, 1962, lecture given at the Fifth Contemporary Education Forum of the Kokuritsu Chōkōminkan), in Kuno, *Seijiteki shimin no fukken*, 28–57.

108. Kuno by this point no longer uses the word *"taishū,"* now employing the term *"kōshū"* instead, indicating that the masses have already become an enlightened public. For a comparison with Maruyama's thought, see Maruyama, "The Theory and Psychology of Ultra-Nationalism," 3–11, 19–23, and "The Ideology and Dynamics of Japanese Fascism," 57–65.

109. Kuno, "Kōdō suru minshushugi to wa nani ka," 30. Maruyama Masao, "The Theory and Psychology of Ultra-Nationalism," 3–11, 19–23. See also Maruyama, "The Ideology and Dynamics of Japanese Fascism," 57–65.

110. Kuno, "Kōdō suru minshushugi to wa nani ka," 42.

111. Ibid., 31.

112. Ibid., 36–37.

113. Ibid., 50.

114. Kuno, "Seijiteki shimin no seiritsu," 17.

115. Reprinted in Kuno's *Seijiteki shimin no fukken* as "Seiji ni sanka suru shimin" (Citizen Engagement in Politics), 23–27.

116. See Matsushita Keiichi, "Shiteki yuibutsuron to taishū shakai," 56–57; and Matsushita, "Nihon ni okeru taishū shakairon no igi" (Objections to Mass Society Theory in Japan), *Chūō kōron* 72, 10 (August 1957): 243, cited by Tsuzuki Tsutomu, "Rokujū-nen Anpo zengo no Maruyama Masao" in *Gendai no riron* 235 (March 1987): 7, 17.

117. Tsuzuki makes a particular point of saying that Maruyama's nationalism must be examined. The fact that the prewar type of nationalism was untenable for postwar Japan, in fact, made the task of forging a new kind of national independence all that more crucial. Despite his image of being someone who idealized the West, Maruyama criticized the "typical Japanese attitude," whether at the national level or at the level of individual psychology, of simultaneously venerating and looking down on the West, indicated by the homonyms *"haigai."* Tsuzuki, "Rokujū-nen Anpo zengo no Maruyama Masao," 9; and interview with Kurihara Akira, November 27, 1990.

118. Barshay, "Imagining Democracy in Postwar Japan," 392; Tsuzuki, "Rokujū-nen Anpo zengo no Maruyama Masao," 10.

119. Interview with Kurihara Akira, November 11, 1990.

120. Barshay, "Imagining Democracy in Postwar Japan," 395.

121. Tsuzuki, "Rokujū-nen Anpo zengo no Maruyama Masao," 14.

122. See Carol Gluck's discussion of "denaturing politics" in chapter 3 of *Japan's Modern Myths: Ideology in the Late Meiji Period* (Princeton, N.J.: Princeton University Press, 1985), 50–53. Gluck claims that politics was "denatured" first of all by "displacing" the term and associating it with selfish, undesirable urges in order to restrict the political activities of any groups that challenged the state's authority. But as she admits, this process did not cure the fever for politics; rather it came out under the rubric of patriotism.

123. Maruyama, "The Theory and Psychology of Ultra-Nationalism," 10. "We find a tendency, then, to estimate morality not by the value of its content, but in terms of its power, that is, according to whether or not it had a power background. In the last analysis this was because the real locus of Japanese morality was not in the conscience of the individual but in the affairs of the nation."

124. Maruyama, "8.15 to 5.19," 51–52. The article is a transcription of a discussion apparently held shortly after June 19. See Andrew Barshay, *State and Intellectual in Imperial Japan: The Public Man in*

Crisis (Berkeley: University of California Press, 1988), 5–11, for a concise discussion of the prewar formulation of the public. As Barshay notes on page 8: "The state, then, sought to bind the 'public' to itself, along with the authority to define the identity and values of its subjects. The centripetal force of this identification was most evident among bureaucrats, where personal, official, and national identity were intertwined with a powerful sense of mission—to civilize the people, to acquire learning for the sake of the nation, to raise Japan's status in the world."

125. Maruyama, "8.15 to 5.19," 51–52.

126. " 'De aru' koto to 'suru' koto" ("Being" and "Doing") was a talk given at the Iwanami Bunka Kōen Kai (Iwanami Cultural Lecture Series) in October 1958. The talk was later serialized in the *Mainichi shinbun* from January 9 to 12, 1959, and published as part 4 of *Nihon no shisō* (Tokyo: Iwanami Shinsho, 1961), 153–180.

127. Maruyama, " 'De aru' koto to 'suru' koto," *Nihon no shisō*, 155. Article 12 reads, "The freedoms and rights of this constitution guaranteed to the people must be maintained by the regular efforts of the people." Article 97 states that basic human rights are "the fruits of the efforts people made over many years to acquire freedom."

128. Ibid., 156.

129. Maruyama, "8.15 to 5.19," 51.

130. The text was published in the *Asahi Journal* 2, 24 (June 12, 1960): 11–17.

131. Maruyama, "Kono jitai no seijiteki mondaiten," *Asahi Journal* (June 12, 1960): 16.

132. Ibid., 15 and 14, respectively.

133. Barshay, "Imagining Democracy in Postwar Japan," 382.

134. Ibid., 394.

135. It was common to blame subservience and acquiescence to authority for the rise of fascism, and when looking for the origins of this attitude, many blamed the prewar state's agrarian ideology for engendering it. Prewar ethics texts portrayed the village as a model of social harmony achieved through obeisance to the headman, whose authority emanated from the local god. This model then served as an allegory for "proper" service to the imperial state. Rural communities were metonymical for the nation; they were society writ small. See Robert King Hall, *Shūshin: The Ethics of a Defeated Nation* (New York: Bureau of

Publications, Teachers College, 1949), 89–90, 132–135. Thus, the postwar task for intellectuals who considered themselves progressive modernists was to break up such *kyōdōtai* (communities) and engender modern, universal values through new social and political structures.

136. Maruyama, "'De aru' koto to 'suru' koto," 159–160.

137. Ibid., 161.

138. Ibid., 163.

139. Ibid., 172.

140. Maruyama Masao, "Patterns of Individuation and the Case of Japan: A Conceptual Scheme," in *Changing Japanese Attitudes towards Modernization*, ed. Marius Jansen (Tokyo and Rutland, Vt.: Charles E. Tuttle Co., 1965), 492–493. As Maruyama writes in the opening pages, this article is a response to the Hakone Conference on the "Modernization of Japan," held August 29 to September 2, 1960, in the wake of the Anpo and Miike protests. The conference participants split along a number of questions: is modernization "value-free"? is it universal or only Western? does it produce cultural convergence? does it necessitate democracy? is it good or bad? However, Western scholars tended to follow Reischauer's line of modernization theory and were hostile to Marxist critiques from the Japanese side.

141. Barshay, "Imagining Democracy in Postwar Japan," 395. See also Koschmann, *Revolution and Subjectivity in Postwar Japan*, 236: "Maruyama does not reify or take as given any of the specific forms of government institutionalization, but rather treats them all as 'fictions' in constant need of subjective reevaluation and intervention. Indeed, his view of democracy as a 'fiction' that is never entirely realized implies a kind of permanent revolution, albeit always securely within the framework of the state."

142. Koschmann points this out in Maruyama's discussion of Fukuzawa's philosophy. "Maruyama's argument here has important implications for democratic revolution. He affirms that modern subjectivity is not merely an epistemological mechanism but also entails an antiauthoritarian form of praxis. When the subject 'renders its own perspective fluid'—and thus undergoes a continuous process of self-transformation—those in power lose control of values and have to recognize the legitimacy of pluralism." *Revolution and Subjectivity in Postwar Japan*, 184.

143. *Tayori* 6 (November 20, 1960): 2, 3. The Liberal Democratic Party refused to reply to any of the queries.

144. *Tayori* 20 (June 20, 1962): 4–14.

145. The suggestion for this viewpoint comes from Guy Yasko's analysis of the Zenkyōtō student movement in Japan in the late 1960s, especially in his description of the activist Tokoro Mitsuko. "The Japanese Student Movement, 1968–1970: The Zenkyōtō Uprising" (Ph.D. dissertation, Cornell University, 1997), 13–14.

CHAPTER SEVEN

1. This is certainly the case with Packard's 1966 book, which is still the only full-length account of the protests, and continues down to more recent treatments such as John Welfield, *An Empire in Eclipse: Japan in the Postwar American Alliance System: A Study in the Interaction of Domestic Politics and Foreign Policy* (London: The Athlone Press, 1988). Wellfield describes the importance of the Anpo crisis as "exposing latent ambiguities in the Japanese-American strategic relationship, the deep fissures within the Conservative camp, the extraordinary organizational power of the Opposition parties and the degree of public support for their neutralist platforms" (137).

2. Arturo Escobar, "Culture, Economics, and Politics in Latin American Social Movements Theory and Research," in Escobar and Alvarez, *The Making of Social Movements in Latin America*, 73. Cited in Abelmann, *Echoes of the Past, Epics of Dissent*, 4.

3. LeBlanc, *Bicycle Citizens*, 16–17.

4. Ibid.

5. David Snow and Robert Bedford, "Master Frames and Cycles of Protest," in Morris and Mueller, *Frontiers in Social Movement Theory*, 133–155.

6. Ellis Krauss, *Japanese Radicals Revisited: Student Protest in Postwar Japan* (Berkeley: University of California Press, 1974). Margaret McKean, "Political Socialization through Citizens' Movements," in Steiner, Krauss, and Flanagan, *Political Opposition and Local Politics in Japan*, 228–273.

7. *Tayori* 34 (June 10, 1965): 2–5.

8. For an analysis of the Sanrizuka protest movement, see David Apter and Sawa Nagayo, *Against the State: Politics and Social Protest in Japan* (Cambridge, Mass.: Harvard University Press, 1984).

9. *Tayori* 52 (August 15, 1971): 2–8. See also Mochizuki Sumiko's report in *Tayori* 57 (March 10, 1974): 4–6 for further articulation of members' reasons for identifying with the Sanrizuka struggle.

10. Opposition farmers thought the new airport might be for U.S. military use. According to David Apter and Nagayo Sawa, the government considered this "a remote contingency at best," despite the Vietnam War. *Against the State*, 211. The possibility, however, was not entirely ruled out. As it turned out, the airport took much longer to construct than originally anticipated, owing to the opposition movement, and the United States pulled out of Vietnam three years before the Narita airport was open to traffic.

11. One particularly instructive example is Tokoro Mitsuko, who participated in the June 15, 1960, action and whose writings heavily influenced the form that Zenkyōtō took, even though she died at the end of January 1968 just as medical students were voting to strike, setting off the takeover of Tokyo University. See Yasko, "The Japanese Student Movement 1968–70," 4–23.

12. Krauss, *Japanese Radicals Revisited*, 92–98.

13. LeBlanc, *Bicycle Citizens*, 128, 156.

14. LaClau and Mouffe, *Hegemony and Socialist Strategy*, 86–87.

15. Neal Learner notes that the percentage of women in the House of Representatives in the Diet is still less than 5 percent, which puts Japan 124th among 131 nations. Neal Learner, "Fighting for Equality in Japan," *The Progressive* 63, 3 (March 1999): 15.

16. See, for example, Frank Upham, *Law and Social Change in Postwar Japan* (Cambridge: Harvard University Press, 1987), 145–156; Mary Brinton, *Women and the Economic Miracle*, 228–234; Yoko Kawashima, "Female Workers: An Overview of Past and Current Trends," in Fujimura-Fanselow and Kameda, *Japanese Women: New Feminist Perspectives on the Past, Present, and Future*, 283–286.

17. One of the few English-language articles about the Zushi issue is problematic in focusing on the antiexpansion mayor Tomino Kiichirō, rather than the housewives' movement that first raised the issue and elected him. See Ken Ruoff, "Mr. Tomino Goes to City Hall: Grass-

Roots Democracy in Zushi City, Japan," *Bulletin of Concerned Asian Scholars* 25, 3 (1993): 22–32.

18. Kurihara Akira, "New Social Movements in Present-Day Japan," *Journal of Pacific Asia* 5 (1999): 10.

19. Havens, *Fire across the Sea*, 55.

20. Ibid., 57.

21. One practical reason for this decentralized structure was to protect the U.S. military deserters that the Japan Technical Committee for Assistance to Antiwar U.S. Deserters (JATEC), composed of Beheiren members, was helping to get to neutral-country safe havens. See Sekiya Shigeru and Sakamoto Yoshie, eds., *Tonari ni dassōhei ga ita jidai: JATEC, aru shimin undō no kiroku* (Tokyo: Shisō no Kagakusha, 1998).

22. Maruyama Hisashi, *"Mini komi" no dojidaishi*, 12.

23. Tsurumi Yoshiyuki, Shunsuke's cousin, said that "our inclination toward concrete action sprang not so much from direct contact with the NLF as from latent dissatisfaction with the bureaucratic and doctrinaire character of the domestic political parties and the organized left wing." "Beheiren," *Japan Quarterly* 16, 4 (October 1969): 445. Cited in Havens, *Fire across the Sea*, 56.

24. Havens, *Fire across the Sea*, 68–69.

25. Yasko, "The Japanese Student Movement, 1968–70," 12–13.

26. Ibid., 6, 11.

27. Ibid., 14.

28. Ibid., 2.

29. Krauss and Simcock, "Citizens' Movements: The Growth and Impact of Environmental Protest in Japan," 197.

30. Krauss and Simcock posit a much more radical philosophical break between the Anpo era citizens' movements and those that followed, seeing the former as having broad, common goals and the latter as categorically different because of their narrow interests and diverse aims. At the same time, they note that merging the "idea" of citizens' movements onto later residentially based environmental movements helped residents' movements legitimize their protests locally, connect with similar movements in other regions, and draw general support from third parties. Ibid., 199, 201–202, 212–214.

31. Miyazaki Shōgo, *Ima, "kokyōsei" o utsu: [Dokyumento] Yoko-hama shinkamotsusen hantai undō* (Tokyo: Shinsensha, 1975), 15–16, 134–141. Miyazaki thus applies the same logic that Kuno employed during the Anpo protests. Kuno defined democracy as a method of solving public problems, and he distinguished private interests, whose scope is limited to the principals involved, from public interests, which are determined by universality of effect and go beyond the interests of the immediate parties involved. Kuno also claims that designation of public and private is not quantitatively determined in terms of majority versus minority. Public means that which benefits the "common wealth." Kuno, "Kōdō suru minshushugi to wa nani ka," 29.

32. Mutō Ichiyo, "The Alternative Livelihood Movement," 4–11.

33. Kurihara, "New Social Movements in Present-Day Japan," 17–20.

34. There is a tendency in new social movement theory to consider movements' development as a result of the society achieving a particular stage of modernization. The resource mobilization paradigm often assumes the necessity of "developed" social and political structures modeled on the postwar West. Even some of the correctives offered by later paradigms focused on identity and participants' ideas and motivations still make the tacit assumption that social movements' self-aware-ness and consciousness as historical actors only occurs in "advanced" countries. (See Alain Touraine, *The Return of the Actor: Social Theory in Postindustrial Society,* trans. Muna Godzich [Minneapolis: University of Minnesota Press, 1988], 66–68.) Hence Escobar's critique that Abel-mann reiterates. See Arturo Escobar, "Imagining a Post-Development Era? Critical Thought, Development and Social Movements," *Social Text* 10:37, cited in Abelmann, *Echoes of the Past, Epics of Dissent,* 5.

BIBLIOGRAPHY

Abelmann, Nancy. *Echoes of the Past, Epics of Dissent: A South Korean Social Movement*. Berkeley: University of California Press, 1996.

Amano Masako. "Kusa no Mi Kai" (The Grass Seeds). In *Kyōdō kenkyū: Shudan* (Collaborative Research on Collective Bodies), edited by Shisō no Kagaku, 269–276. Tokyo: Heibonsha, 1976.

————. "Kusa no Mi no jūroku-nen: Aru shufu saakuru egaita kiseki" (Sixteen Years of the Grass Seeds: Traces Depicted in a Certain Women's Circle). *Shisō no kagaku* (Science of Thought), 115 (special issue 3: Shūdan no sengo shisōshi [Postwar Intellectual History of Groups], 1971): 30–42.

Anpo Jōyaku Kaitei Soshi Kokumin Kaigi Chōsa Iinkai et al., eds. *Rekishi e no shōgen: 6.15 no dokyumento* (Witness to History: Documents from June 15). Tokyo: Nihon Hyōron Shinsha, 1960.

Apter, David, and Sawa Nagayo. *Against the State: Politics and Social Protest in Japan*. Cambridge, Mass.: Harvard University Press, 1984.

Aragaki Hideo. *Tensei jingo 4: 1958.7–1963.4* (Vox Populi, Vox Dei 4: July 1958–April 1963). Tokyo: Asahi Shinbunsha, 1971.

Ariyoshi Sawako. *The Twilight Years*. Translated by Mildred Tahara. Tokyo: Kodansha International, 1984.

Asahi Journal, ed. *Onna no sengo shi I: Shōwa nijū nendai* (A Postwar History of Women I: 1945–1955). Tokyo: Asahi Shinbunsha, 1984.

Asahi Shinbun, ed. *Hōdō shashin shū 1961* (Asahi Shinbun News Photography, 1961). Tokyo: Asahi Shinbunsha, 1961.

Asahi Shinbunsha, ed. *Shōwa 35-nen, Asahi Gurafu ni miru: Shōwa no sesō* (1960—Social Conditions in Shōwa as Seen in Asahi Graph), vol. 13. Tokyo: Asahi Shinbunsha, 1976.

Asanuma Toshinao, Inaba Yoshikazu, Katsumata Jirō, and Nakamura Kiyoshi. "Rōdō kumiai to rōdōsha no jihassei" (Labor Unions and Workers' Autonomy). *Shisō* (Thought), 460 (October 1962).

Auer, James. *The Postwar Rearmament of Japanese Maritime Forces, 1945–71.* New York: Praeger Publishers, 1973.

Barshay, Andrew. "Imagining Democracy in Postwar Japan: Reflection on Maruyama Masao and Modernism." *Journal of Japanese Studies* 18, no. 2 (Summer 1992): 365–406.

——. *State and Intellectual in Imperial Japan: The Public Man in Crisis.* Berkeley: University of California Press, 1988.

Bellah, Robert. "Continuity and Change in Japanese Society." In *Stability and Social Change,* edited by Bernard Barber, 374–404. Boston: Alex Inkeles, Little, Brown and Co., 1971.

Brinton, Mary. *Women and the Economic Miracle: Gender and Work in Postwar Japan.* Berkeley: University of California Press, 1993.

Broadbent, Jeffrey. *Environmental Politics in Japan: Networks of Power and Protest.* Cambridge: Cambridge University Press, 1998.

Buckley, Sandra. *Broken Silence: Voices of Japanese Feminism.* Berkeley: University of California Press, 1997.

Calderón, Fernando, Alejandro Piscitelli, and José Luis Reyna. "Social Movements: Actors, Theories, Expectations." In *The Making of Social Movements in Latin America,* edited by Arturo Escobar and Sonia Alvarez, 19–36. Boulder, Colo.: Westview Press, 1992.

Calhoun, Craig, ed. *Habermas and the Public Sphere.* Cambridge, Mass.: MIT Press, 1992.

Carlile, Lonny. "Sōhyō versus Dōmei: Competing Labour Movement Strategies in the Era of High Growth in Japan." *Japan Forum* 6, no. 2 (1994): 145–157.

Choi, Chungmoo, guest ed. *The Comfort Women: Colonialism, War, and Sex* (special issue). *positions: east asia cultures critique* 5, no. 1 (Spring 1997).

Cook, Haruko Taya, and Theodore Cook. *Japan at War: An Oral History.* New York: The New Press, 1992.

Cumings, Bruce. "Japan's Position in the World System." In *Postwar Japan as History,* edited by Andrew Gordon, 34–63. Berkeley: University of California Press, 1993.

Dirlik, Arif. "Past Experience, If Not Forgotten, Is a Guide to the Future, or, What Is in a Text? The Politics of History in Chinese-Japanese Relations." *boundary 2*, 18, no. 3 (Fall 1991): 29–58.

Dower, John. "The Bombed: Hiroshimas and Nagasakis in Japanese Memory." In *Hiroshima in History and Memory*, edited by Michael J. Hogan, 116–142. Cambridge: Cambridge University Press, 1996.

———. *Empire and Aftermath: Yoshida Shigeru and the Japanese Experience, 1878–1954*. Cambridge: Council on East Asian Studies, Harvard University, 1988.

Duke, Benjamin C. *Japan's Militant Teachers: A History of the Left-Wing Teachers' Movement*. Honolulu: University Press of Hawai'i, 1973.

Duus, Peter, ed. *The Twentieth Century. Cambridge History of Japan*, vol. 6. Cambridge: Cambridge University Press, 1988.

Escobar, Arturo, and Sonia E. Alvarez. "Introduction: Theory and Protest in Latin America Today." In *The Making of Social Movements in Latin America: Identity, Strategy, and Democracy*. edited by Arturo Escobar and Sonia E. Alvarez, 1–15. Boulder, Colo.: Westview Press, 1992.

———, eds. *The Making of Social Movements in Latin America: Identity, Strategy, and Democracy*. Boulder, Colo.: Westview Press, 1992.

Field, Norma. *In the Realm of a Dying Emperor*. New York: Pantheon, 1991.

Figal, Gerald. "How to *jibunshi*: Making and Marketing Self-Histories of Shōwa among the Masses in Postwar Japan." *Journal of Asian Studies* 55, no. 4 (1996): 902–933.

Fujimura-Fanselow, Kumiko, and Atsuko Kameda, eds. *Japanese Women: New Feminist Perspectives on the Past, Present, and Future*. New York: The Feminist Press, 1995.

Fujioka Wake. *Women's Movements in Postwar Japan*. (Selected articles from Tsuji Seimei, ed., *Shiryō: Sengo nijū-nen shi* [Resources: A Twenty-Year History of the Postwar]. Tokyo: Nippon Hyōronsha, 1966]). Honolulu: East-West Center, 1968.

Gayn, Mark. *Japan Diary*. Rutland, Vt.: Charles E. Tuttle Co., 1981.

Gluck, Carol. "The Idea of Showa." In *Showa: The Japan of Hirohito*, edited by Carol Gluck and Stephen R. Graubard, 1–26. New York: W. W. Norton and Company, 1992.

———. *Japan's Modern Myths: Ideology in the Late Meiji Period*. Princeton, N.J.: Princeton University Press, 1985.

———. "The Past in the Present." In *Postwar Japan as History*, edited by Andrew Gordon, 64–95. Berkeley: University of California Press, 1993.

Gordon, Andrew. "Contests for the Workplace." In *Postwar Japan as History*, edited by Andrew Gordon, 373–394. Berkeley: University of California Press, 1993.

———. *The Wages of Affluence: Labor and Management in Postwar Japan*. Cambridge: Harvard University Press, 1998.

———, ed. *Postwar Japan as History*. Berkeley: University of California Press, 1993.

Habermas, Jürgen. *Structural Transformation of the Public Sphere*. Translated by Thomas Burger. Cambridge, Mass.: MIT Press, 1989, 1995.

Hall, Robert King. *Shūshin: The Ethics of a Defeated Nation*. New York: Bureau of Publications, Teachers College, 1949.

Hall, Stuart. *The Hard Road to Renewal*. London: Verso, 1988.

Hane, Mikiso. *Modern Japan: A Historical Survey*. Boulder, Colo.: Westview Press, 1986.

Hara Kazuo, dir. *Yuki yukite shingun* (The Emperor's Naked Army Marches On). Tokyo: Shisso Productions, 1987.

Havens, Thomas R. H. *Fire across the Sea: The Vietnam War and Japan, 1965–1975*. Princeton, N.J.: Princeton University Press, 1987.

———. *Valley of Darkness: The Japanese People and World War Two*. New York: W. W. Norton and Company, 1978.

Hein, Laura. *Fueling Growth: The Energy Revolution and Economic Policy in Postwar Japan*. Cambridge: Council on East Asian Studies, Harvard University, 1990.

———. "Growth Versus Success: Japan's Economic Policy in Historical Perspective." In *Postwar Japan as History*, edited by Andrew Gordon, 99–122. Berkeley: University of California Press, 1993.

Hein, Laura, and Mark Selden, guest eds. *Textbook Nationalism, Citizenship, and War: Comparative Perspectives*. Special issue. *Bulletin of Concerned Asian Scholars* 30, no. 2 (April–June 1998).

Heiwa Mondai Kondan Kai. "Anpo kaitei mondai ni tsuite no seimei" (Declaration on the Issue of Revisions to the Security Treaty). *Sekai* (The World), 176 (February 1960): 12–17.

Hicks, George. *The Comfort Women: Japan's Brutal Regime of Enforced Prostitution in the Second World War*. New York: W. W. Norton and Company, 1994.

Hidaka Rokurō. *1960-nen, 5-gatsu, 19-nichi* (May 19, 1960). Tokyo: Iwanami Shinsho, 1960.

Hosaka Masayasu. *Rokujū-nen Anpo tōsō* (The 1960 Anpo Struggle). Tokyo: Kodansha Gendai Shinsho, 1986.

Ide Busaburō, ed. *Anpo tōsō: 'Sengo shi' o tsukuru daitōsō no kiroku* (The Anpo Struggle: Record of a Major Struggle That Shaped Postwar History). Tokyo: San'ichi Shobō, 1960.

Igarashi Yoshikuni. "The Politics of Transgression: The Mass Social Situation in Postwar Japan." Paper presented at the Association for Asian Studies Annual Meeting, Los Angeles, March 25, 1993.

Inaba Yoshikazu. "Burūsu nanka utau mono ka" (I'll Never Sing the Blues). In *Kokutetsu ni ikite kita* (Living for the Japan National Railways), special issue of *Takarajima*, 58 (November 25): 50–70. Tokyo: JICC Shuppan Kyoku, 1986.

―――. *Densha to rōdō* (Trains and Labor). Tokyo: Doyō Bijutsusha, 1983.

―――. "The Record." *Ōi Shijin* (Poets of Ōi), 25 (July 31, 1961): 26–30.

―――. "Rōdō to hyōgen" (Work and Expression). In *Shi no kakumei o mezashite*, edited by Kokutetsu Shijin Renmei, 161–167. Tokyo: Iizuka Shoten, 1984.

Ishida Takeshi and Ellis Krauss. "Democracy in Japan: Issues and Questions." In *Democracy in Japan*, edited by Ishida Takeshi and Ellis Krauss. Pittsburgh: University of Pittsburgh Press, 1989.

―――, eds. *Democracy in Japan*. Pittsburgh: University of Pittsburgh Press, 1989.

Kageyama Saburō. "Nihon no bunka fūdo ni okeru fujin jaanarizumu no rekishiteki yakuwari to tenbō" (The Historical Role and View of Japan's Cultural Customs in Women's Journalism). In *Fujin jaanarizumu kenkyū* (Research into Women's Journalism), 152–155. Tokyo: Toyota Zaikoku Josei Kenkyū, 1977.

———. *Shinbun tōsho ron: Minshu genron no hyaku-nen* (Discussion on Newspaper Contributions: A Century of People's Expression). Tokyo: Gendai Jaanarizumu Kai, 1968.

Kamishima Jirō, Maeda Ai, and Tetsuo Najita, eds. *Sengo Nihon no seishin shi: Sono saikentō* (A Psychological History of the Japanese Postwar: That Reexamination). Tokyo: Iwanami Shoten, 1988.

Kanba Toshio. "'Anpo tōsō' waga musume kokkai minami mon ni shisu" (The Anpo Struggle: My Daughter Died at the South Gate of the Diet). In *Sengo sanjū-nen* (Thirty Years of the Postwar), *Showa shi tanbō* (Inquiries into Shōwa History), vol. 6, edited by Mikuni Ichirō, 221–246. Tokyo: Kadokawa Bunko, 1986.

Kawashima Yoko. "Female Workers: An Overview of Past and Current Trends." In *Japanese Women*, edited by Kumiko Fujimura-Fanselow and Atsuko Kameda, 271–293. New York: The Feminist Press, 1995.

Kishigami Daisuke. "Ishi hyōji." In *Haraguchi Junzō—Hatachi no echudo, Kishigami Daisaku—Ishi hyōji, Ōtake Ayumu—Shi to hangyaku to shi* (Haraguchi Junzō—Etude on Being Twenty, Kishigami Daisaku—A Demonstration of Will, Ōtake Ayumu—Poetry, Treason, and Death). *Nihon kyōyō zenshu* (Collected Works in Japanese Culture), vol. 16. Tokyo: Kadokawa, 1974.

Kobayashi Tomi. *Kaigara no machi: Koe naki hitobito no deai* (Town of Shells: Encounters with the Voiceless). Tokyo: Shisō no Kagakusha, 1980.

Koe Naki Koe no Kai, ed. *Koe Naki Koe no Tayori* (Correspondence of the Voiceless Voices). Vol. 1: 1960–1970, Vol. 2: 1970–1995. Tokyo: Shisō no Kagakusha, 1996.

———. *Mata demo de aou: Koe Naki Koe no ni-nen kan* (Let's Meet Again at the Demonstration: Two Years of the Voiceless Voices). Tokyo: Tōkyō Shoten, 1962.

Kokutetsu Shijin Renmei, ed. *Shi no kakumei o mezashite: Kokutetsu shijin ronsō shi* (Toward a Revolutionary Poetry: A History of Debates from the Japan National Railway Poets). Tokyo: Iizuka Shoten, 1984.

Kornhauser, William. *The Politics of Mass Society.* Glencoe, Ill.: Free Press, 1959.

Kōsai Yutaka. *The Era of High-Speed Growth: Notes on the Postwar Japanese Economy.* Translated by Jacqueline Kaminski. Tokyo: University of Tokyo Press, 1986.

Koschmann, J. Victor. *Revolution and Subjectivity in Postwar Japan.* Chicago: University of Chicago Press, 1996.

————, ed. *Authority and the Individual in Japan: Citizen Protest in Historical Perspective.* Tokyo: University of Tokyo Press, 1978.

Krauss, Ellis. *Japanese Radicals Revisited: Student Protest in Postwar Japan.* Berkeley: University of California Press, 1974.

Krauss, Ellis, and Bradford Simcock. "Citizens' Movements: The Growth and Impact of Environmental Protest in Japan." In *Political Opposition and Local Politics in Japan*, edited by Kurt Steiner, Ellis Krauss, and Scott Flanagan. Princeton, N.J.: Princeton University Press, 1980.

Kumazawa Makoto. *Portraits of the Japanese Workplace: Labor Movements, Workers, and Managers.* Translated by Andrew Gordon and Mikiso Hane. Boulder, Colo.: Westview Press, 1996.

Kuno Osamu. "Kōdō suru minshushugi to wa nani ka" (What Is Active Democracy?). In Kuno, *Seijiteki shimin no fukken*, 28–57. Tokyo: Ushio Sensho, 1973.

————. "Mittsu no yakuwari" (Three Roles). *Tayori* (Correspondence), 5 (October 20, 1960): 11.

————. *Seijiteki shimin no fukken* (The Restoration of Political Citizens). Tokyo: Ushio Sensho, 1973.

————. "Seijiteki shimin no seiritsu" (The Establishment of Political Citizens). *Shisō no kagaku* 19 (July 1960): 9–17. Reprinted in *Seijiteki shimin no fukken*, 7–22. Tokyo: Ushio Sensho, 1973.

Kurihara Akira. "New Social Movements in Present-Day Japan." *Journal of Pacific Asia* 5 (1999): 7–22.

Kusa no Mi Kai, ed. *Jū-nen no kiroku: Daijūkai sōkai o kinen shite* (Ten-Year Record: Commemorating the Tenth General Assemby). Tokyo: Kusa no Mi Kai, 1964.

————. *Kusa no Mi: Sanjū-nen no kiroku* (Thirty-Year Record of the Grass Seeds). Tokyo: Kusa no Mi Kai, 1984.

————. *Kusa no Mi: Yonjū-nen no kiroku* (Forty-Year Record of the Grass Seeds). Tokyo: Kusa no Mi Kai, 1994.

Laclau, Ernesto, and Chantal Mouffe. *Hegemony and Socialist Strategy: Toward a Radical Democratic Politics.* New York: Verso, 1985.

Learner, Neal. "Fighting for Equality in Japan." *The Progressive* 63, no. 3 (March 1999): 15.

LeBlanc, Robin. *Bicycle Citizens: The Political World of the Japanese Housewife.* Berkeley: University of California Press, 1999.

Lewis, Michael. *Rioters and Citizens: Mass Protest in Imperial Japan.* Berkeley: University of California Press, 1990.

Linhart, Sepp. "From Industrial to Postindustrial Society: Changes in Japanese Leisure-Related Values and Behavior." *Journal of Japanese Studies* 14, no. 2 (Summer 1988): 271–307.

Lipsitz, George. *Time Passage: Collective Memory and American Popular Culture.* Minneapolis: University of Minnesota Press, 1990.

Lu, David. *Japan: A Documentary History.* Armonk, N.Y.: M. E. Sharpe, 1997.

Mainichi Shinbunsha, ed. *Kōdo seichō: Shōwa 31–38 nen* (Rapid Economic Growth: 1956–1963). *Shōwa shi* (A History of Shōwa), vol. 15. Tokyo: Mainichi Shinbunsha, 1984.

Maruyama Hisashi. *Mini komi no dōjidai shi* (A Contemporary History of Mini-Communications). Tokyo: Heibonsha, 1985.

————. *Mini komi sengo shi: Jaanarizumu no genten o motomete* (A Postwar History of Mini-Communications: Seeking the Origins of Journalism). Tokyo: San'ichi Shobō, 1985.

Maruyama Masao. "'De aru' koto to 'suru' koto" ("Being" and "Doing"). In Maruyama, *Nihon no shisō,* 153–180. Tokyo: Iwanami Shinsho, 1961.

————. "Fukusho no setsu" (A Call to Return to the Beginning). *Misuzu* 17 (August 1960): 26–32.

————. "8.15 to 5.19: Nihon minshushugi no rekishiteki imi" (August 15 and May 19: The Historical Significance of Japanese Democracy). *Chūō kōron* (Central Forum), 75, no. 8 (August 1960): 44–54.

————. "The Ideology and Dynamics of Japanese Fascism." In Maruyama, *Thought and Behavior in Modern Japanese Politics,* edited by Ivan Morris, 25–83. London: Oxford University Press, 1963, 1969.

———. *Koei no ichi kara* (From a Place in the Rear Guard). Tokyo: Miraisha, 1982.

———. "Kono jitai no seijiteki mondaiten" (Political Issues in the Current Situation). *Asahi Journal* (June 12, 1960): 11–17.

———. *Nihon no shisō* (Japanese Thought). Tokyo: Iwanami Shinsho, 1961.

———. "Patterns of Individuation and the Case of Japan: A Conceptual Scheme." In *Changing Japanese Attitudes Toward Modernization*, edited by Marius Jansen, 489–531. Tokyo and Rutland, Vt.: Charles E. Tuttle Co., 1965.

———. "Sentaku no toki" (A Time to Choose). *Misuzu* 17 (August 1960): 2–5.

———. "The Theory and Psychology of Ultra-Nationalism." In Maruyama, *Thought and Behavior in Modern Japanese Politics*, edited by Ivan Morris, 1–24. London: Oxford University Press, 1963, 1969.

———. *Thought and Behavior in Modern Japanese Politics*. Edited by Ivan Morris. Expanded ed. London: Oxford University Press, 1963, 1969.

———. "Thought and Behavior Patterns of Japan's Wartime Leaders." In Maruyama, *Thought and Behavior in Modern Japanese Politics*, edited by Ivan Morris, 84–134. London: Oxford University Press, 1963, 1969.

Matsushita Keiichi. "Citizen Participation in Historical Perspective." In *Authority and the Individual in Japan,* edited by J. Victor Koschmann, 171–188. Tokyo: University of Tokyo Press, 1978.

———. "Marukusushugi riron no nijūseikiteki tenkan—taishū nashonarizumu to seiji no ronri" (Changes in Twentieth-Century Marxist Theory: The Logic of Mass Nationalism and Politics). *Chūō kōron* (Central Forum), 72, no. 3 (March 1957): 142–157.

———. "Shiteki yuibutsuron to taishū shakai" (Historical Materialism and Mass Society). *Shisō* (Thought), 395 (May 1957): 43–63.

———. "Taishū kokka no seiritsu to sono mondaisei" (The Formation of the Mass State and Its Problems). *Shisō* (Thought), 389 (November 1956): 31–52.

Matsushita Kenichi, ed. *Shōkai: Gendai ronsō jiten* (Comprehensive Dictionary of Contemporary Debates). Tokyo: Ryūdō Shuppan, 1980.

Matsuzawa Hiroaki. "'Theory' and 'Organization' in the Japan Communist Party." In *Authority and the Individual in Japan*, edited by J. Victor Koschmann, 108–127. Tokyo: University of Tokyo Press, 1978.

McKean, Margaret. *Environmental Protest and Citizen Politics in Japan.* Berkeley: University of California Press, 1981.

———. "Political Socialization through Citizens' Movements." In *Political Opposition and Local Politics in Japan*, edited by Kurt Steiner, Ellis Krauss, and Scott Flanagan, 228–273. Princeton, N.J.: Princeton University Press, 1980.

Melucci, Alberto. *Nomads of the Present: Social Movements and Individual Needs in Contemporary Society.* Philadelphia: Temple University Press, 1989.

Mikuni Ichirō, ed. *Sengo sanjū-nen* (Thirty Years of the Postwar). *Shōwa shi tanbō* (Investigations into Shōwa History), vol. 6. Tokyo: Kadokawa Bunko, 1986.

Minaguchi Kōzō. *Anpo tōsō shi: Hitotsu no undō ronteki sōkatsu* (History of the Anpo Struggle: An Adversarial Summation of a Movement). Tokyo: Shinpō Shinsho, 1969.

Miyazaki Katsuji. "Time to Reevaluate the Security Treaty." *Japan Quarterly* 37, no. 4 (October–December 1990): 416–424.

Miyazaki Shōgo. *Ima, "kokyōsei" o utsu: (Dokyumento) Yokohama shinkamotsusen hantai undō* (Challenging the Notion of "The Public" Today: The Movement to Oppose the New Yokohama Freight Line [Documents]). Tokyo: Shinsensha, 1975.

Miyoshi, Masao. *Off Center: Power and Culture Relations between Japan and the United States.* Cambridge: Harvard University Press, 1991.

Morris, Aldon, and Carol McClurg Mueller, eds. *Frontiers in Social Movement Theory.* New Haven, Conn.: Yale University Press, 1992.

Mueller, Carol McClurg. "Building Social Movement Theory." In *Frontiers in Social Movement Theory*, edited by Aldon Morris and Carol McClurg Mueller, 3–25. New Haven, Conn.: Yale University Press, 1992.

Mutō Ichiyo. "The Alternative Livelihood Movement." *AMPO: Japan-Asia Quarterly Review* 24, no. 2 (1993): 4–11.

Mutō Ichiyo and Inoue Reiko. "Beyond the New Left: Part 1, In Search of a Radical Base in Japan." *AMPO: Japan-Asia Quarterly Review* 17, no. 2 (1985): 20–35.

Nakamura Kiyoshi. "'Ōi Shijin' no katsudō" (The Activities of the Poets of Ōi). In *Kyōdō kenkyū: Shudan* (Collaborative Research on Collective Bodies), edited by Shisō no Kagaku, 191–199. Tokyo: Heibonsha, 1976.

———. "Omeshi kikansha no zangyō" (Overtime for the Emperor's Locomotive). In *Tennō shishu* (Emperor Poem Anthology), 57–58. Tokyo: Origin Shuppan Center, 1989.

Nakane Chie. *Japanese Society.* Berkeley: University of California Press, 1970.

Nihon Senbotsu Gakusei Shuki Henshu Iinkai, ed. *Kike wadatsumi no koe: Nihon senbotsu gakusei no shuki* (Listen to the Voices of Wadatsumi: Writings of Japanese Students Killed in the War). Tokyo: Tōkyō Daigaku Shuppan Kai, 1949, 1952.

Noguchi, Paul H. *Delayed Departures, Overdue Arrivals: Industrial Familialism and the Japanese National Railways.* Honolulu: University of Hawai'i Press, 1990.

Oda Makoto. "The Ethics of Peace." In *Authority and the Individual in Japan,* edited by J. Victor Koschmann, 154–170. Tokyo: University of Tokyo Press, 1978.

———. *Nan demo mite yarō* (I'm Gonna Look at It All). Tokyo: Kōdansha Bunko, 1979.

Ōe Kenzaburō. *Hiroshima Notes.* Translated by Yonezawa Toshi. Tokyo: YMCA Press, 1981.

Ōe Shinobu. "Anpo hantai tōsō o dō hyōka suru ka" (How Does One Evaluate the Struggle to Oppose Anpo?). Section 3, part 3 in *Kyōkasho saiban: Nihonshi no sōten,* vol. 2, edited by Tōyama Shigeki, 204–226. Tokyo: Ayumi Shuppan, 1983.

Ōe Shinobu and Fujii Shōichi, eds. *Sengo Nihon no rekishi* (A History of Postwar Japan), vol. 2. Tokyo: Aoki Shoten, 1971.

Olson, Lawrence. *Ambivalent Moderns: Portraits of Japanese Cultural Identity.* Savage, Md.: Rowman and Littlefield, 1992.

Onnatachi no Genzai o Tō Kai, ed. *Onnatachi no 60-nen Anpo* (Women's 1960 Anpo). *Sengoshi nōto sengo hen* (Notes on Postwar History), vol. 5 (1959.1–1960.12). Tokyo: Inpakuto Shuppansha, 1990.

Ōsawa Shinichirō. *Kohō no shisō: Arui wa chōsei e no shuppatsu* (A Philosophy of the Rear: Or Embarking on a Long March). Tokyo: Shakai Hyōronsha, 1971.

———. "Saakuru no sengoshi" (A Postwar History of Circles). In *Kyōdō kenkyū: Shūdan* (Collaborative Research on Collective Bodies), edited by Shisō no Kagaku Kenkyūkai, 68–92. Tokyo: Heibonsha, 1976.

———. "Shūdan no sengo shisōshi: ko" (Postwar Intellectual History of Groups). In Ōsawa, *Kohō no shisō*, 8–44. Tokyo: Shakai Hyōronsha, 1971.

Ōtake Tsutomu. "Yamanami no kai" (The Mountain Range). In *Kyōdō kenkyū: Shudan* (Collaborative Research on Collective Bodies), edited by Shisō no Kagaku, 118–132. Tokyo: Heibonsha, 1976.

———. "Yamanami no kai: Sake no nomikata to saakuru no hōhō" (The Mountain Range: Ways to Drink and Methodologies of Circles). *Shisō no kagaku* (Science of Thought), 115 (Special Issue 3: Shūdan no sengo shisōshi [Postwar Intellectual History of Groups], 1971): 43–56.

Ōtoshi Shigeyuki. *Anpo sedai sennin no saigetsu: Kokkai totsunyū no hi kara* (The Years of One Thousand People from the Anpo Generation: From the Day They Stormed the Diet). Tokyo: Kōdansha, 1980.

Owada Jirō and Ōsawa Shinichirō. *Sōkatsu Anpo hōdō: Sengo shi no nagare no naka de* (A Summary of Reports on Anpo: In the Midst of the Flow of Postwar History). Tokyo: Gendai Jaanarizumu Shuppankai, 1970.

Pacific War Research Society. *Japan's Longest Day*. Tokyo: Kodansha International, Ltd., 1968.

Packard, George. *Protest in Tokyo: The Security Treaty Crisis of 1960*. Princeton, N.J.: Princeton University Press, 1966.

Painter, Andrew. "The Telerepresentation of Gender in Japan." In *Reimaging Japanese Women*, edited by Anne Imamura, 46–72. Berkeley: University of California Press, 1996.

Parsons, Talcott. *On Social Institutions and Social Evolution: Selected Writings*. Edited with an introduction by Leon H. Mayhew. Chicago: University of Chicago Press, 1982.

Popkin, Samuel. *The Rational Peasant*. Berkeley: University of California Press, 1979.

Prazan, Michaël, and Tristan Mendès France. "Cartoonist Who Challenges Japan's Status Quo." *Guardian Weekly,* February 15, 1998, 16.

Rubin, Jay. "From Wholeness to Decadence: The Censorship of Literature under the Allied Occupation." *Journal of Japanese Studies* 11, no. 1 (Winter 1985): 71–103.

Ruoff, Ken. "Mr. Tomino Goes to City Hall: Grass-Roots Democracy in Zushi City, Japan." *Bulletin of Concerned Asian Scholars* 25, no. 3 (1993): 22–32.

Sabouret, Christophe. "Moves to Redraw the Past Alarm Historians." *Guardian Weekly*, February 15, 1998, 16.

Sakuta Keiichi. "The Controversy over Community and Autonomy." In *Authority and the Individual in Japan*, edited by J. Victor Koschmann, 220–249. Tokyo: University of Tokyo Press, 1978.

Satō Maya. "Anpo tōsō ni sanka shita onnatachi" (Women Who Took Part in the Anpo Struggle). In *Onnatachi no 60-nen anpo* (Women's 1960 Anpo), edited by Onnatachi no Genzai o Tō Kai, 8–31. Tokyo: Inpakuto Shuppansha, 1990.

Scalapino, Robert, and Junnosuke Masumi. *Parties and Politics in Contemporary Japan*. Berkeley: University of California Press, 1962.

Scott, Alan. *Ideology and New Social Movements*. London: Unwin Hyman, 1990.

Scott, James. *The Moral Economy of the Peasant*. New Haven, Conn.: Yale University Press, 1976.

Seiki Kazuko. "Shōhisha undō ni jihassei o" (For the Self-Generation of the Consumers Movement). *Tayori* (Correspondence), 38 (June 15, 1966): 22–23.

Sekiguchi, Noriko, dir. *Sensō Daughters*. New York: First Run Icarus Films, 1989.

Sekiya Shigeru and Sakamoto Yoshie, eds. *Tonari ni dassōhei ga ita jidai: JATEC, aru shimin undō no kiroku* (When Deserters Were Next Door: JATEC, Records of a Citizens' Movement). Tokyo: Shisō no kagakusha, 1998.

Shiba Aiko. "Kangofu—sono hi no watashi" (Nurses—That Day and Me). *Yamanami* 25 (Anpo Struggle special issue) (October 1961): 4–6.

Shibagaki Kazuo. *Kōwa kara kōdo seichō e: Kokusai shakai e no fukka-tsu to Anpo tōsō* (From Peace to Rapid Economic Growth: The Re-vival of International Society and the Anpo Struggle). *Showa no rekishi* (A History of the Shōwa Era), 9. Tokyo: Shogakkan, 1989.

Shibata Shingo. "'Taishū shakai' riron e no gimon" (Doubts Regarding "Mass Society" Theory). *Chūō kōron* (Central Forum), 72, no. 8 (June 1957): 170–186.

Shinobu Seiichirō. *Anpo tōsō shi: Sanjūgo-nichi kan seikyoku shi ron* (A History of the Security Treaty Struggle: A Theory on the Thirty-Five-Day Political Situation). Tokyo: Sekai Shoin, 1961.

Shiratori Kunio. "Gendai no shisō jōkyō to saakuru undō" (The Con-temporary Situation of Philosophy and the Circle Movement). *Yama-nami no kai* 45 (August 1975).

——. *Mumei no Nihonjin: "Yamanami no kai" no kiroku* (Nameless Japanese: A Record of the Mountain Range Group). Tokyo: Miraisha, 1961.

Shisō no Kagaku Kenkyūkai, ed. *Kyōdō kenkyū: Shūdan* (Collaborative Research on Collective Bodies). Tokyo: Heibonsha, 1976.

Shisō Undō Kenkyūjo, ed. *Anpo fūunroku: Sōran jūnen no kiroku* (A Record of the Anpo Situation: Ten Years of Discord). Tokyo: Zen-bōsha, 1969.

Shoop, Donald. "Sunagawa Incident." Ph.D. dissertation, University of Denver, 1985.

Shūdan. See Shisō no Kagaku Kenkyūkai, ed. *Kyōdō kenkyū: Shūdan.*

Snow, David, and Robert Bedford. "Master Frames and Cycles of Pro-test." In *Frontiers in Social Movement Theory*, edited by Aldon Morris and Carol McClurg Mueller, 133–155. New Haven, Conn.: Yale University Press, 1992.

"Sōkan sengen: Sara ni fukaku shūdan no imi o" (Founding Decla-ration: Probing Further the Significance of Collectives). *Saakuru Mura* (Circle Village), 1 (September 1958): 2–7.

Steiner, Kurt. *Local Government in Japan.* Stanford: Stanford University Press, 1965.

Steiner, Kurt, Ellis Krauss, and Scott C. Flanagan, eds. *Political Oppo-sition and Local Politics in Japan.* Princeton, N.J.: Princeton Uni-versity Press, 1980.

Sunday Mainichi, Economist, and Mainichi Graph, eds. *"Anpo" ni yureta Nihon no kiroku* (A Record of Japan Jolted by "Anpo": May–June 1960). Tokyo: Mainichi Shinbun, 1960.

Takabatake Michitoshi. "Citizen's Movements: Organizing the Spontaneous." In *Authority and the Individual in Japan*, edited by J. Victor Koschmann, 189–199. Tokyo: University of Tokyo Press, 1978.

———. " 'Rokujū-nen Anpo' no seishin shi" (A Psychological History of 1960 Anpo). In *Sengo Nihon no seishin shi* (A Psychological History of the Japanese Postwar), edited by Kamishima Jirō, Maeda Ai, and Tetsuo Najita, 70–91. Tokyo: Iwanami Shoten, 1988.

Takeuchi Yoshimi. *Fufukujū no isan* (Legacy of Disobedience). Tokyo: Chikuma Shobō, 1961.

Tanaka Yuki. *Hidden Horrors: Japanese War Crimes in World War II*. Boulder, Colo.: Westview Press, 1996.

Tanigawa Gan. "Teikei no chōkoku" (Overcoming the Form). In *Minshushugi no shinwa* (Myths of Democracy), 7–41. Tokyo: Gendai Shichōsha, 1966.

Tayori. See Koe Naki Koe no Kai, ed. *Koe Naki Koe no Tayori*.

Togawa Isamu. *Kishi Nobusuke to hoshu antō* (Kishi Nobusuke and Conservatives' Secret Strife). *Shōwa no saishō*, vol. 5. Tokyo: Kōdansha, 1982.

Tōkyō Daigaku Shokunin Kumiai, ed. *6.15 zengo: Ichō namiki kara kokkai e* (Before and After June 15: From Ginkgo-Lined Streets to the Diet). Tokyo: Tōkyō Daigaku Shokunin Kumiai, 1960.

Touraine, Alain. *Return of the Actor: Social Theory in Postindustrial Society*. Translated by Myrna Godźich. Minneapolis: University of Minnesota Press, 1988.

Tōyama Shigeki, ed. *Kyōkasho saiban: Nihonshi no sōten* (The Textbook Suit: The Issue of Japanese History). 2 vols. Tokyo: Ayumi Shuppan, 1983.

Tsuji Kiyoaki, ed. *Seiji* (Politics). *Shiryō: Sengo nijū-nen shi* (Resources: Twenty Years of Postwar History), vol. 1. Tokyo: Nihon Hyōronsha, 1967.

Tsurumi Kazuko. *Social Change and the Individual: Japan before and after the Defeat in World War II*. Princeton: Princeton University Press, 1970.

Tsurumi, Shunsuke. *A Cultural History of Postwar Japan*. London: Kegan Paul International, 1987.

———. *An Intellectual History of Wartime Japan, 1931–1945*. London: Kegan Paul International, 1986.

———. *Jiron, essei* (Current Views, Essays). *Tsurumi Shunsuke chōsa-kushu* (Collected Works of Tsurumi Shunsuke), vol. 5. Tokyo: Chikuma Shobō, 1976.

Tsuzuki Tsutomu. "Rokujū-nen Anpo zengo no Maruyama Masao" (Maruyama Masao before and after 1960 Anpo). *Gendai no riron* 235 (March 1987): 5–18.

Uno, Kathleen. "The Death of 'Good Wife, Wise Mother'?" In *Postwar Japan as History*, edited by Andrew Gordon, 293–322. Berkeley: University of California Press, 1993.

Upham, Frank. *Law and Social Change in Postwar Japan*. Cambridge: Harvard University Press, 1987.

Usui Yoshimi, ed. *Anpo 1960: Nihon seiji no shōten* (Anpo 1960: The Focus of Japanese Politics). Tokyo: Chikuma Shobō, 1969.

Vogel, Ezra. *Japan's New Middle Class*. 2d ed. Berkeley and Los Angeles: University of California Press, 1963.

Watashitachi no Rekishi o Tsuzuru Kai, ed. *Ikiru genten o motomete: Shufu no taiken shita Shōwa shi* (In Search of a Living Origin: A History of Shōwa through the Experiences of Housewives). Tokyo: Akebono Shuppan, 1978.

Weinstein, Martin E. *Japan's Postwar Defense Policy, 1947–1968*. New York: Columbia University Press, 1971.

Welfield, John. *An Empire in Eclipse: Japan in the Postwar American Alliance System: A Study in the Interaction of Domestic Politics and Foreign Policy*. London: The Athlone Press, 1988.

Wilkinson, Thomas O. *The Urbanization of Japanese Labor, 1868–1955*. Amherst, Mass.: University of Massachusetts Press, 1965.

Wolf, Margery. *Women and the Family in Rural Taiwan*. Stanford: Stanford University Press, 1972.

Yamabe Emiko. "Shufutachi no Anpo: Sanka shinakatta shufu hyakunin no koe kara" (Housewives' Anpo: From the Voices of One Hundred Housewives Who Did Not Participate). In *Onnatachi no 60-nen*

Anpo (Women's 1960 Anpo), edited by Onnatachi no Genzai o Tō Kai, 35–51. Tokyo: Inpakuto Shuppansha, 1990.

Yamada Munemitsu, ed. *Anpo to kōdo seichō* (Anpo and Rapid Economic Growth). *Dokyumento Shōwa shi* (Shōwa History Documents), vol. 7. Tokyo: Heibonsha, 1975.

Yasko, Guy. "The Japanese Student Movement 1968–70 : The Zenkyoto Uprising." Ph.D. dissertation, Cornell University, 1997.

Yayama Tarō. "The Newspapers Conduct a Mad Rhapsody over the Textbook Issue." *Journal of Japanese Studies* 9, no. 2 (Summer 1983): 301–316.

Yoshimoto Takaaki. "Gisei no shūen" (An End to Fictions). In *Minshushugi no shinwa* (Myths of Democracy), 43–76. Tokyo: Gendai no Shichōsha, 1966.

INDEX

Abelmann, Nancy, 13–14, 220n. 22
Acheson, Dean, 169
Acorns (Donguri). *See* Tanashi-Hōya
  Acorns
All Japan Labor Union Congress
  (Zenrō), 174
alternative livelihood cooperatives,
  142
Anpo generation, 34–35, 200–201
Anpo Hihan no Kai. *See* Committee
  to Criticize the Security Treaty
Anpo protests: attempts to control,
  37, 46, 102, 153, 173, 192,
  253n. 72; bystanders' role in, 77,
  102, 148–149, 157, 160; diversity in, 5–6; geographic spread
  of, 76–77; June 4 general strike,
  37, 42, 155–156; June 10
  Hagerty incident, 37; June 15, 2,
  36–39, 43–44, 46–48, 76, 102,
  103–106, 161–163; legacies of,
  8, 17–18, 22, 54, 197–198,
  200–201, 206–209, 211;
  May 19, 1–2, 16, 21, 26, 42,
  150–152, 163, 167, 186; media
  coverage of, 19–21, 40, 41,
  47, 77, 106, 150, 163, 245n. 7;
  organization of, 21–22, 173–
  176; portrayal as communist
  conspiracy, 19, 155, 217n. 4,
  222n. 12; significance of, 17,

53–54, 195–198; student
  involvement in, 17, 103, 158;
  violence in, 39, 44, 45–47, 48,
  103, 106, 158–159, 161–163
Anpo treaty (U.S.-Japan Security
  Treaty): articles of, 16; contradiction with the Constitution,
  16, 169–170; forcible ratification
  of, 16, 25–26, 41, 42, 51, 137,
  148, 150, 164; negotiations on,
  24; stipulations of, 25, 170,
  224n. 31
anti-bases movements, 171; Girard
  case, 251n. 65. *See also*
  Sunagawa protests
anti-Vietnam War movement, 54.
  See also Citizens' Federation
  for Peace in Vietnam
Article 9 (of the Japanese Constitution), 16, 168–169; text of,
  220–221n. 1
Asahi shinbun: coverage of Takeuchi
  Yoshimi's resignation, 182; and
  Joint Declaration of Seven Newspapers, 50; local editions of, 130;
  and origins of the Grass Seeds,
  40, 52, 112, 127–129, 138
Asanuma Inejirō, assassination of,
  192
atomic bomb victims, 30, 119–120,
  237n. 17, 238n. 18

ABOUT THE AUTHOR

WESLEY SASAKI-UEMURA is associate professor of Japanese history at the University of Utah. He received his Ph.D. from Cornell University in 1993. Published works include an article in the journal *positions* titled "Tanigawa Gan's Politics of the Margins in Kyushu and Nagano."